RURAL SOCIAL WO

An international perspec

Richard Pugh and Brian Cheers

First published in Great Britain in 2010 by

Policy Press
University of Bristol
1-9 Old Park Hill
Bristol BS2 8BB
UK
t: +44 (0)117 954 5940
e: pp-info@bristol.ac.uk
www.policypress.co.uk

North American office:
Policy Press
c/o The University of Chicago Press
1427 East 60th Street
Chicago, IL 60637, USA
t: +1 773 702 7700
f: +1 773-702-9756
e:sales@press.uchicago.edu
www.press.uchicago.edu

© Policy Press 2010

British Library Cataloguing in Publication Data
A catalogue record for this book is available from the British Library.

Library of Congress Cataloging-in-Publication Data
A catalog record for this book has been requested.

ISBN 978 1 86134 720 6 paperback
ISBN 978 1 86134 721 3 hardcover

Cover design by Qube Design Associates, Bristol
Front cover image: www.istock.com
Printed and bound in Great Britain by Cromwell Press, Trowbridge

Contents

Acknowledgements

We would like to record our appreciation of the suggestions made by Glen Schmidt at The University of Northern British Columbia and material provided by Leslie Brown at The University of Victoria, Canada.

Introduction

Most texts on rural social work are written with a particular national context in mind and rarely address an international readership, though, of course, they may provide valuable information and ideas that can be adapted to other settings. In contrast, this book draws upon a wider range of international research, theory and practice in rural social work with the aims of:

- establishing the diversity of rural practice contexts;
- disseminating information about interventions and models of practice in rural areas;
- promoting the development and inclusion of rural perspectives in practice for the education, recruitment and deployment of rural workers.

Some aspects of rural practice have been well researched but there are areas where we lack empirical evidence and instead have to rely upon theoretical speculation, descriptive accounts of practice and our own personal observations. Accordingly, it is also our intention to point up areas for future research and development.

This book is primarily written for those who practise and teach social work in what might be called 'European-influenced' systems of social service in predominantly industrial capitalist societies. That is, the forms of social work found in Australia, Canada, the UK, the US and most of the countries of Western Europe: countries where there is a history of state and voluntary provision for personal social services and where there are well-established traditions of professional social work education. These countries tend to have highly urbanised populations clustered around large cities and towns. While the most distant and remote rural areas may have suffered population decline, in many of these countries substantial numbers remain living in rural areas. In some countries there is evidence of counter-urbanisation as increasingly affluent workers move into the more accessible rural districts surrounding towns and cities. The United States of America provides a striking example of the paradox of urbanisation and overall population growth. The US Census Bureau (2000a) has estimated that while around 78% of the population live in urban metropolitan areas, the remaining 22%, a surprising 55 million people, still live in rural districts (Daley and Avant, 2004). So while the proportion of the total population living in rural areas may have declined considerably since 1900, the actual numbers living there have more than doubled (Lohmann and Lohmann, 2005).

While some parts of this text may have relevance for practice in other countries such as Brazil or India, in many places the most pressing welfare priorities for rural populations require interventions directed towards more fundamental needs: for clean water, satisfactory housing, basic health care and education. While religious organisations may provide some rudimentary services in the countryside, formal social service provision is typically scarce or non-existent, and most people rely primarily upon their family and immediate community for support when needed. In such countries, the primary goals for social action and welfare development may be targeted at the broader community, but, as this book will make clear, we do not think that it is necessary to make a rigid distinction between social programmes and community development aimed at larger groups and populations, and personal social services geared towards the particular needs and problems of individuals and families. Indeed, a key proposition of this book is that this division, which is most evident in the UK, and can also been seen in Australia, Canada and the US, can obstruct effective intervention in rural problems.

At the outset, we acknowledge that the idea that there is something that can be described as rural social work is not one that is universally accepted or recognised. There is a well-established tradition of rural social work in the US and the term is widely recognised in Australia and Canada, but in the UK and on the European mainland it is much less commonly used to describe a specific area of practice. This is largely because the demands and problems of rural practice remain under-recognised, but it is also a consequence of a number of other factors. Levels of urbanisation and population density are much higher in many European countries, and so the needs of rural populations may be socially and politically marginalised. The fact that the majority of social work teaching and research is located in urban institutions may also contribute to under-recognition, while in some countries the prevailing systems of social intervention do not recognise social work as a distinctive welfare profession in the first place (Schilde and Schulte, 2005).

We begin this book with the notion of rural social work as a descriptive term. That is, one that simply identifies the location and context of social work practice in rural areas. From a descriptive point of view, the term 'rural social work' has as much utility as, say, describing work with children and their carers as child and family social work. For us, the term 'rural social work' does not mean that all problems and situations in rural places are the same. We do not suppose that rural problems can be addressed with one set of methods and approaches, and we certainly do not propose any overall theory about doing rural social work. Indeed, a central theme of this book is that rural communities are diverse and the ways in which personal and social problems are experienced by rural dwellers can vary from one place to another, and, consequently, may require different responses according to the particular contexts in which they have arisen. As Fluharty (2002) memorably commented some years ago, 'If you've seen one rural community you've seen ... one rural community' (cited in Lohmann and Lohmann, 2005, p xxii). Nevertheless, we think the term rural social work has merit in directing attention to some key questions about how social work is practised in non-urban areas. For example, is the practice of social workers in rural areas distinctively different from that in urban areas, and, if not, should it be?

Our experience from practice and research is that social workers in rural areas often find that their professional training has not adequately prepared them for the challenges they face. For example, most discussions on professional confidentiality are premised upon the assumption that social workers typically work in formalised one-to-one situations in urban areas and are unlikely to have any other social contact with service users. In urban areas, the size of the local community and the density of population usually make it relatively easy to establish and maintain confidentiality. In contrast, a woman in a rural area who is subject to violence from her male partner cannot simply walk into a women's aid centre in a small rural town without wondering whether her visit will be observed by someone who knows her, and who might make assumptions about why she is going there. This is not simply an issue about her desire for privacy, but one that may bear directly upon her safety, as a visit might have very risky consequences if it became known to her abusive partner. The point is that the risk of further violence may be exacerbated by the lack of anonymity in a small community, yet few social work programmes devote more than cursory attention to some of the specifics of rural practice.

If social work policies, practices and training are premised upon the unwitting and unrecognised assumption of an urban setting, then the result will be that some of the factors that bear upon service provision and upon personal and social problems in rural areas will be neglected. Our concern is that while there are some excellent examples of professional preparation around the world, in general most social work students will receive little, if any, specific preparation for rural practice. Consequently, they may arrive in rural posts with little knowledge of the existing literature and research and be poorly prepared for their practice (Locke, 1991). In the absence of well-founded knowledge, they may feel that they are 'making it up as they go along' (Cheers, 1998).

Problems of definition

Most texts on rural social work attempt to get to grips with the question of what is meant by rural social work, and there are two approaches that can be taken to this. The first approach, and the one that is most commonly encountered, is to attempt to define what 'rurality' is. That is, to define the rural place or setting. The second approach is to attempt to define the field of practice. That is, to establish what, if anything, is distinctive about rural social work.

Defining rurality

This approach, which has been widely used in rural sociology and rural policy, typically attempts to establish a definition of rurality based upon a single demographic criterion such as population density, the size of rural settlements, their geographical location or the time that it takes rural dwellers to travel to work or access public services. Mono-dimensional definitions, which are widely used by government agencies and researchers, may draw upon existing data sets to map relationships between particular demographic features and data on a range of social indexes of health, welfare, income, crime, educational attainment, employment and so on. Certainly, it seems a reasonable contention to suggest that some aspects of social work practice in the remoter Scottish islands may be rather different from those in a large city like Glasgow, or that workers practising in the northern areas of Canada, where there are few roads and where travel may necessitate lengthy journeys or even air travel, face some different issues than those working in a metropolitan area like Toronto. The advantages of using a single clear criterion seem obvious. It appears to allow clear generalisations and statements to be made about rural places, rural problems and potential solutions. There are also what might be termed residual definitions, such as the one formerly used by the US Census Bureau (2000a) (see also www.nysdot.gov/divisions/policy-and-strategy/darb/dai-unit/ttss/repository/ua_2k.pdf and www.rupri.org/dataresearchviewer.php?id=38 or www.census.org), where rural is everything that is not otherwise defined as urban or metropolitan.

There are extensive technical debates about the merits of different sorts of definition and some writers have also attempted to distinguish between rural and remote areas. They contend that remote areas tend to have distinctively different characteristics because of their distant locations. However, little evidence is adduced to show that there are sustained and consistent differences between remote rural districts and other rural areas. Nevertheless, there may be merit in descriptively signalling the facts of distance and isolation and their potential impact upon the context of practice with the term 'remote'. For instance, although we are not persuaded that a conclusive definition is necessary or possible, it is important to recognise that in remote areas with small populations lone or solo working may be commonplace as social work teams may be small or non-existent, and that as a result social workers may be more likely to practise in a generic or generalist manner.

There are several drawbacks, with these sorts of mono-dimensional definitions, the most obvious being the validity of the definition used. For example, when the size of the community is used, there can be highly contentious debates about what size counts as a rural community, should it be 2,500 or 10,000 or maybe even 20,000 people? While a community of 2,500 might be termed a rural village in a UK context, because it may be located only a few miles away from another community or even a larger town, it may lack many of the facilities one might find in a similar-sized community in say rural Australia or Canada. A further difficulty is that while each definition may capture one aspect of rurality very well, each one ignores other dimensions that may be more significant in particular situations. Thus, a definition based upon geographical remoteness would not take into account the size of a community or the opportunities for regular employment, yet it may be these features of a particular village or small town that impact most upon the life chances and the problems faced by its inhabitants. Furthermore, the experience of life in such places may differ greatly according to the prevailing political climate in terms of the degree of economic and social support given to a particular community. Unsurprisingly, some writers on rurality often conclude that the existing definitions are inadequate and that perhaps a 'compound definition' (Halfacree, 1993), maybe one that combines two or more of these criteria, should be established (Olaveson et al, 2004). One example of a compound definition reported by Olaveson and her colleagues is that of Cleland (1995) who devised a complex index for the US that measured rurality on 11 dimensions and arrived at an overall rating from zero (least rural) to 19 (most rural). However, they noted that when 'applied to each state, it creates an unusual measure of degree of rurality for some states … Wyoming the most sparsely populated state, scores a 3' (Olaveson et al, 2004, p 15). Of course, it is possible that an index like this would be much more representative of people's perceptions of rurality if it were applied to somewhat smaller areas.

Another difficulty in attempting to establish mutually exclusive definitions that allow clear-cut statements about whether an area is either rural or urban is that such either/or categorisations do not capture the complexity and variability of rural communities. We agree with Ginsberg, who in reference to the work of Coward et al (1994), contended that 'scholarship on rural areas is sometimes impeded by efforts to create dichotomies as ways of understanding the differences between rural and nonrural areas' (1998, p 6). In our view, attempts at definitive demarcation are unhelpful because they presuppose that there is some enduring essential or intrinsic feature of 'rurality' that can be found in all rural communities. Whereas, as we will argue throughout this book, the diversity of rural areas, together with the crucial importance of how variably people may subjectively experience the place and their position within the community, makes such suppositions difficult to sustain. Attempts at definitive categorisation, which presume that there are some homogeneous features of rural life invariably signalled by the distinction, are often contradicted by the direct and detailed knowledge that social workers gain from working with diverse individuals and groups, people whose position within their communities may not be easily subsumed under the broader definition. Furthermore, policies and practices based upon assumptions of sameness/similarity can lead to inappropriate provision that neglects the needs of some people, especially those from minority groups.

Implicit in many definitions is the idea that something changes about the way communities work and how people live within them as one moves across the definitional boundary marker. Thus, the marker of size or distance is also regarded as a reliable indicator of social characteristics. While we may have subjectively experienced such changes, there are considerable difficulties in deciding objectively where precisely to draw the lines of definition in terms of size or distance. It seems presumptuous to try to 'fix' rurality in these ways without clear evidence that the dynamics of rural life vary reliably as one moves to a larger or smaller place, or nearer or further away from a large centre of population.

Our view is not that definitions are irrelevant or unimportant. Indeed, they may be extremely significant when politicians, government and funding bodies are making decisions about resources and service priorities. Our reservation is that not only do they tend to aggregate some very variable aspects of rurality, but they also direct attention away from other fundamentally important aspects of rural life. Therefore, we are appreciative of Martinez-Brawley's attempt to 'transcend the classic debate' (2000, p xx) about defining rurality, which led her to use, instead, the term 'small communities'. We also wish to move beyond a discussion of the demographics of rural life into a broader appreciation of the social dynamics of rural life. Nonetheless, we think that rural workers should familiarise themselves with the sorts of definitional criteria that are being used in their localities, if only to challenge and problematise them.

Defining the practice

The second approach is much less common and is often not explicitly stated in terms of a definitional issue, but it centres on the question: 'In what ways is rural social work different from urban practice?' Locke and Winship (2005) suggest that there are five recurrent and significant themes in the literature on rural practice:

- Generalist practice – that is, being 'skilled in working with individuals, families, small groups, organizations and communities' (Locke and Winship, 2005, p 6).
- Community development – they note that as early as 1933 Josephine Brown was calling for rural workers to embrace both casework and community work.
- External relations – that is, relations with significant people outside of the immediate issue, such as local politicians and other influential actors.
- Cultural influences – sensitivity to the particularities of local rural cultures as well as to the needs of minority groups.
- Desirable characteristics of workers – these include a visible commitment to the local community and the capacity to work without much professional support.

In contrast to this thematic approach there have been a number of empirical studies in Australia and the US that have tried to establish whether rural work is different. Some have compared rural practice with that employed in urban areas and have generally concluded that there is little difference between rural and urban practice (Grant, 1984; Whitaker, 1986; Puckett and Frederico, 1992; York et al, 1998). Nonetheless, because most of these studies have predominantly focused upon existing patterns of service provision rather than upon the existence of, or need for, particular skills, they are unlikely to show significant differences. Indeed, as we have noted elsewhere:

> Descriptive comparative studies such as these are unlikely to show major rural–urban differences because they are based upon current work practices which are largely determined by prevailing social care structures, practitioners' world views, and paradigms emphasised in mainstream professional literature and education programs.... Descriptive studies miss the heart of the matter ... they treat practitioners as if they float free of their social contexts. This may work for much of urban practice where practitioners spend their working hours dealing with people who they will never come across in other roles. But the assumption does not hold where they live in the same small community as their clients. Social care practice is not merely influenced by the rural context – practice and practitioners are integral parts of that context. (Cheers, 1998, p 220)

The problem may be that existing studies have looked at the wrong sorts of things (Locke, 1991). Unsurprisingly, studies into the ways in which services are provided in rural areas tend to find service patterns that replicate the assumptions and structures found elsewhere in social work practice. Perhaps more attention should be paid to what individual social workers actually do, but as even their daily practices are likely to reflect broader organisational factors, this approach may not prove distinctive either. Interestingly, a non-comparative study by Gumpert et al (2000, cited in Lohmann and Lohmann, 2005) found that most rural workers thought that there were some distinctive characteristics of rural communities that impacted on their work. The features they noted included extensive networks of local knowledge, a suspicion of outsiders and a slower pace of work with clients.

We need to develop our knowledge of the ways in which rural workers may modify their practice or manage other more personal aspects of their lives. Thus, the second point in this quotation about social context is crucial, for it is this aspect of rural work that seems to be most significant in identifying what might be different about rural practice. It raises a number of interesting questions about how rural workers, especially those who live and work in the same place, manage issues about confidentiality, personal safety, their work and their social lives, and how they relate to the wider community as well as how it relates to them.

There may be few, if any, social work skills that are unique to rural contexts, but we think that there are reasonable grounds for supposing that workers may need to apply their skills differently and to do so with knowledge of the social dynamics of rural communities. The most obvious feature of these dynamics is the more personalised basis of formal relationships in rural areas and the need to be aware of the wide social networks that exist in small communities. In many small communities, it is often possible to know most other people within them, either directly or indirectly, and this creates some fascinating dilemmas for workers and clients who may find it difficult to keep a clear separation between their professional role and their personal life. However, even these dynamics are not exclusive as they may also occur in some urban areas. For instance, neighbourhood workers, especially those working in encapsulated areas like public housing projects or districts that are partially isolated from the larger urban area by virtue of their geographical location, perhaps separated by a river or railway line, have reported similar dilemmas. Furthermore, when such issues do arise in urban practice they may not be fully recognised, reported or researched.

The second important point to note is that while studies that have specifically sought to examine possible differences between urban and rural practice have not found conclusive differences, this may well be the result of looking simply at the services that are provided rather than asking whether these are what is required. That is, if urbanist assumptions about service provision are simply enacted in the design and planning of rural services, it is not surprising that empirical investigation reveals few differences. The question might be better framed as not 'In what way are services different?', but rather 'To what extent should they be different?' (Cheers, 1998).

To summarise, our position is that rural social work is a term that usefully identifies a set of issues and concerns around social work practice in non-urban areas. However, it does not identify an exclusive set of characteristics that can only be found in rural areas, though we do think that there are some features that are more commonly encountered there. Practical experience of rural social work encourages practitioners to look again at questions of context, and it is this appreciation of the social dimensions of local practice that is often more consciously acknowledged than is the case in urban practice. Indeed, rural social work has an important role in reminding 'mainstream' practice of something that is often overlooked, but always remains evident to those who work in rural areas: specifically, that social context and the dynamics of communities matter. Ultimately, the sorts of questions and issues that interest rural practitioners also have relevance for social work practice in other locations.

Appreciating rural contexts and rural problems

We have already noted that one difficulty with the attempts to define rural is that they tend to assume some enduring or essential features of rurality that may not actually exist. Thus, all writers on rurality are faced with the question of how to write about some of the more common features of rural life without presenting these things as if they were universal characteristics. While most social work texts on rurality acknowledge some of the technical problems of definition, and clearly recognise the political and service consequences that can follow from different sorts of definition, they do not seem to recognise the sociological significance of this problem of definition. This 'slipperiness' of definition is a direct consequence of the fact that there are many different ways of understanding and representing rurality and these ways of seeing and understanding the countryside do not solely arise from objective and empirical 'facts'. Indeed, Murdoch and Pratt have warned that 'we should be extremely wary of attempts to definitively define the rural ... [because any definition] is saturated with assumptions and presuppositions' (1997, p 56). The point is that all definitions are socially constructed and so will vary according to the perceptions and positions of those who construct them.

It is crucial that social workers recognise that the ideas we have about the countryside may be shaped and influenced by a wide range of assumptions and even idealisations about rurality. Some of these ideas may have a long history. For example, when Marx and Engels in the 1870s (1972) saw the countryside as a place of oppression, ignorance and poverty and, consequently, welcomed the urbanising effects of capitalism, they were not alone in representing rural life as being backward, basic and uncultured. Indeed, the assumption of the superiority of city life is still evident in the contemporary usage of the words 'urbane' and 'rustic', which imply that those who live in rural areas have somehow been left behind and are socially isolated from the wider society. In many industrialised countries there may be ambiguous or even conflicting ideas of rurality and rural life. In an earlier text we noted that:

> there are multiple idealisations within countries as well as considerable variations between different countries. In much of Europe the countryside is often seen as a largely unchanged and unchanging place, an unspoiled pastoral landscape dotted with quiet rural communities. A place of family origin before urbanisation ... [and] more recently

with the growth in disposable incomes and leisure time ...
as an urban playspace.... What seems to be less common in
Europe and more widespread in popular culture in North
America is the representation of rurality in terms of notions
of ruggedness, individuality and pioneering spirit.... Thus,
the idealised historical representation is not so much a
picture of the countryside as a place of origin, of peace
and stability, but is one featuring the hardships and hazards
endured, and of nature tamed. (Pugh, 2001, p 44)

Different sorts of representations of rurality are important because
they may have a wider significance in terms of ideas about how the
countryside should be used, about who lives there and about how
rural life should be lived. These ideas can have a powerful symbolic
and political significance and may be used to make statements about
identity and nationality. For example, Sibley has pointed out that in
England the countryside is seen by some people as having a 'sacred'
quality that is the essence or heart of Englishness, a quality that at various
times is seen as being threatened and 'endangered by the transgressions
of discrepant minorities' (1997, p 219) such as the urban working
class, gypsies, migrant workers and so on. Writing about the sorts of
assumptions that are made about First Nation communities in Canada,
Dickson-Gilmore and La Prairie make the point that:

Aboriginal communities are too often viewed as the
romanticized last bastions of 'noble savages' or as deeply
impoverished, highly dysfunctional entities in desperate
need of the benevolent aid of outsiders. These extremes
deny and distort reality. (Dickson-Gilmore and La Prairie,
2005, p 228)

The point is that idealisations do not accurately represent social
realities. When idealisations are used to promote a sense of belonging
or nationality, or even when it is assumed that rural communities are
essentially groupings of similar people, or at least groupings who share
a common worldview and common norms, it is less likely that other
aspects of social differentiation will be recognised and appreciated. In
fact, the apparent homogeneity of rural communities is often contrasted
with the more obvious diversity of urban areas to make a point about
social cohesiveness. One result is that the recognition of forms of
discrimination, such as racism and homophobia, is much less likely to
occur if idealisations of rural communities ignore these forms of social

difference in the first place. Furthermore, the comparative 'invisibility' of some problems among dispersed and remote communities, such as family violence, poverty and drugs, may lead to the conclusion that these problems are largely urban issues. Clearly, if people's perceptions are that there are no black or other ethnic minorities living locally, or, alternatively, no violent abusers or substance misusers, then it follows for many of them that there cannot be a local need or local problem.

So, to return to the point about what sorts of generalisations we might be able to make about rurality in relation to rural social work, without assuming that these things are universally the case, there are six features that have been widely noted in the rural literature:

- the existence and needs of some rural dwellers tend to be unrecognised or are understated;
- rural populations are typically under-served by welfare services;
- rural infrastructures are weaker, that is the availability or presence of other services such as affordable housing, effective transport systems and so on is reduced;
- employment opportunities are restricted, either because of the rural location and/or the changing rural labour market;
- poverty and poorer life chances are more common in the most rural areas;
- rural services generally cost much more to deliver.

Much of the literature makes the point that rural problems are often similar to those found in urban areas but notes that these problems may be experienced differently because of the rural location. For instance, Rollinson and Pardeck in a review of rural homelessness in the US (2006) noted that family violence appeared to be much more commonly reported in rural than urban homelessness. Many of these features interact with each other, and it is often the case that problems in rural areas are exacerbated by the fact that rural dwellers may have fewer public and private resources available to deal with their problems. Unsurprisingly, rural people often appear to have relatively low expectations of welfare services in the first place. Additionally, some individuals and groups may experience systematic neglect, while others suffer from institutionalised racism in their contacts with human service agencies.

Throughout this book we wish to persuade readers of the complexity and variability of lived experience and so avoid making any simplistic assumptions about what other people's lives are like. As we shall see later, for example, being black or gay in the countryside may well be experienced as being an exposed and risky position, but we should not assume that this is so for all those who may be thus identified. The dynamics of small communities, which can certainly heighten feelings of isolation and vulnerability, can also permit different and more positive sorts of local response and adaptation. Moreover, the political context within which rurality is constructed can also have a significant bearing on how the wider society responds to rural problems. For example, in countries where urbanisation is a more recent phenomenon and where many people have more recent rural origins there may be a much more sympathetic appreciation of the needs of rural communities and their people. Seen in this more sociological way, the rural context in which rural social work is undertaken becomes a fascinating place. The countryside, far from being a separate dimension of social life, can be seen to have a complex relationship with the wider society. Most important, it helps us to understand how the idealisation of the 'rural' impacts upon our perceptions of social problems, upon our ideas of who 'belongs' in the countryside and, ultimately, upon whose needs are recognised.

The content and structure of the book

Three core themes run throughout this book. The first is the recognition of the diversity of rural contexts and rural lives. The second theme is the contention that successful rural practice requires a sound appreciation of local context. The third theme is that this diversity plus the contextual knowledge of particular places and communities logically leads to a rejection of any 'one size fits all' solution. Thus, not only do we reject the implicit urbanist assumptions that underpin some approaches to practice, but we also contend that no rigid distinction in practice should be made between personal social services and more community-focused interventions. Although welfare services in some countries may organisationally distinguish between the two broad approaches to practice, we think that this is an unhelpful separation which unnecessarily restricts the range of possible interventions.

This book is divided into two parts. Part One, entitled 'The experience of rurality', has five chapters that establish the general context of rural social work and review the experiences of minority individuals and groups in rural areas and the sorts of service responses that have been made to them. Chapter 5, the final chapter in this section, summarises and reviews some of the general problems and possibilities of rural practice. Part Two of the book is entitled 'Developing rural practice'. Chapters 6 and 7 set out two broad approaches to developing and providing rural social services, focusing first upon the delivery of personal social services and then addressing community-oriented approaches. We have presented these approaches separately for clarity although our view is that, in practice, rural social workers may need to use a range of interventions from casework to community development. Chapter 8 then reviews the education and training, recruitment and retention of rural practitioners. The book ends with a short conclusion that summarises the main themes of the book and offers some pointers for developments in education, research and practice.

Part One
The experience of rurality

ONE

Contexts of practice

Introduction

At the start of this book we emphasised the importance of understanding the diverse rural contexts in which social work is conducted. This chapter reviews five dimensions that can be used to understand and analyse these contexts:

- geography
- demography
- economy
- political and structural dimensions
- community.

In setting out these key dimensions we do not provide a comprehensive review of every relevant factor, but, instead, signal features that will help rural workers to think about the nature of their own local contexts and how these might impact upon the lives of the people and communities they serve. Although there is considerable variation within and between different countries, there are some common themes that can be usefully identified from the literature and the research on rural communities. These key dimensions can also influence how practice is planned, organised, funded and delivered, and may be used comparatively to appreciate similarities and differences between rural contexts. A careful appreciation of different contextual dimensions may help identify which factors appear to be most relevant or significant in particular places, and avoid the mistake of assuming that if an initiative has succeeded in one rural area it will also do so in another. The final part of this chapter reviews some of the different approaches to conceptualising and studying rural communities.

Geography

The term 'geography' is used here to refer to the physical location and patterns of settlement in an area. The remoteness of a place or its landscape may make it more difficult to travel to, or to move around the area. Features such as hills and mountains, river valleys and dense forest, can add considerably to the distance and journey times required to access local services, and the impact of other features, such as harsh or changeable weather conditions, may not always be immediately evident to a visitor or newcomer to an area. To a summer visitor, the stormy winter weather of the North Atlantic that results in many island communities from Scotland to Norway being cut off for days at a time can be hard to imagine. Climate can affect how local people interact and their expectations of each other, and in harsh climates there may be tacit understandings of what neighbours are expected to do for each other, or even for strangers, which might not be common in more temperate regions. Travelling in the hot, dry conditions of the Australian desert regions or the freezing conditions of northern Canada can be difficult and hazardous for workers and clients alike.

Access to natural resources is usually the primary reason for settlement, as early settlers farmed, mined, quarried, fished, hunted and harvested an area. These resources may still be important, but in many places their significance has diminished. Some settlements owe their origins to their favourable location for transport links such as river crossings and mountain passes, or for vital supplies of water and food. Nevertheless, physical features alone do not provide a sufficient basis for understanding places. The ways in which individuals and communities have responded and adapted their lives to these geographical factors are key to understanding local contexts and, also, for identifying similarities or differences between places.

Physical obstacles to travel are often accompanied by relatively poor transport infrastructure, with poor roads and few other links such as railways and airfields. Rural areas differ greatly in the availability of public transportation, though generally people rely heavily upon private transport to get to school or work, to shops or to access other services. High rates of car ownership mean that rising costs such as fuel prices and associated taxes, licences and maintenance costs have hit rural people hardest, especially those in the more remote settlements. Rising costs may also limit people's capacity to use their vehicles as freely as they wish, and may impede access to services. In countries where the increasing marketisation of public services has resulted in reductions in public subsidy for transport in rural areas, more people are likely to need their own transport to access services that are becoming more distant from them. Some rural dwellers, especially the poor and those who may need social services the most, can be characterised as 'reluctant owners', and there is evidence that the rural poor spend a higher proportion of their limited incomes on transport than their urban counterparts (RDC,

1996; Cloke et al, 1997). This creates a self-reinforcing cycle, where the withdrawal of services increases the need for car ownership, which in turn further depletes already inadequate or marginal household resources and pushes people further into poverty.

Rural settlements vary widely with respect to how distant they are from larger towns and cities where services may be located. Generally the living standards of rural people in regard to indices of health, education, and social and material well-being diminish the further their settlement is away from larger population centres. The reasons for this are complex, and include such things as higher prices for goods and services, decreased or more distant social and support networks, and reduced opportunities for participation in the wider society through entertainment, recreation, and cultural and political activities. Reduced access to services is a major reason for lower living standards and numerous studies of health and social service usage have produced evidence of 'distance decay' (Cheers, 1998; Giarchi, 2007). That is, the further away potential users live from the point of service, the less likely they are to use services. This effect has been shown to operate even for emergency and critical services and has marked negative effects upon overall health outcomes (Deaville, 2001; Asthana et al, 2003). Social geographers have attempted to devise ways of measuring these effects and have identified several dimensions of relative access, such as distance from larger settlements, availability and regularity of public and private transport, travel costs and resources to meet them, road conditions, and geographic and climatic conditions. An example of this sort of approach can be seen in the work of Griffith in Australia who developed a comprehensive way of measuring relative access to services and its association with factors such as remoteness (Griffith, 1994). Distance decay is likely to be exacerbated by the increasing centralisation of services that is occurring in some rural areas (Mungall, 2005).

Settlement patterns have major implications for rural social work and human services. Service delivery is generally cheaper and access easier in more densely populated areas. Where smaller settlements are clustered around significant regional centres that are large enough to support a range of point-specific services, these can be supported by some outreach and satellite centres. In contrast, service delivery and access is more difficult in sparsely populated areas with dispersed settlement patterns, especially when efficient transport and road systems are non-existent or unreliable. These circumstances require different and innovative service models, such as satellite services and networks (see Chapters 6 and 7). Thus, settlement location and size are important variables influencing the nature of rural social work practice. In the case of some indigenous peoples, dispersed local populations present some interesting challenges. For instance, in Anmatjere in Central Australia, there is a settlement that has a central cluster of people, buildings, infrastructure and services as well as several 'camps' that community members move between.

In many places, access, especially to information about services, has been improved by technological advances. For instance, improvements in landline telephony have increased coverage, enhanced privacy through the reduction in party lines and, of course, provided access to cable and satellite services including television and the internet. The rapid adoption of mobile telephony in developed countries is now being mirrored in many less developed countries as set-up and sign-on costs have diminished, and in the most remote communities, improved satellite systems have also improved communications. Some rural people now have easier and more reliable access to information and services such as tertiary education, medical diagnosis and counselling services. Self-directed and telephone-assisted parenting training programmes have had some success in this regard (Sanders, 1999). These developments mean that people can now participate more effectively in geographically dispersed social, business and political networks, and this aspect may become increasingly significant for people who lack local peers, or whose capacity to engage with what is available is limited in some way, such as by their age or caring responsibilities. Nevertheless, the uptake of new technologies can be hindered if there are few local opportunities to access training in computer skills, and it remains the case that the poorest and most marginalised groups are the least likely to have access to these technologies (Bowden and Moseley, 2006). Furthermore, improvements in electronic communication may lead to reductions in local public and private services and, paradoxically, increased access costs for poorer people. Moreover, many remote areas still do not have mobile phone coverage or broadband internet access, or, if they do, have much higher costs for these services.

Demography

Straightforward comparisons of rural demographics between countries are hindered by the different classificatory systems used around the world, but it is evident that the distribution of populations between rural and urban areas varies within and between countries. For instance, the rural proportion of the overall population in the UK is estimated by the Office for National Statistics as being around 20% in England and around 36% in Wales (ONS, 2004). However, in the most rural localities the local proportions are much higher with around 57%, 70% and 36%, respectively, in the most rural areas of Scotland, Wales and England (Pugh, 2000). In contrast, US data for 2000 showed that just under 21% of the total population were living in rural areas (US Census Bureau, 2000), and a closer examination of these data in terms of most and least rural areas shows some surprising aspects of distributions and size. For example, while California has around 10% of its population in rural areas, the actual numbers living in the countryside are still substantial and exceed the total populations of several smaller states. Furthermore, across the US 'the proportion living outside any "organized" place (small town or village) is almost four times the number of rural people living in towns and villages of 2,500 or less' (Lohmann and Lohmann, 2005, p xv). Indeed, Ginsberg noted that over 55 million people in the US live in rural areas (1998). In Australia, around 14% of the population live in settlements of less than 1,000 inhabitants, with considerable variation between the states and territories (ABS, 2002).

During the 19th and 20th centuries most Western nations experienced long-term population movement from rural to urban areas as industrialisation progressively concentrated capital, production and employment in and around the major cities. In many countries, the mechanisation of farming and other primary industries, together with increasing specialisation in agricultural production, which reduced the demand for rural labour and eroded the viability of small farms, also contributed to the drift to urban areas (Perkin, 1969; Bodor et al, 2004). However, there were particular factors that operated uniquely in some places, and these are sometimes identified as 'push' and 'pull' factors. For example, in Ireland the potato famine greatly reduced the rural population and 'pushed' many into migration, as did the clearances of small croft farmers to make way for sheep in Scotland. On the other hand, the discovery of gold in California and Australia, like the abundance of fish off the coasts of north-east America and eastern Canada, were clearly important 'pull' factors.

In recent years there has been some reversal of the overall trend as the phenomenon of counter-urbanisation has been recorded in some places. This is most evident in the increase in populations in rural areas close to larger urban centres and also in popular locations rated for their quality of life (Champion, 1989; Allinson, 2003). Some writers have suggested that the recent interest in counter-urbanisation has overemphasised the trend and overshadowed some of the other powerful drivers for rural population change, such as economic and social decay, and young adults moving away to seek education and employment (Stockdale, 2004). Nevertheless, in Britain most rural areas that have sustained their populations owe this to internal migration (Buller et al, 2003; Hartwell et al, 2007). The most common reason for counter-urbanisation seems to be the preference of relatively affluent professional workers for rural living, but the development of greenfield sites for light industrial development in rural areas also plays a part. In the UK, the proportion of the rural workforce involved in manufacturing increased from 1971 to 1991 to the point where it was only slightly lower than the national average (Champion and Watkins, 1991). There has also been some inward movement into the more remote areas of Ireland, Scotland and Wales due to the growth in tourism and rural leisure activities, and also from people seeking alternative lifestyles. As we shall see later in Chapter 4, the movement of people into and out of settlements can alter the social dynamics of a community, and also bring new social problems to them. For instance, in Australia, from 1971 to 1991 the rural population increased faster than the urban rate (Castles, 1995). As with most rural indicators, these broad trends mask more detailed population movements. High-growth rural areas included retirement destinations, provincial cities with a broad economic base located in agricultural growth areas, other provincial cities distant from larger competing centres, the fringes of metropolitan areas that were previously rural settlements, and some inland townships serving as destinations for declining hinterland populations (Salt, 1992, 2001).

Overall population densities vary considerably between countries, as shown in Table 1.1.

Table 1.1: Population density

Country	People per square kilometre
Australia	2.6
Canada	3.2
New Zealand	14.9
United States of America	31
South Africa	39
Eire	59
France	110
Germany	232
United Kingdom	246
India	336

Note: Data are estimates for July 2005, taken from the *United Nations World Populations Prospects Report* (UN, 2004).

However, these overall density figures can be misleading as within particular countries there may be some surprising features when one looks at the more detailed patterns of settlement. Canada, one of the world's largest countries, has most of its population concentrated within 300 km of the US border (Bodor et al, 2004). Similarly, Australia, with one of the lowest densities overall, is one of the most urbanised countries in the world. Most of the population lives in three main coastal strip areas, with nearly two thirds of the population living in a major city (ABS, 2009), while the huge interior 'desert' region that encompasses around 80% of the total land mass remains very sparsely populated (Australian Government, 2001). Even within smaller countries there may be very significant variations. For example, while the local government district of Kensington and Chelsea in London has a density of 13,609 people per square kilometre, the least populated areas of Wales and Scotland have densities of 25 and 8, respectively (ONS, 2002).

Ethnicity and diversity

The ethnic composition and diversity of a settlement may have significant implications for its social dynamics, and, of course, upon local needs and social services. Generally, the range of ethnic diversity tends to be smaller in rural areas, and in many places the numbers of people from ethnic minority groups are also smaller than in more diverse urban areas, though the discovery of new natural resources such as oil and gold may lead to sudden and large inflows of more diverse migrant workers. In some countries like Australia, Canada and the US, indigenous people constitute significant proportions of local populations in some places. In Australia indigenous people are more likely to live in more rural and remote areas (Castles, 1995; Bodor et al, 2001). For instance, while around 90% of the overall Australian population live in 2.8% of the total land area, indigenous people are more sparsely distributed across the country. Approximately 50% of indigenous people live in cities and in areas surrounding urban areas, while the rest live in rural areas, with around 26% living in more remote places (HREOC, 2006). In more recent times, indigenous Australians have been returning to traditional homelands, to areas that have often lacked physical and social infrastructure such as water, power, transport facilities, and health, human and education services (OND, 1994). In Canada and the US, the patterns of settlement are more varied; while some First Nation people live on reservations adjacent to large urban areas like Phoenix or Montreal, others like the Navajo are spread over very large rural areas. One consequence of these differing distributions can be seen in some indicators of rural health and well-being that may reflect the extreme disadvantages suffered by indigenous people generally rather than any other intrinsic rural–urban differences. Every rural area of the UK has some minority ethnic population within it, though the proportions vary greatly from less than 1% to around 7% (Denham, and White, 1998; de Lima, 2004; Dobbs et al, 2006). For example, the 1991 Census indicated that there were over 33,000 people living in small villages and the wider countryside who self-identified as 'Afro-Caribbean' (Office of Population Censuses and Surveys, 1992), while Jay (1992) estimated that there were between 26,200 and 36,600 people who might be perceived as black living in south-west England. There are also others, such as Poles, Ukrainians, Germans and Italians, usually ex-service personnel or ex-prisoners of war and their families, who are often overlooked, and some, like gypsies and travellers, whose presence, insofar as it is noted, is almost always regarded as problematic and contentious (Cemlyn, 2000). While there are considerable differences in the experiences of minorities in rural areas within and between different countries, the most common experience is of relative disadvantage compared to other local ethnic groups, and comparative social and political 'invisibility' (Jay, 1992; de Lima, 1999; Dhalech, 1999; Avant, 2004; Chakraborti and Garland, 2004). They also suffer many disadvantages with respect to most social, economic, material and health indicators (further information can be found in Chapter 3). So, even when ethnic minorities constitute significant elements of the local population, their aspirations and problems may receive comparatively little social and political attention, and, consequently, welfare services remain ignorant of their needs or, alternatively, respond inadequately to them (Carlton-LaNey, 1998; Pugh, 2004a, 2004b).

Age structures and family patterns

Overall, rural population characteristics generally mirror national trends such as an ageing population, smaller families, increasing family diversity and higher divorce rates (Buller et al, 2003). Consequently, rural–urban demographic differences are often relatively small and certainly not as great as many people seem to believe, although as one might expect there are variations between countries and regions (Lowe and Speakman, 2006). Generally, the reduction of traditional forms of employment coupled with changing aspirations has led to young people and younger families leaving rural areas. This has resulted in a demographic shift towards an older population as people of working age and school-leavers seek employment and education elsewhere

(Salt, 1992; Bone et al, 1993; Rolley and Humphreys, 1993; Cheers and Yip, 1994; Buller et al, 2003; Hartwell et al, 2007). However, there are exceptions. For instance, in Australia there are proportionately more children under 17 years, fewer young adults from 17 to 25 years, especially women, more adults between 30 and 55 years, more married couples and nuclear families, and fewer divorced, separated and widowed people in rural than urban areas (Castles, 1995). In contrast, in the UK, there are also relatively fewer youth from 18 to 29 years and fewer young children up to four years in rural areas (Denham and White, 1998). In comparison with national figures, Australian indigenous settlements and populations have relatively more children, young people and families than other kinds of settlements, and fewer older people because of significantly reduced lifespans. Some indigenous settlements also have a preponderance of women for most of the year as the men seek employment elsewhere.

Economy

Changes in local, regional and international economies can have considerable social, political and material repercussions in rural settlements. This section outlines some of the most significant changes and their possible consequences for rural settlements in industrialised countries. Rees commenting on the British context made some points that are relevant to the rural economies of other industrialised nations:

> Changes in rural employment structures are central to any understanding of the reality of rural social life. On the one hand they reflect profound shifts in the nature and organisation of capitalist production and, more specifically the widely differing types of locality. On the other, employment changes themselves have resulted in radical developments in terms of rural class structures, gender divisions, the forms of political conflict occurring in rural areas and, indeed, of the complex processes by which 'rural cultures' are produced and reproduced. (Rees, 1984, p 27)

Social workers need to understand how these broader forces may shape the lives and the life chances of those whom they seek to help. For example, without an understanding of how changing employment patterns may impact upon traditional gender roles, workers might fail to see how these changes may influence the dynamics of social relationships within families. Furthermore, social workers who become involved in local social planning and development initiatives may need to have some appreciation of the economic situation and potential of the community. It should be noted, however, that while a strong local economy may play an important role in the sense of well-being in a community the relationship is by no means straightforward (Stedman et al, 2004).

Economic changes and their impact on employment and population

The relative importance of agriculture and other primary industries as a source of employment declined significantly in most industrialised countries during the 20th century. For example, in 1991 only 24% of Australian rural workers were employed directly in agriculture, forestry and fishing (Castles, 1995), while by 2000 in the US, less than 1% of the total workforce was involved in farm-related employment (Lohmann and Lohmann, 2005). There are many reasons for this decline in farming and farm employment, which vary across countries. They include:

- The continuing mechanisation of agriculture and the industrialisation of farm practices, which led to a decline in demand for rural labour as farms have become larger, more specialised and more efficient.
- Farms becoming more capital intensive requiring more borrowing and thus becoming more vulnerable to increases in interest rates, production costs and declining commodity prices.
- Increasing internationalisation of trade and the loss of export markets. For example, many Commonwealth countries like Australia and New Zealand and former colonies in the West Indies have lost the preferential access to markets that they once had. The impact of the GATT (General Agreement on Trade and Tariffs) and the agricultural policies of the European Union have also reduced the level of local or national protection that countries have been able to give to farmers.
- Local exigencies such as cattle and crop diseases, and climatic conditions. In Australia from the 1970s to the 1990s, for instance, prolonged droughts in conjunction with rising production costs, falling commodity prices and high debts forced many primary producers to leave the industry.
- Changing consumer preferences have reduced the demand for some agricultural products, for example, the consumption of sugar and meat.

These changes have led to depopulation in some rural areas. For instance, as the number of Australian farms declined from 200,000 in the mid-1960s to 120,000 in the mid-1990s (Cribb, 1994), many rural settlements and regions suffered serious population decline, especially those with less than 1,000 people in the more sparsely populated inland areas (Henshall Hansen Associates, 1988; Salt, 1992). Depopulation on this scale has considerable knock-on effects, reducing the viability of both private and public sector enterprises and services as local demand diminishes and the costs of delivery become concentrated upon a smaller population base. Governments and non-government organisations may withdraw infrastructure (for example, public transport) and services (for example, education, financial services, health provision). Politically, too, there can be significant effects, for as the power of the rural constituency diminishes it may become harder for rural people to persuade regional and national governments to address their concerns (Van der Ploeg et al, 2000). One Dutch employee of the Farm Union expressed his frustration at calls for greater diversification:

> Everybody seems to agree on these issues, but do they know what they are talking about? Can a farmer have 50 campsites on his farm? Everybody starts to protest if you want that, even though a farmer needs to have this scale in order to make it profitable.... It is essential to offer people real opportunities instead of talk, otherwise rural policy remains half-baked. (cited in Boonstra, 2006, p 309)

In the UK a survey undertaken by the National Federation of Women's Institutes (NFWI, 1999) found that nearly 500 post offices and 1,000 shops had closed in rural villages in the previous decade, with 30% of villages being left without a shop. Such withdrawals of service may then increase access costs, which tend to impact most upon people on low incomes. Population decline may also weaken community solidarity, and reduce the effectiveness of local social networks and support systems. The weakening of the local infrastructure may intensify the processes of decline, resulting in further community disintegration and impoverishment. Weak local economies typically result in increased unemployment, poverty, and health and other social problems. An Australian study of families displaced from their farms found that males were especially at risk of losing self-esteem and social standing and of dissatisfaction with their jobs, housing, social networks and social support systems (Bryant, 1991). Many countries have noted higher rates of stress and suicide among farmers and agricultural workers, and, in some areas, drug misuse and other problems such as family violence seem to have increased (Hawton et al, 1998; Kelly and Bunting, 1998).

These broad economic trends can be mitigated by local and national factors. For example, in the US subsidies for wheat farmers have ameliorated some of the economic and social impacts of market internationalisation. Similarly, while overall figures point to a decline in traditional forms of rural employment, more specific local data often show that agriculture and its associated industries such as food processing, packing and canning, abattoirs, livestock services, haulage, agricultural machinery and other farm supplies, as well as other primary extractive industries like forestry, quarrying and mining, remain important features of the local economy. Often, other forms of employment have become much more significant, such as work in health and welfare services, in the utility companies supplying water, electricity and telecommunications, on military bases (Boyle, 1995), and in other public services and government bodies.

Settlements with a narrow industry base, centred on a single industry such as mining, are more vulnerable to economic recession. Such places often have relatively homogeneous populations and flat social structures, with occupational communities of predominantly unskilled, semi-skilled and/or working-class people. Economic slumps in such places can result in a more widespread deprivation. Nonetheless, even in more diverse local economies, recession in particular industries can result in pockets of deprivation as their residents may still have relatively few alternative sources of employment, as their low incomes, scarce financial resources and low levels of education and qualifications reduce their occupational mobility. Their needs may be ignored or marginalised if the wider community is flourishing.

Some settlements have sustained their economies by exchanging one narrow economic base for another (for example, agriculture to aquaculture) or by broadening it a little by adding another industry. While such changes might bring short-term economic stability, they remain vulnerable to fluctuations in the long term, and the introduction of new industries usually brings other significant changes. Indeed, in some instances the economic shift brings with it significant social and political effects. Local people who lack the skills required by the new industry, and lack access to retraining opportunities, including those who cannot leave or do not wish to do so, may be at risk of long-term unemployment and poverty (Bone et al, 1993). While rapid economic growth may bring benefits to some local people, it can also have negative effects for others, especially the disadvantaged, through higher prices, increased rents, accommodation problems, transportation difficulties and a range of social problems (Bone et al, 1993). Furthermore, rapid population growth in boom towns frequently results in increasing crime rates as social norms and community cohesion are weakened (Freudenberg and Jones, 1991).

The changing nature of work

Settlements with fluctuating economies arising from changing external market conditions, or environmental influences such as droughts and floods, may rely upon a seasonal and casualised workforce. Sometimes these shifting demands for labour result in the extended employment of women, indigenous people and other ethnic minorities, and sometimes it is provided by itinerant and migrant workers. The long traditions of migrant labour, legal and illegal, in agriculture in the south-western states of the US continue. Hanson (2007) has estimated that around 24% of farm workers are illegal migrants and contends that they have filled an important gap in the US economy, where there is a shortage of unskilled labour. The use of migrant labour in rural areas is becoming more widespread as Mexican farm workers who were once largely employed in the southern Border States adjoining Mexico are now employed in farms and factories as far north as Minnesota. In 1999, just over a third (34%) of agriculture workers in the UK were seasonal or casual workers and the expansion of the European Union to include several former soviet bloc countries has seen large numbers of Polish, Lithuanian and Slovak workers moving into agricultural employment in the UK (TUC, 2004; Gilpin et al, 2006). A study of migrants from Eastern Europe working in Wales noted their 'apparent willingness to work long hours, tolerate poor conditions and work for low rates of pay in order to maximise their earnings' (Wales Rural Observatory, 2006a, p 10). It also found some evidence of poor and overcrowded housing conditions and a lack of access to health services, partly from lack of knowledge and partly from lack of interpreting services.

In areas where small farms predominate whose income cannot sustain a household, part-time farming and fishing combined with other part-time employment is commonplace. Studies in Australia, New Zealand and the UK have found that increasing engagement in 'pluriactivity' has accompanied declining farm incomes (Benediktsson et al, 1990; Le Heron et al, 1991; Denham and White, 1998). The sorts of off-farm activity used to earn additional income include contracting, ploughing, harvesting, hedge-cutting, haulage and landscaping, while on-farm activities include cottage industries such as crafts, eco-tourism, farm shops, golf courses, caravan sites, bed and breakfast and holiday rentals

(Le Heron et al, 1991; Pugh, 2000). Denham and White (1998) found that 'homeworking', or working for oneself in one's own home, often for very poor rates of pay, had increased in the UK. One consequence of this expanding range of employment is that the working hours of both men and women in rural areas of the UK and Australia have increased (Alston, 1991; Cloke et al, 1997).

Across Western Europe women have become an increasingly important part of the agricultural workforce, constituting 54% of part-time workers and 40% of the seasonal and casualised workforce (Whatmore et al, 1994; Little, 2002). The changing nature of work has had some interesting gendered effects, although rural sociologists are divided about their significance. The survival of many small farms has been dependent upon the continuance of some traditional patterns of social roles (Brandth, 2002; Price and Evans, 2006), but the involvement of women in non-traditional work and divisions of labour is thought to erode patriarchal gender relations in rural families (Pettersen and Solbakken, 1998; Little, 2002). Although a UK study (Chapman et al, 1998) found that rural women's wages were growing faster than those of rural men, and faster than those of women in urban areas, their average level of earnings was lower to begin with. The increasing use of computer-based technologies and the shift to employment in service industries has tended to increase the opportunities for women, and, generally, they have been quicker than men to seek further education and training to improve their incomes. These changes can have liberating effects for women, as this respondent to a researcher on family violence noted:

> When I knew it was crunch time, I knew I would be in a position where I would eventually have to support the kids ... and I hadn't been involved with the business much because he pushed me out. I did a [business] course and ... other courses and I built my skills up and ended up running that business in 12 months. I ... knew eventually he would pull the pin; and I just had to get as much as I could under my belt before he did.... He made it clear that if I left I would be dealing with it all on my own and I didn't have a profession.... I am glad I stayed for that 12–18 months because of what I did I walked straight into a job within two weeks and that made so much more difference and I felt straight away I can do this. (Wendt, 2005, p 216)

Political and structural dimensions

The national political contexts within which rural affairs are considered vary in two important dimensions. The first is the degree of autonomy allowed at local and regional levels. Even in regard to the Common Agricultural Policy (CAP) of the European Union it is evident that different countries have implemented these in different ways (Greer, 2005). Moreover, in Western European countries where the principle of subsidiarity is embodied in government, that is, the notion that central government should not do anything that can be better or more appropriately done at a lower level of government, or be done by some other body or by people for themselves, local government tends to have more independence in determining local policies and priorities (Chamberlayne et al, 1999). For instance, Hetherington and her colleagues (1997) noted that child protection practice in Belgium was much less centrally driven than it is in the UK, and that consequently social workers had much more professional autonomy in case decisions. Consequently, rural concerns may be more readily addressed in countries where federal or devolved systems of government permit considerable local independence at state or province level.

Regional development organisations can wield considerable power as distributors of funding for economic development and may play a critical role in sustaining the economic viability of rural settlements (Cheers et al, 2007; McDonagh et al, 2009). In many countries, these regional agencies are also important sources of funding for community and social development. For this reason, social workers and their agencies need to know how to access funding and contribute to their policies and plans. The economic and political marginality and general impoverishment of some regions may result in a compliant workforce and a rather uncritical consideration of planning proposals emanating from regional development organisations and local authorities (Cloke et al, 1997). This environment can be exploited by governments and private interests for unpopular, harmful and politically sensitive activities such as nuclear production, dumping of weapons and nuclear waste, high-pollution operations such as coal-driven power stations, chemical works, quarrying, refuse disposal and landfill. Such proposals frequently result in community divisions between those who stand to gain, such as potential employees and landowners, those who want to 'preserve' the countryside and those in the region's traditional primary industries (Murdoch and Marsden, 1994).

The second way in which political contexts vary is in the degree of general responsiveness of national governments and politicians to rural concerns. Halhead (2007) notes that in Scandinavia and many of the Accession States, village activism and rural movements are often spurred by a 'democratic deficit' as local people find governments unresponsive to their representations. Although the importance of agriculture to national economies has declined in most industrialised countries, there are still significant differences in its political significance within them. For instance, in France, where many city dwellers still have links to rural areas, there is considerable sympathy at a national level for the problems of French farmers, whereas in the UK, whose population became highly urbanised much earlier, most people have lost their local links and farming generally receives little sympathy beyond the particular catastrophes of diseases like foot and mouth or BSE ('mad cow disease'), which may threaten urban populations. Rural social policy has, historically, taken second place to agricultural policy though important political shifts are taking place in some countries. In Australia, Britain, New Zealand and North America, it has been suggested that a new politics of rurality is beginning to emerge in which the former dominance of agricultural interests is being replaced by a broader view of what matters in rural life (Woods, 2006). For example, debates about land use have become broader discussions that incorporate environmental issues, amenity value and social effects. Woods notes that:

> The provision of public services to rural areas has been returned to the political agenda by the combined efforts of neo-liberal state restructuring and an increasingly vocal rural population, including both in-migrants who expect urban levels of service and established residents concerned at the gradual dismantling of rural infrastructure. (Woods, 2006, p 584)

In many countries threats to rural services such as closures of schools and post offices are presented as threats to the very continuance of communities (Robinson, 1990) and in countries as diverse as Canada, Finland, Germany, Hungary, Ireland, Sweden and the US, there has been considerable resistance to such moves (Woods, 2006). Indeed, the comment made by one protester in Nebraska sums up the general feeling very well, 'Forcing the closure of schools in rural Nebraska will have a consistent result – towns and villages will become poorer, smaller, and less viable communities' (cited in Woods, 2006, p 588). In some instances resistance has been successful, such as in Canada where a plan to close some 5,000 rural post offices was halted by a vociferous public campaign.

This dimension of responsiveness to rural concerns can be examined at a very local level where it may be evident that some issues, like racism or family violence, are marginalised by local politicians who do not recognise, or do not wish to recognise, that these phenomena exist in their community. Indeed, the presumption that there are problems but 'not round here' obstructs many efforts to develop services, and as a result other groups who may be relatively 'invisible' among the more dispersed population of rural areas, such as those in poverty, people with mental health problems, and gay men and lesbians, may also find that their presence is not recognised either. For instance, in a study of the Barossa Valley area of South Australia, Wendt (2005) found that family violence was unacknowledged by many people, either because it challenged powerful networks based on gender, family, religion, business and socio-economic status, or, alternatively, was a threat to local cultural attitudes that ascribed great value to preserving the family unit and the family name.

The focus and the organisation of social welfare systems in many Western industrialised nations tend to disadvantage rural residents in a number of ways. The overriding emphasis on individuals and families rather than whole communities undervalues relationships between individual and community well-being, and also underplays the importance of building and sustaining the capacity of rural settlements to respond to local needs. Social issues are often isolated from their economic, social and cultural contexts and this is compounded by a categorical, or 'silo', approach to welfare provision. This is where the organisational fragmentation of policies and agencies makes it difficult to respond in a coordinated way to the interconnected nature of rural issues (Cheers, 1998). In highly centralised political systems, such as in Australia and the UK, urban-based central government departments, rather than local government and community-based organisations, hold sway over many crucial areas of policy and provision, and are often insensitive to rural concerns and lack understanding of rural contexts. This is often evident in the way in which ideas about what should be done or what works are implicitly based upon assumptions of an urban context (Pugh, 2006, 2007). A common problem in many countries is that funding for public services is often based upon general population statistics such as population density or size, without any consideration of the additional costs of rural services or the specific needs that communities might have.

The increasing influence of neo-liberal approaches to social policy and welfare provision, which espouse minimal government intervention in the market and human affairs more generally, has led to reduced social protection and welfare in many countries (Esping-Anderson, 1990; Mishra, 1999). The marketisation of social welfare arrangements, through strategies such as privatisation, the purchaser–provider split in provision, competitive tendering for public services and an emphasis upon regulation through performance indicators and output targets, has had deleterious effects generally and has also impacted negatively upon rural contexts (Walsh, 1995; Lane, 2000; Herbert-Cheshire, 2003; Warner and Hefetz, 2003). For example, competitive tendering may lead to increased administrative costs for agencies, which may be disproportionately burdensome for small local agencies. They risk closure or being taken over by larger national and state-wide organisations, with the result that local, contextual knowledge can be lost.

A review of the effects of market welfare approaches on rural service agencies in Australia by Cheers and Taylor (2005) found that:

- the viability of many small, settlement-based service agencies was being threatened, which decreased access and choice for users while at the same time increasing costs for them;
- additional yet unfunded costs were being borne by local agencies, who spent time doing administrative paperwork and positioning their organisations to ensure their survival, rather than ensuring that services meet local needs;
- small, local agencies were finding it increasingly difficult to compete with larger organisations and were amalgamating or forming alliances, or, alternatively, were being squeezed out or subsumed by these larger bodies;
- agencies were finding cooperation and service coordination more difficult as competitive tendering was creating friction, division and mistrust among them;
- the advocacy capacity of community-based groups had been curtailed by funding restrictions, the requirements of service-level agreements, reductions in funding to peak bodies and by government strictures;
- funding according to outcome-based benchmarks disadvantaged rural settlements as they were less responsive to local conditions.

Overall, local ownership and control over service development and delivery was being transferred to large, external organisations that were less well positioned to understand and relate to local needs, priorities and perspectives. Similarly, control over service models, structures and methods was being transferred to government funding bodies through increasing emphasis on vertical accountability of services at the expense of 'horizontal accountability' to local people and organisations (Martinez-Brawley, 2000). These trends had significantly reduced community and user participation in service development, management and delivery.

Community

While some aspects of settlement may be readily apparent, that is, their location, geography and so on, the presence of community may not be so easily noted. It should not be assumed that all settlements are necessarily single communities, although many are, this is not always the case and common exceptions include places where there:

- are indigenous and non-indigenous communities, or two ethnic communities living in the same place;
- is an indigenous community whose membership spans several settlements;
- is a community whose members move among several settlements or are partly nomadic, such as the Sami people in Northern Scandinavia.

The concept of community is often defined in terms of the sense of identity that people have of being bound together by association, shared relationships and common interests or culture. However, social scientists have had enduring debates about the reality or the merits of the concept (Delanty, 2003), partly because, as Newby states:

> Social scientists who seek to analyse the concept of community therefore have to wade through thickets of sentiment and emotion ... attempts to define the term have been fraught with difficulty, not least, one suspects, because almost any definition will do violence to a number of deeply held beliefs about its essential qualities. (Newby, 1994, p xi)

The history of these debates reveals some interesting shifts in the ways that communities are presented and studied (Charles and Davies, 2005). Many early studies of rural communities tended to stress the internal stability and cohesiveness of local life and documented the ways in which this was being changed and threatened by the wider world.

Some of these studies were subsequently criticised for being partial and highly subjective accounts that tended to idealise rural communities and ignored some of the real divisions and problems that existed within them. Nonetheless, this theme of the decline of community has a long history and can still be found in some accounts today despite the fact that often it is 'sustainable only if selective, romanticised views of the past are adopted' (Crow and Allan, 1994, p 3).

This raises an interesting question as to why this occurs. The most immediate possibility is that the image that an outsider has of a community may be a product of her or his expectations and so is prone to presumptive bias. Alternatively, what is learned about a community from studying it and talking with its members may not be a completely accurate account of what life is actually like within it. Researchers have often recognised that their presence has its own effects and that this might limit their access to some aspects of community life, thus most have tried hard to build trust and acceptance with local people. However, the problem may be a more fundamental one, which is that what people tell themselves and others about their community is not always a social reality simply because the notion of community itself serves vitally important functions for them. These beliefs may not always be accurate in terms of the social practices that people actually undertake, but they have an important symbolic role. For example, the notion that some people belong to a community while others remain outsiders is often a significant factor in maintaining a sense of internal cohesion, membership and belonging (Cohen, 1982). As we shall see in Chapter 2, these divisions may be enduring or relatively short-lived but can be an important social dynamic in small communities, particularly when they become organised around language, ethnicity, religion or class. Thus, community may be a socially constructed notion that may not entirely reflect local life, but nonetheless provides important information about the nature, history and self-perceptions of local people.

This way of looking at communities can help social workers to better understand the important role that narratives play in local life and in constructing their community (Bridger et al, 2001; Cheers et al, 2003). Such narratives can construct and preserve a heritage and may also be used to mobilise a community to defend itself against recurring threats, or to react to new circumstances. For instance, one study in a small country town identified a heritage narrative that community leaders used to motivate residents to work together to establish a community bank in response to the loss of commercial banking services (Kennedy, 2004). Several decades earlier, the community had saved the town from flooding by working together to build banks of sandbags, and this story was used metaphorically to mobilise support for a new sort of 'bank'. Of course, not all narratives originate within the community. It is interesting to note that many countries that followed policies of de-institutionalisation did so with some implicit and somewhat idealised assumptions that communities could provide care (Williams, 1989). In many cases, these were often erroneous and sexist assumptions about the capacity of families to provide such care, and many writers have noted that the majority of informal care is in fact provided by women, who pay a high price for their efforts, as the very fact of being a carer predisposes them to increased chances of ill health, poverty and isolation (Brown and Smith, 1993; Hooyman and Gonyea, 1995). Thus, shifting the locus of care also shifted the burden from the state to families and to women in particular (Bulmer, 1987). Similarly, in Canada, the assumptions that underpin some developments in restorative justice and 'sentencing circles' in indigenous communities have been criticised for failing to take account of the lack of social justice that prevails within them. The very conditions that lead to high rates of crime in some communities, especially against women and children, also undermine the community stability and social practices that would secure its success (Dickson-Gilmore and La Prairie, 2005).

A social constructionist approach can also help social workers understand why there may be disjunctions between what a community thinks and says about itself, and what exists and how people behave. For example, a youth needs study in a popular Australian tourist destination (Bone et al, 1993) identified a dominant narrative promulgated by some community leaders that local institutions such as sports clubs, churches, families and youth clubs were meeting the needs of youth. A secondary narrative was that the youth who slipped through this net were primarily unemployed transients from southern cities. However, the researchers found that most of the unemployed, unoccupied youth were actually local people. These findings subverted the dominant narrative and were resisted by local government. Consequently, a development group was formed and this mobilised a latent narrative, which was that ultimately youth problems were a matter for local community organisations and not the council, and over the subsequent two years it secured more than AU $2 million for youth facilities and services.

In recent years, most studies of community have sought to avoid the problems of selectivity and romanticisation and have attempted to present a more complex and nuanced picture about how communities work, and in which the conflicts and divisions that exist within the community are identified and analysed. For example, Jedrej and Nuttall in a study of rural repopulation in Scotland noted how 'Local people may also feel resentment towards incomers who involve themselves in tourism development and are therefore perceived to be exploiting a locality' (1996, p 167). They also show how the term 'white settler', which was formerly used in the colonial context of the British Empire in Africa and Asia, has come to be used pejoratively of urban incomers, and the English in particular.

There has also been a revival of interest in studying communities empirically as social entities based upon social networks and relationships (Charles and Davies, 2005). What is most interesting about many of these studies is that despite the frequent bemoaning of the decline of community, they often show that while there have been changes, most notably in the decline in occupational communities revolving around a particular workplace or industry, durable and significant networks of kinship, belonging and association remain active in many places (Crow and Allan, 1994). Although academics will continue to debate the concept of community, there is little doubt from their research that many rural people still see it as having meaning, often expressing it in terms of family, common interests, a shared sense of belonging and a common interest in the well-being and development of the community as a whole (Cheers et al, 2007). Some studies that have examined the social practices that constitute communities have concluded that much of this is undertaken by women, who operate patterns of mutual support and reciprocity to support and protect their families. For instance, a study of child protection reporting in rural Australia found that while men might play a part in noting the possibility of abuse, women were most often involved in the actual reports to child protection agencies (Manning and Cheers, 1995).

Finally, a number of writers have attempted to identify the ways in which people in a place interact with the wider society. Within the literature on rural communities and rural social work, much use has been made of the concepts of vertical and horizontal ties between people, communities and organisations (Warren, 1963; Martinez-Brawley, 2000). Vertical links exist between a community and the local and state governments, welfare organisations and other government-funded bodies that contribute to its social and economic well-being and development. They provide access to information about social, economic and political change beyond the community and to external resources, expertise, power and decision-making. Vertical links can bring external resources into a community, which, in turn, can help to revitalise local organisations and stimulate the commitment of local people to community and economic development (Luloff and

Wilkinson, 1979; Martin and Wilkinson, 1984; Wilkinson, 1989, 1991). Indeed, a review of rural development projects in several countries concluded that the state is a necessary partner because it provides resources and expertise, and sets the policy and regulatory framework within which the non-government sector must operate (Midgley et al, 1986). In contrast, horizontal links within communities provide mutual support, social cohesion and integration, energy and resources, which contribute to effective community and social fields and social well-being. Some observers argue that horizontal ties in many communities have been weakened over recent decades by increasingly dominant vertical ties as small communities become more integrated into national and global social trends and phenomena (MacPherson, 1994; Sher and Sher, 1994).

Conclusion

In this chapter we have introduced different dimensions of the geographic, demographic, economic, structural and social contexts of rural settlements. This has involved a degree of generalisation across rural contexts as we recognise that it is not possible to analyse each dimension in depth, or to address the potential diversity of local factors that operate within them. So, three concluding points arise from these inevitable limitations:

- First, the diversity of rural settlements and communities both across and within countries means that rural social workers and their agencies should always seek to develop their own analyses of local contexts. For instance, while general statistics concerning demographic features of the population may be useful for broad outline service planning and development, there is no substitute for detailed analysis of the particular locality, which can sometimes reveal significant variations from the general picture.
- Second, rural contexts are not fossilised and fixed entities, they are subject to changes from within and without their boundaries, and should be properly viewed as dynamic places. As in urban areas, change is always present though its effects may not always be recognised or fully acknowledged locally or externally. Rural social workers, however, are often well-placed to observe the impact of social and economic forces upon the lives of those whom they serve, and their own embeddedness and appreciation of the locality should help them to avoid the error of decontextualisation where personal

problems may be mistakenly perceived as having individual origins and individualised solutions.

- Third, a sophisticated and informed appreciation of local context frequently leads social workers to recognise that they cannot provide their services in isolation from other agencies, organisations and decision-making bodies. In many instances, they need the support, understanding or resources of these other actors to successfully achieve their objectives. Often the decisions that have the widest ramifications for rural settlements and their people are not made in welfare agencies, but in community and business fields such as local government, development organisations and chambers of commerce. Thus, social workers and their agencies should try to ensure that their professional knowledge of local social issues is included in decision-making in all sectors, and that local planning responds to the needs of those whose interests may be marginalised socially and politically.

TWO

The social dynamics of small communities

Introduction

The social dynamics of life in small communities impact upon people's lives, their problems and their understandings of their difficulties, as well as their views about how these might be best addressed. Social work in rural communities may not be completely distinctive from practice in urban areas, such as housing projects or encapsulated 'urban villages' (Meert, 2000). However, because small communities are where most rural work takes place, these social dynamics are likely to be more frequently encountered, which is why workers in rural areas need to develop an awareness of these factors and their potential significance.

There have been many sociological and ethnographic studies of small rural communities, and as we noted in regard to different fashions in community studies in Chapter 1, their focus has shifted over the years from largely descriptive accounts through to more critical examinations of how communities work (Crow and Allan, 1994). Most of these studies are single case studies that provide insights into the dynamics of the particular communities studied, but rarely permit well-supported generalisation to other settings. Some of the work included in this chapter is cited because it identifies and illuminates particular social dynamics whose relevance to other settings has, inevitably, to be judged by the reader.

Perhaps one of the most common dynamics in small communities lies in the tension between the comparatively high social visibility and social knowledge that people have of each other, and the need to sustain everyday social life and avoid divisive or unmanageable conflict. Cohen contends that:

> Because people know a great deal about each other ... [they] have to behave in particular ways – to conceal certain things, to restrain others. They have to accord with the conventions of intimate society and, at the same time, they have to resist

the tensions inherent in the too-close existence of small-scale society. (Cohen, 1982, p 11)

He points out that if social order and stability are to be preserved individuals must, through a variety of mechanisms, 'somehow subordinate individuality to communality' (1982, p 11). So for example, in the Scottish island community that he studied, which had an 'equalitarian' culture, individual assertiveness was generally unwelcome. He noted that, 'Even in the closest social association, relations of inferiority and superiority are rarely expressed, although they may well be tacitly recognised' (1982, p 11). Of course, in communities with different cultures, different perceptions will exist in regard to particular aspects of behaviour and social comportment. For example, in many small communities, and often in indigenous communities, the avoidance of shame is a powerful factor in maintaining compliance with normative expectations. Nevertheless, one of the most commonly noted features of small communities seems to be the more personalised basis of formal relationships between social workers and clients (Ellen Walsh, 1989; Ginsberg, 1998; Galbreath, 2005). This largely arises from the increased likelihood of contact with each other as they go about their ordinary lives outside of the professional encounter. This may be reinforced by a normative expectation that interpersonal relationships should be conducted in a friendly and less formalised manner.

In this chapter, we introduce some of the key factors that operate in small communities and show why social workers might need to develop some understanding of gender roles, ideas of belonging and place, gossip, and social visibility and confidentiality. The latter part of the chapter looks at some of the important challenges facing workers who live and work within small communities and draws on previously published work on dual relationships (Pugh, 2007a).

Gender roles

Research into gender roles in rural areas reveals a tendency towards some rather traditional ideas and practices (Campbell et al, 2006). Little (2003), in an interesting paper on the relationship between gendered identities and the construction of rurality, argues that rural places are characterised by highly conventional ideas. For example, masculine and feminine identities in rural areas are seen to have some enduring characteristics, with rural men being assumed to be 'fit, strong, powerful and healthy' (2003, p 405), while their wives are expected to be 'level headed, practical, sensible and loyal' (2003, p 412). Little, like many other writers, argues that these gendered identities play an important role in sustaining rural communities, and, particularly, in sustaining family farming (Prugl, 2004; Heather et al, 2005). Indeed, Price and Evans (2006) contend that the survival of small family farms at a time when divorce rates are so high depends, first, upon farming men making a good choice of partner, and, second, upon the avoidance or suppression of women's legal rights. They argue that not only do rural women keep the farm going with their direct labour and paid work outside of the farm, but they are also expected to be financially silent partners. That is, not to extract their share of the funds during the marriage, or even at its dissolution if it should break down. Thus, they may feel themselves to be locked into the marriage because of these financial considerations, which may include consideration of their children's inheritance too. Price and Evans (2006) contend that at a time when many young farm women seem to be rejecting the traditional patrilineal assumptions of inheritance and family farming, the suitability of a future wife becomes a pressing issue, especially when the survival of the family business could be threatened by marital breakdown. For instance, one embittered Welsh farmer stated: 'Too many women coming into farming are gold diggers now.... She was my wife, but she had no right to anything from the farm. I've passed it on to my sons. She would have ruined me if she could' (Price and Evans, 2006, p 291). Therefore, to sustain farming, it is not enough for farmers to find a wife, they must find the 'right' sort of wife.

Little contends that farm women not only sustain the rural household and reproduce the family, but also control the 'disorganised heterosexuality of the bachelor farmers' (Little, 2003, p 414), in the sense of organising and socialising these men, men who to outsiders may appear uncouth and unsophisticated. One young woman said of such a farmer:

> He's a lovely bloke, but if you could see the way he lives....
> He lives with his mum and dad. Mum doesn't really have her teeth in for much of the time and his dad I just couldn't understand because he was so broad Yorkshire ... the kitchen has a cold tap in it and a stone trough like a horse's drinking trough which is their sink. He lives in the middle of nowhere, so maybe it's fair enough that he's got these entrenched attitudes. (Little, 2003, p 413)

Heather and her colleagues (2005) writing of rural Alberta in Canada contend that while economic instability in farming has affected both men and women, its effects upon women are more pronounced, as they are more likely to become more involved in direct labour upon the farm, or to seek other forms of income and employment. They note that the women in their study accepted some aspects of traditional conceptions of their role, while resisting others:

> They were proud of their ability to manage a heavy workload and of their contribution to farm and community, but perceived their efforts as unrecognised. They dreamed of having more time to themselves. They were aware of the impact that their workload had on their health, but regarded this as a temporary situation. When the farm was struggling to survive, the community was also threatened, and it was the caregiver, the woman, who took on the additional work. (Heather et al, 2005, p 91)

Alston (2003), in research into women's roles in rural Australia, noted the prevalence of gendering in the organisational culture of agricultural associations, which was often buttressed by sexist remarks. The result was that women were seen in very stereotypical ways and their efforts trivialised or overlooked. Prugl (2004), in a review of women's role and position in German agriculture, suggests that the modernisation of family farming has resulted in a loss of power and status for women, and that this is mirrored in the increasingly lengthy hours that they work. Her point is that as women have become needed as a flexible workforce they have lost control of their work and their own income. However, the larger the farm, the less likely women were to play a part in direct labour upon it. Nonetheless, their contribution to farm incomes through the provision of other services, such as farm holidays, food, riding lessons, guided tours and so on, has increased. Prugl concludes that gender continues to be a key regulatory factor in the division of labour, power and income.

If rural areas are perceived by young women as restrictive in terms of personal opportunity then unsurprisingly they may seek opportunities elsewhere. Indeed, there is evidence from a number of countries that men are less likely than women to move away from their home area (Kasimis et al, 2003), and that those who stay tend to be less well qualified and have lower social mobility than women who migrate (Dahlstrom, 1996; Ní Laoire, 2001). The results of these differential patterns of attainment and migration can be seen in areas where there is a mismatch between the numbers of men and women, and consequent difficulties for local men seeking a partner. In rural areas experiencing depopulation there are often higher rates of unmarried men relative to unmarried women over the age of 45 years (Haase, 1999).

Much research suggests that for men, the struggle to survive in farming is, as Ní Laoire states, 'a struggle to retain one's identity as a man' (2001, p 232). Reviewing a range of studies, she contends 'that it is the conjunction of rural restructuring processes and the challenges to the traditional masculine order that makes the situation of some rural men so precarious' (2001, p 233). Australian and Japanese studies (Yamamoto, 1992; Burnley, 1995; Baume and Clinton, 1997) also indicate that rural men are more likely to commit suicide. Similarly, a US study in Alabama also noted that rurality was strongly linked to suicide rates (Zekeri and Wilkinson, 1995). It appears that relatively socially isolated rural men, whose social and economic position may be under threat because of farm problems, unemployment and the lack of other opportunities, and who also feel powerless in other regards, perhaps in the face of increasing bureaucracy from government agencies, may be the most vulnerable to feelings of hopelessness and, thus, be at risk of suicide. There is also some evidence that, for men, being married is protective of suicide risk (Ní Laoire, 2001). Some idea of the sense of beleaguerment felt by farmers in depopulating areas was evident in the statement made by one young Irish farmer who said 'We're the last generation here. There will only be trees after us' (Ní Laoire, 2001, p 228). The point is that losing a farm is not simply losing a job, it can mean leaving a way of life, losing a home and perhaps facing the end of a family tradition. The increasing vulnerability of farming is evident in many countries, and research in Norway showed that there was no longer an automatic assumption of sons following their fathers in working the farm, as there had been a shift from the idea of inheritance as a duty, to inheritance as a choice (Villa, 1999).

Place and belonging

'Place' refers both to the geographical sense of an area that people hold in their minds and to the social territory that exists within that physical location. Newcomers to rural areas may be surprised by the extent to which local people have a much larger sense of 'home' territory, often extending far beyond the immediate boundaries of their settlement. Place:

> is a subjective phenomenon which varies according to individual perceptions of space, boundaries, insiders and outsiders, social roles, and social networks. The idea of place

> extends from ideas about what is 'home' and what it should look like, through to ideas about social significance, that is, the relative significance of different people in a person's social landscape. (Pugh, 2000, p 26)

Cohen (1982) suggests that belonging to a place or locality is typically mediated through networks of kinship, neighbourhood, friendship, occupation and belief. Indeed, in many small communities the ideas that people have about the 'place' they live in are often strongly linked to their ideas about their own identity and social position, and to those that they have about other people. This is often expressed most clearly when distinctions are made between insiders and outsiders, or between locals and incomers in an area. However, it is a mistake to assume that such distinctions are permanent and fixed, as the boundaries of identity and acceptance may shift rapidly, or may be drawn differently according to circumstances. For example, in Labrador in Canada, Plaice observed how the descendants of mixed Indian, Inuit and European people shifted the way in which they identify themselves as native or non-indigenous 'white' Canadians according to the circumstances (1990).

In their Scottish study Jedrej and Nuttall (1996) found that although everyone seemed to agree that there were 'locals' and 'incomers', they did not agree about who they were, nor did they necessarily share common perceptions of the significance of the distinction. For example, they had no common idea of what forms of local culture were potentially threatened by the presence of incomers. In contrast, Emmett (1964) in her study of a Welsh village found that local people who were predominantly Welsh-speaking commonly saw monoglot English incomers as a threat to their language and culture, and this view continues in some places. Besides this immediate perception of cultural diminution, it is often the case that when indigenous or older languages are supplanted by newer ones, the significance of place names becomes diminished and, thus, the personal, historical and cultural meaning associated with places is eroded (Nuttall, 1992). While conflicts between locals and incomers over such things as local development and land use are commonly noted, there are instances where these distinctions are made, but the attitude towards the incomers is positive. This happens, for instance, when their arrival, and subsequent consumption or contribution, helps to sustain local services, such as shops, schools and health care facilities.

Jedrej and Nuttall note that 'the vocabulary of "locals" and "incomers" is a complex and deeply embedded metaphor providing the terms in which people express and give meaning to the experiences which constitute their lives' (1996, p 12). They also identify how a sense of place can be 'amplified in the presence of strangers' (1996, p 7), but note that these powerful metaphors of belonging and non-belonging are not necessarily related to the empirical facts of population. They cite Lumb's work, (1982) noting that 'incomers may be numerically significant but socially insignificant, or numerically insignificant but socially significant' (1996 p 6), and that, furthermore, the simplistic notion of a homogeneous resident population receiving differentiated incomers was in many cases untenable. For example, Lumb had found that among the people who were perceived as 'locals', three quarters of them had lived in other places at some point in their lives. Where such distinctions of belonging are made it is commonplace to find incomers being castigated for their lack of knowledge or the crassness of their social behaviour, especially in regard to the subtleties of local gossip and social networks. This sense of cultural incompetence is manifest in the statement made by one rural dweller in Wales that incomers:

> don't know how to behave. They drive the wrong cars, put up the wrong curtains, and create pretty front gardens that just don't fit in. In the village they don't know how to greet people, how to have a real conversation. Some of them want nothing to do with us, and others would like to be part of the community, but only if they can be in charge of what goes on. They just don't know how to belong, even when they try very hard to fit in. (Cloke et al, 1997, p 150)

Resentment, as we shall see in Chapter 3, may be the direct result of colonising behaviour, especially when indigenous inhabitants become marginalised or directly excluded by more powerful incomers. Even the language of resistance to colonisation may be adopted in other settings, for example, as we noted in Chapter 1, in Scotland the term 'white settler' has been used to derogate English settlers.

The assumption of a simple dichotomy of membership/non-membership in rural communities may oversimplify a more complex reality, and may also miss other significant divisions within a community, such as those of kinship, class, occupation and religion. The problem with trying to make a simple distinction between insiders and outsiders is that it reduces the complexity of social location to a simple dichotomy of 'in' or 'out'. But this may not be how most people experience their social situation in rural communities, where the lived experience may be of a much more fluid and contingent set of possibilities. Fitting in is not just an external process applied to individuals, it also has a subjective element too. It is a process that takes place in the mind of the incomer, as their self-identification changes. Burnett describes this as a negotiated process of belonging, meaning that acceptance and belonging are not simply established through interactions with other people, they are also actively constructed internally in a person's self-consciousness. For example, 'I just call myself local now. I don't feel like an incomer any more. I did at first, but not any more ... now I feel part of the community here' (Burnett, 1996, p 26). Most incomers to rural communities are aware of their status and realise that if they wish to be accepted they have some work to do. For example, Robinson and Gardner (2006) report the experience of a Portuguese woman, who decided that she needed to learn some Welsh to avoid being excluded. Burnett (1996) also suggests that women are more conscious of the need to develop a deeper knowledge of the community and usually work hard to acquire this. However, it should be noted that incomers may choose not to integrate (Burnett, 1996). Interestingly, a UK study of social housing in rural areas found that many newcomers 'were not particularly interested in fitting in with village community life, but instead focused on their own social networks, such as family and friends, that may be geographically dispersed' (Bevan et al, 2001, cited in Chakraborti and Garland, 2004, p 135).

Belonging is never a permanent accomplishment that can simply and solely derive from lengthy local residence or kinship. Its status is contingent, being dependent upon conduct and upon the external circumstances that surround individuals. Disruptive or non-conforming behaviour can lead to a change of status, while changes in the external environment can problematise the position of previously secure individuals. For example, a member of a visible ethnic minority who has previously found themselves accepted or tolerated may find that their position becomes less secure as the political currents of racism in the wider society may be expressed in local fears about increasing numbers of outsiders.

Frankenberg (1957), in a classic study of a small community, observed that incomers were often used to undertake roles that might be divisive if undertaken by a more established local resident, for example, leading local resistance to an unwanted planning application. This observation has been confirmed in a number of other studies which note how this strategy might serve useful functions (Emmett, 1964; Cohen, 1982; Jedrej and Nuttall, 1996). It may be a safe way of promoting change within the community, for the blame can be attributed to the outsider if things go wrong. Jedrej and Nuttall also note that incomers, lacking intimate knowledge of others in the community, often have little choice but to:

> treat everyone equally. This is an attribute which residents find very useful in matters affecting those interests which they do hold in common (water, roads, bus stops, sewage etc ...) and incomers will soon find themselves on Community Councils, School Boards, District Councils and the like, representing the community.... Incomers may find this flattering and presume that it is indicative of their integration into the 'community', or, less generously, may talk about the 'apathetic locals', when actually their worth lies in their ambivalent position in so far as they are residents in the settlement but yet are also not part of 'the community'. (Jedrej and Nuttall, 1996, pp 99–100)

As one incomer ruefully noted, 'You think you're doing something for the community, but you just end up being criticised and put down all the time' (Jedrej and Nuttall, 1996, p 178).

The significance of understanding place and belonging is not simply relevant to how we understand the behaviour of people towards each other in small communities, it is also relevant to understanding the social position of social workers. This can be seen in the attempts made by many clients in rural areas to 'place' the worker, that is, to get some idea of who the worker is in relation to other people in their community. Thus, workers may be expected to answer questions or provide information about themselves that would rarely be sought in an urban setting. This might include information about local links, previous experience, family background and local knowledge, which may then be used to 'check out' the worker, to establish what other people think of him or her and, crucially, to decide whether, and to what degree, to engage with the worker. Zur (2006) sees self-disclosure, whether deliberate or unintentional, as an inevitable part of working in rural communities. He argues that familiarity in rural communities plays an important role in establishing trust and the personalised assessment of the worker may be more important than professional credentials or formal status in establishing an effective working relationship. However, judgements may also be based upon other aspects of social workers' activities, so that when they engage with or act as advocates for unpopular causes or people, such as substance abusers, ethnic minorities, travellers and gypsies, their own social position may become a reflection of the status of those whom they seek to help.

Gossip and local talk

Most accounts of rural life make some reference to talk and gossip in small communities, but rarely analyse its functions. Typically gossip is presented as a wholly negative feature indicative of backbiting and division within a community, and it is the case that those whose position in a community may be marginal or 'different' in some way, frequently report their experience of gossip as an oppressive phenomenon. Our view is that local talk and gossip should be recognised as important channels of information by which people learn what might be going on in their community. However, gossip certainly makes rural lives more visible for, as Parr and her colleagues note, 'it extends the observant gaze' (2002, p 3) of the small community and facilitates the sharing of information among people who want to know what is happening within it.

Gossip by its nature is often shared in private domains, such as within the home or in telephone conversations, but it is also shared within more public venues, such as the local market, bar or pub, church, community centre or workplace. For those who feel vulnerable in some way, knowledge of these places and the talk that goes on within them can create anxiety about what is being said, and may inhibit them from entering, or even passing by, such places. One man, speaking of the Highlands of Scotland described the area as 'the valley of the twitching curtains' (Parr et al, 2002, p 4). Parr and her colleagues note that while gossip is not always intended to be negative, as some people do show concern for others, there is nonetheless 'a strong perception that community gossip leads to exclusionary social actions and practices' (Parr et al, 2002, p 9). However, this is a rather limited view of what could be seen as an essential or necessary phenomenon, as gossip may also have a crucial role in the avoidance and resolution of conflict in small communities, where relationships need to be sustained over time, and where it may be difficult or undesirable for people to speak too freely, or to directly confront others with criticism or dissent:

> The indirect transmission of one's opinions or concerns via other people may be a more effective way of communicating in situations of potential conflict without the risks of direct contradiction or loss of face. Furthermore, apart from its cathartic effects in terms of the opportunity to ventilate one's frustrations, the act of telling a third party provides a way of testing one's views and offers the other person the opportunity to 'shape' the dialogue. Gossip in rural

communities like gossip in any community, offers the opportunity for people to say something and to see if it has any effect on the behaviour of others without necessarily having to 'own' it. (Pugh, 2000, p 32)

Emmett (1964) thought that gossip was the currency of social relationships, which could be traded and swapped. She found that the villagers in her study had developed elaborate strategies for maximising their own local knowledge. In anything but the most intimate conversation, she found that villagers would almost always reply to a direct question with the response 'I don't know'. 'Not knowing' was a strategy that had many uses, it could be used to 'keep face' by pretending not to know information that might be potentially embarrassing or shameful. For example, Emmett noted that illegitimate children were often reared by their maternal grandmothers and were brought up to think of the grandmother as their mother and their true mother as their sister. While other people in the community would know the true origins, nevertheless, this sort of arrangement, or fiction, was accepted and supported. So, while the facts of the legitimacy were widely known, the community generally acted as if this were not the case. For instance, in conversation the ages of children or the date of a marriage might only be vaguely stated, and so this form of 'not knowing' allowed people in the village to live with their 'transgressions'. People who were involved in irregular behaviour might be informally teased about it, but would not necessarily be reproached. Not knowing was a formal politeness, but was also a useful strategy for finding out what others might know, as well as a strategy for doing business. For example, a man might pretend not to be interested in a deal, or seem to be unaware of current prices, but then at a crucial point in the discussion could suddenly reveal his interest or knowledge in such a way as to give him a bargaining advantage to undercut or reduce the price.

Although gossip generally may not be as widespread and pervasive as people assume, it nonetheless remains a powerful phenomenon in that many people will act as if it were so (Burnett, 1996). There is little doubt that it has a normative function in shaping behaviour and plays a complex role in revealing events and allowing evaluative comment and judgement, but surprisingly little has been written as to how social workers might understand and engage with local talk and gossip. Green and Mason, in regard to the possibility of hearing unsolicited information about people, state that 'Rural welfare workers must make professional judgements about this, or create some barriers to receiving and using such information' (2002, p 39), but offer little advice as to how these things might be done. Should our judgements about unsolicited information be made on the basis of the reliability of the informant or some consideration of their motives, or should they involve some weighing of the risks and benefits to other people? If we cut ourselves off from local networks we may be perceived as distant, unfriendly and remote. An inquiry into what had gone wrong when a number of children on the remote Scottish island of Orkney were removed from their homes into public care heard from one witness that:

> It is highly desirable that they [social workers] should both know the community, its character, traditions and customs and be known by those whom they are there to serve. The trust and confidence which each should have in the other cannot be effectively secured if the social worker appears as a remote occasional visitor who does not in any sense belong to the area. (Clyde, 1992, p 340)

In one Australian case, a woman who was being labelled as a 'druggie' was in danger of losing a custody battle with her ex-husband because of erroneous perceptions about her and her new partner. When the social worker involved heard the rumours he was unable to contact the woman to see what she wanted to do, but decided to quash the local rumours anyway. Later, when she learned of his intervention, the woman thanked him (Cheers, 1998). Another example of responding to gossip was reported by Turbett (cited in Pugh, 2006) where the erratic behaviour of a mother with epilepsy who had recently moved into the community was mistakenly perceived by some locals as being evidence of drug misuse. This perception skewed their response to both her and her family, who were seen as incomers with no local connections and undeserving of local housing or services. Although the woman and her family did not realise what was being said, local workers heard the rumours, and thought that if she was introduced to a local mental health support group, other people in the community would soon begin to understand her situation and learn of her links to the locality, and the hostility would diminish. She joined the local service user group and local perceptions quickly became much more sympathetic and helpful towards her. In both these examples, workers had to consider how best to respond to harmful gossip and whether they should adhere to strict notions of confidentiality. Martinez-Brawley is unequivocal in stating that 'the social worker has an ethical responsibility ... to correct misinformation in the social environment that might adversely affect the client' (2000, p 280). While the content of the gossip in both these cases was negative and stigmatising, the fact of its existence alerted social workers to what was happening. In the first case, the worker deliberately breached confidentiality, in the second, informed by their understanding of social dynamics, they circumvented the need to do so.

In other circumstances, gossip may be explicitly considered for its protective functions in terms of alerting workers to people at risk. For instance, during some research into child protection registrations, one worker in a predominantly rural area in reply to a question as to whether he agreed with the decision to deregister a child said that he did not, but added that it did not really matter because 'everyone knows about her anyway', meaning that he thought there was little chance that any further indications of risk would go unnoticed and unreported (Pugh, 2006). Indeed, in many places where there is a strong sense of affiliation, people will often informally report their concerns about other people. Delaney and Brownlee (1995) noted that rural workers in northern Canada often faced a problem in having access to too much information (cited in Schmidt, 2000). There may also be expectations that workers, too, will operate within these informal networks of knowledge and this can lead to dilemmas as social workers may experience considerable pressure to share information within their community, especially when it concerns issues of safety and risk. Green (2003a) noted that a worker who had to undertake work with a released child sex offender would be bound by professional expectations of confidentiality, but would nonetheless be subject to criticism if this person reoffended, as people might well think that the worker was able to provide some protection for her/his own children while the rest of the community carried on without this awareness of potential risk.

Social visibility, reputation and confidentiality

The higher social visibility of people in rural communities, where workers and clients, their partners and families, and even their vehicles, may be recognised as they go about their business, means that people are aware that their behaviour, and possibly their problems, are likely to become known about by other people. Parr et al (2002) suggest that there are two dimensions of visibility in rural communities. The first is the direct observation of the activities of other people, where actions and behaviour are more obvious than in urban settings. Indeed, they make the point that it is the fact of knowing people and having repeated opportunities to witness what they do that allows onlookers to notice changes in routines and demeanour. The second is the distribution of knowledge of one's activities to social networks. As one young man said, 'That's the problem it doesn't matter where you are, I get caught, it doesn't matter what I do, somebody sees me! We were in Dunvegan one night and I thought, nobody is going to see me over here, got back and ... Somebody had seen me!' (Parr et al, 2002, p 5).

This awareness of gaze, as well as feelings of shame, can inhibit potential service users from seeking help, as they do not wish to reveal their problems to the wider community. Even when other members of the community know of a person's problems, such as mental health difficulties, this may still pose a problem as individuals may feel that they are under scrutiny and ascriptions are being made based upon repeated observations. One man said, 'It's a place you can go in there and folk will read you, you often don't have to say anything', while another woman commented that 'if you are seeing people on a daily basis, you do notice changes' (Parr et al, 2002, p 7). Consequently, people with mental health problems may adopt strategies for avoiding the gaze of others, such as altering their shopping habits or their journeys. They may also develop ways of 'passing', by managing their behaviour by 'putting on a front' to avoid unwelcome attention. In some cases, the fear of rejection or of hostility can lead individuals to effectively exclude themselves from social contact. The stigmatisation of people with mental health problems in rural areas is widely reported as a barrier to seeking help and treatment (Barbopoulos and Clark, 2003; Findlay and Sheeham, 2004). However, local responses are by no means predictably negative, as judgements about individuals will usually be based upon the extent to which they are seen as belonging to the local community. Philo et al noted that 'Locals with mental health problems are more likely than incomers to be tolerated, though repeated illness or odd behaviour may lead to exclusion from the community support networks' (2003, p 6).

Individuals and families, too, may develop ways of offsetting the potentially negative perceptions that others may have of them and their problems. In a study of Belgian rural villages, Meert (2000) described some of the strategies that poor families used to avoid further economic and social marginalisation. As one might expect, some of these strategies operated within kinship networks, where there was often an element of reciprocity in the strategy adopted. For example, an elderly farmer gave a female relative food in exchange for her cutting his hair and mending his clothes. However, other 'illicit' strategies might involve part-time, unofficial work 'off the books', to avoid taxes or loss of welfare benefits, or poaching rabbits and collecting wood from municipally owned land. Meert noted that some of the poorer farmers avoided contact with the local welfare agency because other farmers sat on its council. Presumably, this avoidance was based upon some sense of shame or failure, since this is commonly observed in studies of selective welfare benefits. Miller, writing about rural areas in the US, notes that bartering, that is, the 'culturally acceptable ... exchange of goods or services in lieu of payment' (1998, p 59), might be a possible way in which a poor family might pay for social services. Although there is not much evidence to indicate whether this might hold for other rural areas, Zur (2006) also notes the significance of barter and gifts in rural communities and among some cultural groups such as Native Americans, where the symbolic exchange is a means of expressing gratitude and maintaining respect. From our own experience, we have also witnessed the significant role that exchange and reciprocity can play in preserving a client's sense of self-worth and signifying that, aside from their current difficulties, he or she is in all other respects a socially competent person.

In small communities, confidentiality may be compromised by existing networks of knowledge and relationships between people, and by the informal witnessing of contact and association between already known persons. There is often a mutual appreciation by social workers and clients of the fact that confidentiality, which is often assured or assisted by relative anonymity in larger urban populations, is more difficult to establish, and perhaps more difficult to maintain. For example, simply to be seen visiting someone's home, or for a client to be seen entering a local office, provides opportunities for gossip and speculation. One example of pre-existing knowledge and contact occurred in the practice of a rural counsellor working in the area where he had grown up, when he realised that the partner that his male client was referring to in his sessions was a former girlfriend. In this instance, the worker initially decided that as the sessions were not primarily focused upon relationship issues that he could continue with his work, but later as the focus of the client's problems shifted, he and his supervisor decided that it was not appropriate to do so.

Clients who realise that knowledge about their problems is likely to emerge informally will sometimes deliberately breach confidentiality by revealing information about themselves to sympathetic people, so that their preferred version of events is made available, rather than a less helpful version that might arise through local gossip. An example of such construction of narrative was evident in a case where a young teenager, who had been hospitalised following severe physical abuse by the father, was concerned that local people in the community, and, in particular, other children at school, did not become aware of the real reason for admission. Thus, a story was concocted that provided an alternative explanation for the stay in hospital. This story was then proffered by the child and tacitly supported by the social worker and the class teacher.

Dual and multiple relationships

Social workers in urban areas are much less likely to come into contact with their clients outside of their work, and even if they do meet, it is often likely to be no more than a passing acquaintance in a street or supermarket. The separation of their lives is usually ensured by the size of the population that surrounds them, and the likelihood that they will live in different districts. In contrast, in small communities in rural areas there may be many occasions where their paths may cross. Social workers who live and work in small communities have to manage some interesting dynamics, in terms of how they relate to their clients and to other people as they go about their personal and professional lives, and many writers on rural social work have noted that living and working in the same place poses some unique challenges (Miller, 1998; Green, 2003a; Galbreath, 2005; Schmidt, 2005; Pugh, 2006; Bodor, 2008). The terms 'dual relationships' and 'multiple relationships' are commonly used to describe these situations.

In the US, there has been a vigorous debate about the propriety and appropriateness of such relationships, but following extensive pressure from rural practitioners and researchers (Reamer, 1998), there has been a shift towards a more pragmatic acceptance of the possibilities of dual relationships. The National Association of Social Workers (2003), in the US, has stated that:

> Social workers practicing in rural areas must have advanced understanding of ethical responsibilities. Not only because dual relationships and multiple relationships are unavoidable but also because the setting may require that dual or multiple relationships be used and managed as an appropriate method of social work practice. (Cited in Galbreath, 2005, p 107)

However, in many other countries the problems are barely recognised within social work, though practitioners in community development have always understood the merits of properly conducted dual relationships, especially in their humanising effects upon worker–client relationships (Gallaway, 1996; Cheers, 1998).

Some of the other challenges of rural practice are more widely acknowledged (Cheers, 1998; Ginsberg, 1998; Martinez–Brawley, 2000).

In particular, many writers have noted the importance of consistency of personal presentation across different social settings and have noted the problems of attempting to maintain professional distance. For example, Ellen Walsh, writing from a therapeutic perspective in the US, noted that 'A clinician's willingness to behave in authentically personal ways with clients … is an especially useful quality … in communities that place a high value on integrity' (1989, p 587), while, in the UK, Pugh noted that:

> in smaller communities, people may have more opportunities to observe each other's behaviour in a range of different situations and are thus, well placed to observe discontinuities between the personal style and manner that is used within work and their behaviour and presentation elsewhere. Workers who may wish to maintain a professional 'distance', or even mistakenly, some sense of 'mystique', will find it difficult to do this, because their 'otherness' and professional power may visibly be seen not to extend to other aspects of their particular rural context. (Pugh, 2000, p 102)

People in rural communities may well have expectations of workers that go beyond those typically faced by their urban counterparts. Zapf (1985) has described this as a pressure for 'role integration' where public and private lives and personae are expected to be congruent and consistent (cited in Schmidt, 2000). Lehmann's empirical study of Australian social work managers in rural areas reported that they 'expressed a sense of exposure to scrutiny and spoke of the multiple roles that they were aware of in their daily lives … [which] led to a sense of increased pressure to fit within the range of acceptable role behaviours' (2005, p 367). One of the ways they dealt with the pressures of being judged and being subject to the 'high level of informal exchange across role boundaries' was to be 'emotionally guarded' (2005, p 367) with their own staff, as well as with people outside the office. Social workers who seek to avoid feeling compromised may decide to opt out of many local social activities. This can be an effective strategy, but they run the risk of being thought of as stand-offish, and this self-isolation may cut them off from other sources of social support and information, and may diminish their effectiveness in situations where they might wish to call upon local help in their work.

Rural workers who are unable to rely upon the anonymity of personal life that might be easily achieved in a populous urban area may be faced with a dilemma. They cannot easily maintain social distance from their clients by relying upon a neutral or detached professional persona, for this may run counter to local expectations and obstruct the building of trust, and may be perceived as pompousness or insincerity. Some clients may be embarrassed by coming into contact with their worker in other settings and may manage the risk of such discomfort through avoidance, effectively helping the worker with the problem of social distance. Our experience is that in situations where service users know and respect local workers, and are confident that confidentiality will not be compromised, they will frequently initiate conversations in non-formal settings and out of hours (Cheers, 1998). Although social work agencies may expect employees to maintain a clear boundary between working and social life, such contacts cannot be easily avoided (Turbett, 2004). Locally, social workers' credibility will not be judged solely upon the quality of their work, but will also be based upon perceptions of their personal conduct in other areas of life, such as recreation and child-rearing practices. Thus, choices about personal presentation extend beyond the immediate work situation.

In small communities, it is not unusual to be invited to weddings and family parties, or to attend other local events at which people who are already known to the worker will be present. Again little guidance is available in social work literature as to how to manage such invitations or occurrences. Zur (2006), writing as a therapist, notes the importance of invitations to ceremonies, rituals and life events, and argues that therapists should attend them as rejections can be highly disruptive of the therapeutic relationship. For Zur, the test of the propriety of acceptance is simply the traditional test of whether the client's welfare is being served. However, for social workers, decisions in such situations are far from being so easily resolved, especially when they are expected to perform statutory duties in regard to child welfare and mental health, tasks, which can leave them vulnerable to social isolation, social pressure or even personal threats and violence (Green et al, 2003; SWIA, 2005). Dilemmas about participation in local social life, difficult though they may be for the incomer, are even more pressing for workers returning to practise in the areas from which they originate, where they may have extensive networks of relationship and pre-knowledge.

There is a considerable literature aimed at assessing the benefits and risks of dual and multiple relationships (Borys and Pope, 1989; Pope and Vetter, 1992; Gottlieb, 1993; Kagel and Giebelhausen, 1994; Younggren, 2002; Galbreath, 2005), but one of the most useful schemas is put forward by Valentich and Gripton, who recognise that professional regulations 'are not detailed enough to anticipate every situation that may arise in practice' (2003, p 11) and suggest making an assessment of the following factors in making decisions about dual relationships. These are:

- the vulnerability of the client;
- power differences between workers and clients;
- risks for the client;
- risks for the professional/worker;
- benefits for the client;
- benefits for the professional/worker;
- clarity of professional boundaries;
- the specificity or diffuseness of the professional role;
- the accessibility of alternative resources;
- community values and cultural norms.

Valentich and Gripton also state that 'appropriate boundaries in helping relationships are set and maintained by decisions and concrete actions taken by the helper throughout, and after the relationship ends' (2003, p 11). For example, Zur (2006) suggests that those who work in situations where dual relationships are inevitable should help their clients to recognise that incidental encounters can arise, and so should help them to consider what responses they might prefer when they encounter the therapist outside of the office.

Conclusion

In this chapter we have outlined some of the most significant social dynamics that may be encountered when working in small communities. Social workers in rural areas need to understand some of the complexities of gendered relationships, not simply to avoid unwittingly reinforcing traditional conceptions, but to become aware of some of the pressures and changes that are taking place, and that may be being played out in the lives of those with whom they work. Similarly, an understanding of ideas of place and belonging can help us to understand why some people's problems are met with a sympathetic response, while those of other people are received with indifference or hostility. The consciousness that people who live in small communities have of the social gaze of other people is a pervasive aspect of rural life that has consequent effects upon people's willingness to engage with welfare services. It is in these circumstances that the judgements that local people make about social workers and their general social comportment become highly significant factors in enabling and delivering social services. However, as we have shown in the latter part of this chapter, there are a number of challenges and tensions inherent in social work practice in rural communities. What is clear is that a conception of confidentiality which 'derives from the 'patient–physician model, where the relationship is essentially dyadic, one-to-one' (Swain, 2006, p 101) cannot be satisfactorily sustained in practice settings where there is a need to engage with, and address, a wider social audience.

The social dynamics of small communities also challenge notions of professional neutrality and detachment. Martinez-Brawley has noted that while social work is a profession where 'confidentiality and detachment are valued in the name of objectivity ... [and where] the assumption is that if the worker knows a client on personal terms, the worker cannot be "objective" about that client' (2000, p 81), this separation of the worker from the community and its members is often not possible. The assumption that objectivity follows from detachment is also open to challenge. Over the past two decades there have been a number of theoretical and political challenges to the idea that professional neutrality is achievable or desirable. Various emancipatory perspectives, such as feminism, anti-discriminatory practice and disability activism, have challenged assumptions of expertise and power and, as Miller (1998) has noted, have reduced the formal distance between clients and workers and legitimated self-disclosure and social integration into communities.

THREE

Indigenous peoples: dispossession, colonisation and discrimination

Introduction

This chapter reviews the experience of indigenous peoples, that is, those who are also referred to as aboriginal or native peoples. It identifies some of the major populations of indigenous peoples living in rural areas within Westernised welfare structures, including: the Aborigines and Torres Strait Islanders of Australia; the Māori of New Zealand; the Inuit, Métis and the First Nations (Indians) of Canada and the US. Currently, the proportions of these indigenous peoples in the respective national populations are: 15% in New Zealand, 4% in Canada, 2% in Australia (Statistics Canada, 2008) and 1.5% in the US (US Census Bureau, 2002). In many countries, the recorded numbers of indigenous people have risen as more people have been willing to identify themselves as such. There are other smaller groups whose history and circumstances have similarities and who may face similar difficulties in securing justice and equitable provision in welfare services, such as Native Hawaiians and other Pacific Islanders, the Sami people of Scandinavia and, of course, other descendants of the older indigenous populations in Europe. It can be difficult to accurately establish the relative position of some of these groups, either because information is not collected or because it remains undifferentiated. This is the case with Native Hawaiians where there is a tendency to conflate data about their situation with that of other Pacific Islanders (Mokuau et al, 2008).

There are different conventions and sensibilities in different countries regarding the terminology used to identify these peoples. In Australia, the capitalised term 'Aborigine' is widely accepted by Aboriginal people, and widely used by government departments, politicians, academics and journalists to refer to people who are native to mainland Australia and Tasmania. Aborigines are distinguished from Torres Strait Islanders originating from the islands north of Cape York, though both are Indigenous Australians. Elsewhere, even in its lower-case form, the term 'aboriginal' is not widely used in ordinary speech. In the US, the term 'Red Indian' is widely thought to be derogatory, and there has also been a move away from the use of the word 'Indian' to the preferred terms of 'First Nation' or 'Native Americans'. Nonetheless, it should be recognised that some of the people identified by these terms continue to describe themselves as Indians or American Indians (see www.nativeamericans.com), and some elements of the ideas of the 'Red Power' liberation movement in the 1960s, together with the traditional spiritual belief in 'walking the Red Road', remain influential in a range of spiritual and self-help initiatives and the language used within them (see Gross, 2003; www.care2.com/c2c/group/AITOTRR). Interestingly, in Canada the government provides explicit advice and direction on the preferred nomenclature (INAC, 2004), and the term 'aboriginal' is becoming more widely used as a politically and socially neutral, and inclusive, term (Chartrand, 1991; Martel and Brassard, 2006). There is also variation in the usage of the word 'indigenous', with commentators in many countries using the lower-case form, but in Australia the capitalised form is preferred. In this chapter we use the lower-case form generally and adopt the capitalised forms of both 'Indigenous' and 'Aboriginal' when referring specifically to an Australian context. Clearly from a social work perspective, sensitivity to the sometimes changing nomenclatures being used is important and the best advice is to ask what people's preferences are, as these may differ from one tribe or band to another, from generation to generation, and, of course, from different levels of political opinion and awareness of identity between different people.

Indigenous peoples, though diverse in origins and cultures, have in common the experience of European migration into their land, and, subsequently, the experience of colonisation and oppression. In many places the dispossession of land removed the freedom to gather and cultivate, hunt or traverse it, and led to loss of livelihood. The treatment of indigenous people by Europeans often encompassed marginalisation and neglect, but extended most notoriously to enslavement, suppression and genocide. Given these dreadful experiences the very fact of the survival of local indigenous people itself is remarkable and is a testimony to their resilience. However, the costs have been high and the negative consequences of social disruption, deculturation and dispossession continue for many people. Unsurprisingly, it has been noted that indigenous strategies of self-preservation commonly include self-isolation and separation (Weaver, 1998; Gross, 2003), preferring to maintain culture rather than succumb to assimilation. The persistence of memories of injustice and feelings of anger have also played a part in maintaining resistance as well as a consequent mistrust of government and 'white' agencies, including social workers and researchers (Weaver, 1998; Gross, 2003).

This chapter begins by identifying some common themes in the experiences of indigenous peoples in Australia, Canada, New Zealand and the US. It then briefly reviews some basic information about the main groups and notes particular issues and problems. The chapter switches to a general review of the social policy and welfare responses made by governments to indigenous peoples and concludes with some key observations about the implications for social work practice with indigenous peoples. Further implications for models of practice are picked up in Chapters 6 and 7.

Common themes in the experiences of indigenous peoples

Although initial contacts between Europeans and indigenous peoples were not always marked by conflict and oppression, the early instances of accommodation and tolerance that did occur were often superseded by conflicts over natural resources and territory as the numbers of early Europeans increased and spread. As new migrants seized, settled, farmed, mined and exploited the 'new' land, traditional native patterns of hunting and gathering, including the intermittent or seasonal cultivation practised by some indigenous people, became more difficult or impossible to sustain. The nomadic or semi-nomadic life of some people became impossible or was severely curtailed as land was claimed, fenced and defended by Europeans.

Indigenous peoples exposed to contact with Europeans were sometimes overwhelmed by new diseases for which they had little resistance. In some places, indigenous peoples were pressed into forced labour, while in others they were forcibly relocated, often to less hospitable and unfamiliar territory. Those who resisted European settlement and expansion were sometimes captured and relocated, but in some countries they were brutally killed, sometimes with the explicit aim of extinguishing them as a people (Stannard, 1992; Trudgen, 2000).

The dehumanisation and derogation of the original inhabitants was underpinned by European assumptions about the cultural and racial inferiority of indigenous peoples. Later in the 19th and early 20th centuries these notions were sometimes justified by mistaken interpretations of Darwin's theory of natural selection or by reference to the fallacious assumptions of eugenics. The perception of indigenous peoples as backward, uncivilised or a sub-human species, or as commodities to be exploited, ultimately provided the rationalisation for countless acts of aggression, treachery and debasement (Malik, 1996). Many Europeans with a sense of their own cultural superiority saw little merit, and often some threat, in the persistence of traditional patterns of authority and decision-making, and usually did their best to undermine or usurp them. Even when Europeans aspired to live in peaceable contact with native people, this rarely endured as Europeans often broke the treaties they had made and any adaptations were usually a one-way process of linguistic and cultural accommodation to European ways, as indigenous peoples were encouraged, or forced, to cease their traditional ways of life.

The suppression of traditional languages and cultures, typically through the inculcation of religion and education (Adams, 1997), has had enduring effects, most notably in destabilising family and community life (Dixon and Scheurell, 1995; Shewell, 2004). In the US, an Indian Commissioner speaking at the establishment of the Phoenix Indian School in 1891 stated that 'It's cheaper to educate Indians than to kill them' (Morgan, 1998). The removal of children from their families, either temporarily through their education in boarding schools in Australia and the US, or permanently through fostering and adoption as in Australia where they were often placed as cheap labour with white families, not only removed them from the kinship of their communities, it attempted to destroy traditional cultures and supplant them with new ideas, habits and beliefs.

In the US, the reactions of Indian children and their families varied considerably; many were distraught at the prospect of separation and parents were often reluctant to let their children go, or having done so, wanted them back. Paradoxically, the experience of education at the schools in some cases strengthened a sense of common Indian identity and so contributed to the pan-Indian political movement for liberation (Adams, 1997). Learning 'white ways' also provided some of the tools for resistance through political activism and legal challenge (Gross, 2003). Some schools were harsh places and most had strict discipline, but the presence of Indian teachers and some more enlightened teachers could often ameliorate the worst effects (Davis, 2001). Nonetheless, these policies of removal and cultural replacement exposed children to economic exploitation, as well as physical and sexual abuse in their new 'homes' (Weaver, 1998; Smith, 2007; Roberts et al, 2008).

In Canada, the schools seemed to have been much harsher places, with many children dying from diseases such as tuberculosis. A report by Dr Peter Bryce to Department of Indian Affairs Superintendent Duncan Campbell Scott in April 1909 indicated that the death rate of Indian children in the schools was very high, reportedly some 40% (cited in Truth Commission into Genocide in Canada, 2001). There is also contentious evidence that children were subjected to illegal and abusive medical procedures (Truth Commission into Genocide in Canada, 2001). All this took place against a wider backdrop of repressive legislation and policy, which included a law enacting the forcible sterilisation of native girls in Alberta (Smith, 2007).

Bringing Them Home (HREOC, 1997), an Australian inquiry into the 'stolen generations' of Aboriginal children, has documented the scale and the damage done to those who were forcibly separated and removed from their families. Indeed, the Human Rights and Equal Opportunity Commission in Australia noted that while the discriminatory laws had long gone:

> as far as Indigenous people are concerned, their children continue to be removed through the child welfare and juvenile justice systems. Due to the entrenched disadvantage and ongoing dispossession of Indigenous Australians, contemporary laws continue to discriminate against Indigenous families where raising children is concerned.
> *Aboriginal families continue to be seen as the 'problem', and Aboriginal children continue to be seen as potentially 'saveable' if they can be separated from the 'dysfunctional' or 'culturally deprived' environments of their families and communities.* (HREOC, 2001)

The historical consequences of contact with Europeans and the subsequent mistreatment and exploitation not only destroyed traditional ways of life and undermined established patterns of social control, but within some groups had enduring effects in diminished parenting capacity, weakened kinship and community networks, and reduced capacity for self-help (Gross, 2003; Shewell, 2004). Moreover, continuing problems with poverty and crime have severely impacted upon the life chances of members of some communities (Eversole et al, 2005; McNeish and Eversole, 2005). Historically, access to new foods, especially those high in sugar and carbohydrates, together with changes in lifestyle, led to poorer health chances for many indigenous peoples. The contemporary causes of poor health are linked to a number of factors, including poor diet in infancy, overcrowding, poor-quality accommodation, low income levels arising from poverty and unemployment, reduced access to health care, and poor education levels linked to low uptake of health information. Health problems arising from obesity, smoking and excessive alcohol consumption are also commonplace in some groups. Sadly, problems of inter-group and intra-family violence and abuse also appear to be common among some groups (Greenfield and Smith, 1999; Robertson, 2000; Memmott et al, 2001; Gross, 2003; Stanley et al, 2003; Sacred Circle, 2005; Hunter, 2008). However, it should be noted that there is considerable variation both within and between different indigenous groups, communities and families.

The age profile of indigenous populations is usually younger than the rates of the general population, because of higher rates of fertility (the number of children born to each mother) and lower life expectancy. Infant mortality rates (the numbers of deaths of children in their first year of life per 1,000 live births), which are thought to be good indicators of general welfare, typically show that indigenous peoples have higher rates than the non-indigenous majorities.

Traditional expectations and intergenerational cohabitation in extended families in many indigenous societies means that child care is seen as a wider responsibility than just the preserve of the parents (DFACS, 1994). The problems of poverty, poor health and lower life expectancy also result in many children being raised in part by people who are not their blood parents. While there are many positive benefits to this broader involvement in terms of substitution, extensive kinship networks and support, there can be drawbacks too. Fuller-Thomson and Minkler (2005) noted that American Indian and Alaskan Native grandparents involved in raising grandchildren were themselves often poor, in poor health, with disabilities and living on reservations with limited support from services. For instance, they found that a third of such grandparents were living below the poverty line yet only a quarter of these were receiving public assistance.

Questions of apology, indigenous identity, formal recognition and reparation by the state are crucial issues for many indigenous peoples. For some peoples, this has taken many years, and for some it is still not established (Havemann, 1999). For instance, only in 2008 did the Australian government formally apologise to Aborigines and Torres Strait Islanders. In the same year, the Canadian government also apologised for the harm inflicted by the residential school system. In some instances, self-identification and recognition by an indigenous community that itself has been recognised are sufficient grounds for individual legal recognition. This recognition is usually based on the explicit recognition of ancestry, historical records of residence, and sometimes upon active participation within the indigenous community and its culture. Nevertheless, some indigenous peoples have yet to establish this status for themselves, and consequently individuals may have to make their claim for recognition in some other way, perhaps by direct appeal to the government or through the legal system. The question of whether individuals will seek recognition is not simply about having the means, or the option, to do so, it also depends upon their own perceptions of their identity, its status and any consequent benefits or risks that may arise from recognition. This can be seen in microcosm in a small study of aboriginal women prisoners in Canada, where Martel and Brassard (2006) found that while some women were proud of their identity or saw clear advantages in expressing it, others declined to assert it, or were ashamed to admit it.

The significance of recognition extends beyond the question of personal and group identity, as in some countries it brings political rights and entitlements beyond those of other citizens, such as exemptions from some civic duties. For instance, the recognition of 81% of Canada's North American Indians who are registered under the Indian Act as Status Indians confers tax exemptions for work carried out on reserved land. However, the situation of Métis peoples is less clear-cut. Although the term 'Métis' has some legal definition, being included in the constitutional identification of First Nations people (which also identifies Indians and Inuits), it is still not a completely unambiguous situation. In the past, the term 'Métis' was sometimes used to refer specifically to the descendants of the Red River Métis, who were perceived by outsiders as having a distinct identity and culture, whereas the lower-case term 'métis' was used generically to describe any person of mixed Indian and European heritage. However, in 2002, the Métis National Council stated that 'Métis means a person who self-identifies as Métis, is of historic Métis Nation Ancestry, is distinct from other aboriginal peoples, and is accepted by the Métis Nation' (MNC, 2008). Individuals who meet these criteria can register as Métis through local registration processes, and although this does not yet confer any further constitutional rights, a Supreme Court decision in 2003 began to establish rights for hunting and harvesting (MNC, 2008).

The question of whether status is self-declared or formally recognised can also have a bearing on political representation and participation in political processes. In some countries formal recognition is externally ascribed, but in New Zealand where the status of Māori is self-declared, they have a choice as to whether to enrol to vote at parliamentary elections on a Māori roll or a General roll. The numbers registered on the Māori roll determine how many Māori seats there are in Parliament, and at the election the enrolled Māori voters select their preferred candidates for these seats. In Australia, the enfranchisement of Indigenous people to vote in federal elections was only granted in the 1962 Commonwealth Electoral Act, and Queensland was the last state to grant this right in 1965 (AEC, 2007). However, it was not until the 1967 referendum that Indigenous peoples were properly included in the national census and the Commonwealth was given the power to make laws in the interests of Indigenous peoples.

An examination of the question of sovereignty and the duties and obligations of national governments to indigenous peoples points up some significant differences between countries and peoples, especially in the degree of self-governance permitted and the robustness of the constitutional arrangements that underpin them. In Australia, for instance, until recently Indigenous peoples had some limited self-governance through ATSIC (the Aboriginal and Torres Strait Islander Commission) established in 1990. Although ATSIC operated under the auspices of Australia's national government, it was an elected body that allowed Indigenous peoples to have a direct influence on policies for their communities and did not replace their general right to vote in national elections. ATSIC was abolished in 2005 amidst controversy, and most of its responsibilities were taken over by other government departments. While there were some divisions of opinion about the merits of ATSIC among Australia's Indigenous peoples, there was general dismay about how this was done. Much of the focus at the time was on the competence and record of ATSIC's leadership, though the formal justification proffered was that it would be better not to have Indigenous affairs operating in a bureaucratic backwater, but instead have these operations fully incorporated within mainstream government departments. This 'mainstreaming' of Indigenous social policy through the absorption of specific initiatives into broader mainstream governance has raised a number of critical concerns, most notably in regard to: the possible loss of specialist capacity; the risk that minority issues might be subsumed by broader concerns; the reduction in democratic influence; and a reduced capacity for self-governance, as elected delegates were replaced with political appointees (Altman, 2004).

In contrast, the founding of the self-governing body in Nunavut, Canada, in 1999 was based upon two Acts of Parliament and the creation of a new territory and permitted a far greater degree of self-government, with powers ranging over health, education, culture and economic affairs (see www.assembly.nu.ca). While the Commissioner is appointed directly by the Canadian National Government, this role is largely symbolic and effective political authority is vested in the Legislative Assembly of Nunavut with the Premier and an Executive directly chosen by the elected representatives. The powers of the Assembly are largely the same as those of provincial government throughout Canada, except that the territorial assembly cannot vary its own constitution, cannot sell public land (this remains a federal decision), cannot borrow money on credit and cannot allow public companies to become incorporated as private entities.

In the US, the position of American Indians and Alaska Natives is an interesting one as they are regarded as 'domestic dependent nations with whom the US government has a formal trust relationship' (Davis, 2007, p 4), that is, they have retained sovereignty from the early treaties and their rights to self-governance are enshrined in the US Constitution. Subsequent legislation, such as the 1975 Indian Self-Determination and Education Assistance Act and the 1993 Indian Tribal Justice Act, together with Supreme Court judgments, affirmed this status. Tribal governments and tribal bodies have powers over economic development, planning, roads, transportation, water, waste disposal, law enforcement and some levels of justice, and some aspects of education and welfare services. However, tribal government structures and responsibilities vary from place to place as different tribes have sought to reassert their authority in different domains of governance (Davis, 2007; NCAI, 2008). The 1978 Indian Child Welfare Act allowed tribes to have jurisdiction over child welfare cases involving native children on reservations (Weaver, 1998). This not only marked the end of formal efforts to weaken Indian culture, but extended the sphere of influence outside of the reservation in cases where a child is a ward of the tribal court (Gross, 2003). In contrast, in Hawaii, which became a state in 1959, the situation of Native Hawaiians is rather weaker despite several attempts to secure the same level of recognition of sovereignty (Bennett, 2007).

Particular groups

Australian Aboriginals

In the 2001 Australian Census some 410,000 people identified themselves as Aboriginal and/or Torres Strait Islanders, although this is likely to be an underestimate as there would be many Indigenous people among the three quarters of a million people who did not complete this section of the form (HREOC, 2006). While around 53% of all Indigenous peoples live in New South Wales and Queensland, they comprise only small proportions of the local populations at 2.1% and 3.5%, respectively. In contrast, Indigenous peoples comprise nearly

29% of the population of the Northern Territory (HREOC, 2006). Overall, around 80% of Indigenous people report speaking only English at home, though in remote areas many people are bilingual with some 55% speaking an Indigenous language (HREOC, 2006).

The age profile of the Indigenous people is lower than that of other Australians and average life expectancy is generally 17 years less, with the life expectancy from birth in the period 1996–2001 being around 59 years for men and 65 for women (ABS, 2008). Although the causes of poor health prospects as noted earlier are complex, this differential has not reduced much in recent years. Indigenous babies are more likely to have low birth weights and, even though the data are incomplete, infant mortality rates (the numbers of children dying in their first year of life) are significantly higher than the Australian average; perhaps three to four times higher. Indigenous people are much more likely to have cardiovascular illnesses, pneumonia, diabetes, hepatitis, TB and some sexually transmitted diseases (HREOC, 2006). Some, but not all, of these problems are clearly linked to obesity, smoking and substance abuse, including alcohol and solvents like petrol. For instance, roughly half of Indigenous adults smoke compared to about a quarter in the general population. In contrast, some 58% of Indigenous respondents report not drinking any alcohol, compared with 38% of non-Indigenous respondents. Previously it had been thought that those Indigenous people who did drink were more likely to do so at risky levels, but more recent research has not confirmed this. Indigenous people generally have higher rates of mental illness and suicide, and are at greater risk of injuries and deaths from violence (HREOC, 2006).

Indigenous children are more likely to come to the attention of welfare authorities and are over-represented in care (Stanley et al, 2003), especially in long-term foster care, where, despite the formal adoption of the Aboriginal Child Placement Principle, many are still placed with non-Indigenous carers (HREOC, 1997; Ban, 2005). The reasons for this are complex but they include a 'continuing cultural bias against Indigenous modes of parenting, inadequate and inappropriate services for Indigenous families and discriminatory treatment of young Indigenous people before the law' (HREOC, 2001).

Hunter (2008), in a review of the Northern Territory Emergency Response to the high levels of child abuse, also points up the complexity of the situation and concludes that reducing child maltreatment in Aboriginal communities requires, 'both Aboriginal self-determination and extensive consultation between Indigenous and non-Indigenous people working in the field' (2008, p 372).

Māori

The New Zealand census counts the number of Māoris in two ways, by ethnicity and by descent. 'Māori ethnicity' refers to cultural affiliation and the self-identity of respondents, whereas 'Māori descent' refers to ancestry. In 2006, there were some 565,000 people who identified with the Māori ethnic group, but around 644,000 people who were of Māori descent (Statistics New Zealand, 2007; Te Ara, 2008). Although Māoris comprise many different tribal groups, a more unified political identity has emerged out of cultural rejuvenation and resistance to continuing marginalisation (see www.maoriparty.com). Compared to the national profile they are a relatively youthful population, with 35% being under 15 years of age and fewer than 5% aged 65 years and over (Statistics New Zealand, 2007). Most Māoris speak English, but about a quarter also speak the traditional language, te reo Māori, while nearly half of those over 65 are native speakers (Statistics New Zealand, 2007).

European settlement in New Zealand was relatively late and although there were some Europeans prior to the early 1800s their numbers were small and did not grow significantly until the 1840s. However, between 1840 and 1900 Māori people lost much of their land through annexation, seizure and through treaties and land deals, some duplicitous and some probably illegal (TRC, 2008), as European numbers increased from around 2,000 to 700,000 (Te Ara, 2008). Whereas 60 years ago most Maoris lived in rural areas, 84% now live in urban areas (Statistics New Zealand, 2007). The majority, some 87%, live in the North Island, and the highest proportions where Māoris comprise over 60% of the local populations are in the Chatham Islands Territory, in Kawerau, in Wairoa and the Opotiki Districts.

The welfare situation of Māoris compared to the general population is poor. They have poorer educational prospects, higher unemployment rates and are more likely to be in poverty and live in poor housing. Māori infant mortality rates at around 10 per 1,000 births are roughly double those of the general population. Māoris are more likely to have health problems associated with smoking, alcohol consumption, diabetes and misuse of drugs, and have lower life expectancy (Māori Health, 2008). They have higher suicide rates and are more likely to be victims of violence. For example, mortality rates from assault and homicide are three times higher for all Māoris than for non-Māoris. For Māori women the situation is even worse with a rate of hospital admissions from violence five times that of non-Māori females (Māori Health, 2008). Māoris are also over-represented in prison where they comprise nearly half of all inmates (Department of Corrections, 2001; Burton, 2006).

Native Americans

In the US the 2000 census found that 4.1 million people reported themselves as being wholly or partly of American Indian or Alaska Native ethnicity (US Census Bureau, 2002). There are 569 federally recognised tribal groups comprising around 2.5 million people, as well as an unknown number of unrecognised groups. Unsurprisingly, there is 'tremendous variation in how Indians identify themselves' in regard to the wider society (Weaver, 1998, p 209). The largest tribal groups are Cherokee, Navajo, Chippewa, Sioux and Choctaw, and the largest concentrations of Native Americans are found in the states of Arizona, Montana, New Mexico, Oklahoma, South Dakota and Alaska (OMHD, 2008). In the US there are over 300 Indian reservations, but not all tribes have reservations and some have more than one. It is estimated that around 50% of Native Americans live on them. Most of the reservations are in rural areas and some are in remote places, but others are close to major urban centres. The size of reservations varies, with some being only a few square miles, while some of the largest encompass thousands of square miles. For instance, Navajo Nation reservation land in Arizona extends over 18,000 square miles.

The health and life chances of indigenous peoples are worse than the general population, with life expectancy being around five years less (NCAI, 2008), higher infant mortality rates (12 per 1,000 compared to 7) and much higher rates of TB, diabetes, accidental injuries and alcoholism. In addition, both suicide and homicide rates are higher: 70% and 100%, respectively (IHS, 2008). Perhaps the most shocking statistics are the rates of violence against women and children (Greenfield and Smith, 1999; McGillivray and Comaskey, 1999). It has been estimated that 34% of American Indian and Alaska Native women will be raped in their lifetime, with non-Native perpetrators being responsible for around 80% of these assaults. Further, some 61% will be physically assaulted during their lifetime, and homicide is identified as being the third most likely cause of death for American Indian women between the ages of 15 and 34 years. In the period 1979–92, three quarters of them were killed by family members or acquaintances (Sacred Circle, 2005).

In Canada, just under 700,000 people self-identify as North American Indians and in 2006 about 40% of them lived on reservations. Overall, around 46% are living in rural areas (Statistics Canada, 2008). Those living on reservations were more likely to speak an aboriginal language than those living elsewhere: 51% compared to 12% (Statistics Canada, 2008). The North American Indian population in Canada is generally much younger than the non-aboriginal population, and children are twice as likely to be living with a lone parent (31% compared to 14%) and about 8% of children live with another relative such as a grandparent, aunt or uncle (Statistics Canada, 2008). Generally, they are more likely to be living in overcrowded and poor-quality housing.

There are also populations of Métis people, living mostly in the western provinces of Canada and Ontario, but also in the US in Montana, North Dakota and Minnesota. They are descendants of marriages from the mid-1600s onwards between Native Americans and French settlers, as well as some from marriages with English and Scottish settlers. In Canada just under 390,000 people self-identify as Métis (Statistics Canada, 2008). Over the years, Métis developed distinct communities, culture and identities, and their own language, Métif (also known as Michif), a mixture of French and Native American words. Most Métis speak English and many speak French as well, while a small number also speak Métif and other Native American languages, such as Cree. Historically, Métis, who were also known as 'mixed-bloods' and 'half-breeds' (MNC, 2008), were subject to discrimination and dispossession of land similar to those endured by Native Americans. Consequently, many people have hidden or denied their ethnicity, and even today some may be unaware of it. Around 30% of Métis live in rural areas, and overall they have a younger age profile than non-aboriginal Canadians, with some 25% being 14 years or younger compared to 17%. They are more likely to be living with a lone parent than non-aboriginal Canadians: 31% compared to 17%.

Inuit in North America

There are Inuit people throughout the Arctic Circle. In the North American Arctic region there are some 56,000 Inuit living on the southern tip of Hudson's Bay, in northern Quebec, along the northern Labrador coast, in the High Arctic Islands, in the Northwestern Territories, in Nunavut and in northern Alaska and the Canadian land area bordering it. Formerly nomadic, they mostly live in settled communities with hunting parties travelling during the hunting season. They have a common heritage, and five language dialects collectively known as 'Inuktitut' are spoken by 64% of Inuit as a 'mother tongue' (Statistics Canada, 2008). Their culture places great emphasis upon cooperation and the family unit and remains vibrant, with a strong oral tradition of storytelling, singing and dancing. The success of their land and compensation claims with the Canadian government has secured their aboriginal rights, such as the rights to hunt, trap and fish, and it is hoped that these legal settlements will provide a secure economic and political base for their future. Nunavut, which was created in 1999, has established a semi-autonomous region with self-government for the 22,500 Inuit people who live within the territory.

Inuit are more likely to be living in overcrowded conditions and poorer quality accommodation than other Canadians (Statistics Canada, 2008). Inuit infant mortality rates are four times higher than the Canadian average and life expectancy for Inuit men is lower by some 13 years than for other Canadian men. Health chances are generally worse, especially in regard to diseases such as TB and hepatitis, and suicide rates are more than 11 times higher than the national average of 11.8 per 100,000 of population (ITK, 2007). These poorer health prospects are linked to a range of factors including: geographic isolation, higher rates of smoking, inadequate health services, cultural barriers to accessing services, poor sewage disposal in some places and economic factors such as low and inadequate income levels (OMHD, 2008).

Apart from wild food that is harvested or caught, food prices are much higher in the north than elsewhere in Canada, although average incomes are much lower (ITK, 2007).

Social welfare responses: what can be done?

In the US, Gross characterises the history of policy towards indigenous peoples as being one that has focused upon the:

> 'plight' of the Native Americans in order to impose a patently inadequate liberal or conservative response aimed at alleviating this plight by making it more comfortable to bear. The historical intention was never to pursue ... values that might lead to self-determination or political independence for the Indian tribes but to forcibly assimilate them into mainstream American society. (Gross, 2003, p 36)

Unfortunately, this characterisation could be applied to a number of other countries as well. The damage that has been done by these policies is evidenced in the wide-ranging inquiries and extensive reports into mistreatment that have been published, like *Bringing Them Home* in Australia (HREOC, 1997) and the *Report of the Royal Commission on Aboriginal Peoples* in Canada (Royal Commission, 1996).

While these reports have resulted in some public acknowledgement and formal apology, there is still some way to go in the complex matters of reparation, rehabilitation and the codification of explicit rights. For example, in Canada the Assembly of First Nations has been disappointed with the lack of progress on many of the most important recommendations made by the Royal Commission (1996).

The continuance of what some writers have called 'historical trauma' (Brave Heart, 1999; Whitbeck et al, 2004; Evans-Campbell, 2008; Zembylas and Bekerman, 2008), that is, the persistence of intergenerational effects of oppression, can be seen in the relatively high rates of mental distress, intra-family violence, alcohol and drug problems, accidental injury, self-harm and stress recorded in some communities (Ban, 2005). It is clear that attempts to deculturate or assimilate groups and individuals not only have immediate effects on those subjected to forcible strategies of assimilation, but also have enduring consequences in removing some of the most important social resources available to marginalised people under pressure, such as their language, culture and livelihood (Pugh, 1996). This is becoming much more widely understood and so it is not surprising that a common response of indigenous peoples has been to revalue and reinvigorate some aspects of traditional culture in order to recreate a sense of positive identity and pride.

While it may be the case that malevolent motives lay behind the damaging practices of assimilation, it would be erroneous to assume that all of those who established and practised such policies were ill-motivated. Many educationalists and social workers appear to have sincerely thought that their efforts were beneficial. The lesson for us today is one that we have learned elsewhere in our practice with other 'minorities', that well-meant actions considered in isolation from the broader social context often have unintended negative consequences. Pearson (2001/2002), an Aboriginal activist in Australia, argues that Indigenous peoples are being damaged by what he terms 'passive welfare' (cited in Briskman, 2007, pp 224–5), that is, systems of support that are culturally inappropriate and ineffective. While there are many reasons for such poor outcomes perhaps the most pertinent is the perspective that frames such interventions, as Weaver cogently summarises:

> Issues such as what is labelled as a problem, the origin of problems, the target of interventions, appropriate interventions, and desired outcomes are all grounded in a

particular belief system that may be incongruent with the belief system of the client. (Weaver, 1998, p 204)

A telling example of this can be seen in research into family violence in an Aboriginal community commissioned by an Aboriginal women's organisation in Ceduna, South Australia, Weena Mooga Gu Gudba Inc, who wanted to better understand the issues and develop strategies to reduce it (Taylor et al, 2001; Cheers et al, 2006a). Local Aboriginal people saw family violence as incorporating a wide range of abusive behaviour among different people, including physical and emotional abuse of women and children, fighting between families and other groups in the community, name-calling, violence perpetrated by street gangs, psychological abuse, spiritual abuse, disregard and neglect of Elders, and government policy and interventions undermining Elders' authority. Rather than point to patriarchal structures and the power of men over women, Indigenous understandings locate family violence within colonisation, dispossession, displacement, disempowerment and erosion of Indigenous culture as these affect all members of the community. Family violence is inseparably intertwined with other issues, such as unemployment and poverty. Consequently, the Western perspectives being used to construct policies and services for family violence in Indigenous communities, with their narrow focus upon individual culpability within patriarchal structures separated from any other understanding of social context, may result in ineffective solutions as they will not encompass a multi-stranded, community-wide and coordinated response among agencies, or be grounded in local Aboriginal culture (Taylor et al, 2004).

Unsurprisingly, a key feature of writing and research on indigenous peoples is the importance of recognising and understanding their belief systems and world views, especially in regard to notions of kinship, network and place in the natural world (Coates et al, 2006). Although spiritual beliefs do of course vary widely in indigenous cultures, many beliefs emphasise the importance of the interconnectedness of everything in the world, including natural forces, animals, humans, the land and so on. Typically, they stress the need for harmony and balance in all connections and relationships. Consequently, what may be seen as problematic, what is seen as a 'cause' and what are perceived as appropriate solutions or forms of help, will be grounded in individual and group beliefs and values.

In a discussion of Australian Aboriginal understandings of the term 'community', Cummins and her colleagues (2008) make the point that while non-Aboriginals may use the term simply to describe the people who live in a place, for Aboriginal people the term is more problematic. For instance, they may understand that they will need to be identified as a community in a particular place in order to receive services, but culturally may embrace a much larger understanding of place, so that where you live is not necessarily your 'place'. Family relationships and kinship networks not only transcend particular places but are also based upon other affiliations that go beyond blood relationships, such as the responsibilities that derive from one's totem (Cummins et al, 2008, p 46). Furthermore, even the conception of who is 'family' differs as this quotation indicates:

> A term that I struggle with is the non-Indigenous use of the term 'extended family' to explain Aboriginal family relationships. When I was growing up I had eight or nine mothers and grandmothers and all of that, and so I took it for granted that all these people had different responsibilities to the children. That's how we grew up. But when I went away from my home I had to learn a whole new language. (Cummins et al, 2008, p 48)

For Cummins and her colleagues, 'roles and responsibilities are all tied up in how the community functions. If the roles and responsibilities are not intact then community is not able to function' (Cummins et al, 2008, p 49). Accordingly, attempts at interventions that do not engage with local conceptions of family and social networks, personal roles and responsibilities, belief systems or understandings of the world are unlikely to succeed or have any enduring benefits.

The problem of simply imposing Western perceptions upon the situations of indigenous people is most apparent in the different understandings of mental distress and mental health. It has long been recognised that not only is there cultural variability in symptoms, but also considerable variability in ideas of causality, and hence in what is seen as an appropriate response or treatment (Patel et al, 1995; Gilbert, 1999). Even resilience, which is typically conceptualised as an individual characteristic with some relational aspects, such as secure attachment and staying in school, has been shown to be supported and expressed in different ways in different cultural contexts (Ungar, 2008). Again, it is the tendency of Western perspectives to decontextualise personal behaviour from its social and cultural location that is most problematic. Indeed, as Evans-Campbell notes in regard to the notion of historical trauma, while the empirical basis of this notion is not yet well established, the fact that it has been so readily accepted by many people within American Indian and Alaska Native communities indicates that 'its descriptive power strongly resonates with those to whom it is meant to apply and ... it is capturing an important part of their individual and community experience that other models miss' (2008, p 317). She also notes that while the focus of most studies so far has been upon the negative effects associated with trauma, some have identified positive effects resulting from survival and adaptation, such as enhanced family and community ties.

For some years now there have been attempts to avoid ethnocentric presumptions about practice, especially in attempts to promote a more culturally aware and sensitive social work practice. These efforts typically aim to educate and train workers in particular knowledge and skills for working with specific groups or communities of people (Castex, 1994; Green, 1999; Hart, 2002; Hurdle, 2002; Green and Thomas, 2005), although some writers propose more generic approaches (Dana et al, 1992; Pinderhughes, 1997). There are also differences in what is claimed by different writers. Some aim for cultural competence, while others, recognising that this might be an overly ambitious or even unattainable goal, more modestly aim to develop a culturally informed practice. Weaver's work in the US has focused on those who work with Native Americans, but its concluding recommendations could be generalised to other circumstances. According to Weaver, the culturally competent social worker should:

- understand and appreciate diversity among and within Native American populations;
- know the history, culture and contemporary realities of specific Native American clients;
- have good general social work skills and strong skills in patience, listening and tolerance of silence;
- be aware of his or her own biases and need for wellness;
- display humility and a willingness to learn;
- be respectful, non-judgemental and open-minded;
- value social justice and decolonise his or her own thought processes (Weaver, 1999, p 223).

Generalised, these are helpful exhortations that in themselves would do much to reduce the scope for ill-informed and damaging interventions, but there are risks in some approaches to cultural competence. In some accounts there is a tendency to assume that cultures are homogeneous and universally shared by all members of a community, whereas even a moment's reflection upon our own personal situations will quickly allow the recognition that different people for a wide range of reasons may have different attachments to the dominant culture, and may selectively apply, modify or disregard particular traditions. For instance, Green and Thomas point out that 'there is a spectrum of culture and tradition that varies from person to person. Some people that live on the reserve will be traditional and follow the teachings of their culture and tradition. Others will not' (2009, p 15). There is also a tendency to treat culture as a rather static and fixed entity, but it is evident that cultures in terms of attitudes and practices not only change, but do so with some rapidity at times. Thus, training materials for cultural competence may be irrelevant in particular circumstances, or may quickly become outdated and inaccurate. Consequently, there is a risk that workers, having received such training, may assume that no further learning is necessary.

Another approach to the problem of uninformed and culturally insensitive practice is to develop a workforce that mirrors the populations that it serves by recruiting and training practitioners from local indigenous groups. In Australia, there has been some criticism of same-group recruitment where it has been perceived either as a means of incorporating and, thus, disempowering indigenous advocates, or as means of avoiding giving proper self-determination (Briskman, 2007). Nonetheless, it is generally the case that indigenous people are more likely to access services when the staff are from the same group, as this should ensure familiarity with local culture and, where necessary, linguistic capacity in the local language. For instance, the Ceduna family violence report referred to above recommended that local Aboriginal men be appointed as counsellors for violent men and given appropriate, culturally based training (Taylor et al, 2001). In another example, reported in detail in Chapter 7, much of the success of the Far West Aboriginal Enterprise Network has been due to the skills, networks, cultural embeddedness and cultural knowledge of the local Aboriginal woman who was appointed as the community developer. However, as Gross points out, 'to be Native is not a sufficient condition for enhancing the chances that ... interventions will work' (2003, p 40).

While workers having a similar identity and culture is likely to prove valuable, there are many other factors that bear upon the likelihood of success. For example, people with problems that are perceived as being stigmatising and shaming may be unwilling to share these with social workers who are members of their own group. There is also some evidence from studies of interpreters that they may be unwilling to accurately convey information that they feel will reflect poorly upon their own group (Baker et al, 1991). Some of the pressures of anyone living and working in the same community were noted in the preceding chapter, but indigenous workers may feel additional pressure to be role models. This may conflict with their own perceptions of themselves as anything other than equals within the community (Green and Thomas, 2005). Of course, these possibilities should not lead to a rejection of same-group recruitment, but they do indicate the need for a more developed understanding of what is needed and what the possible dynamics of such interactions may be in terms of contacts with potential service users and also within the agency itself. There is also a risk that the recruitment of same-group workers can result in the 'ghettoisation' of indigenous issues when non-native workers and the agency withdraw from active engagement and leave everything to same-group workers, whose work then becomes isolated from the mainstream of concerns within it. In Canada, there have been some successful initiatives in developing culturally informed training programmes for both native and non-native workers (Morrisette et al, 1993; Bodor and Zapf, 2002; Bella and Lyall, 2004). Issues of recruitment and training will be further developed in Chapter 8.

Much more common are attempts to develop particular practice initiatives that are responsive to cultural context. Either through the adaptation of mainstream interventions or, as in the case of family group conferences, from the utilisation of existing traditions and practices among indigenous peoples. For instance, in Canada an alternative aboriginal justice scheme, the Toronto Community Council Project, was developed to divert aboriginal adult offenders from the justice system. In a review of its operation Proulx (2003) contended that not only was this a more culturally appropriate system, but it also had good outcomes with nearly two thirds of offenders wholly completing the 'dispositions', and reduced rates of recidivism. Nevertheless, such developments should not be initiated or appraised uncritically. There are a number of potential problems in developing approaches to decision-making that involve the wider social group. There have been concerns that family group conferencing might lead to 'mother-blaming' or undue pressure upon weaker family members. In regard to 'sentencing circles' and innovations in restorative justice, there are concerns that they: may suppress victims' voices, may not protect their interests, may result in very different outcomes for similar offences and may lead to overly lenient outcomes for serious offences (Dickson-Gilmore and La Prairie, 2005).

In Hawaii, there have been a number of interventions based upon traditional Hawaiian practices (Hurdle, 2002). These include, for instance, Ho'oponopono, a family conflict-resolution process that has some similarity with the family group conferencing models developed in New Zealand, and Ho'opono Ahua'a, a community development project that initiated a range of developments based upon traditional values, including a child care centre and health promotion programme.

Perhaps, the best known and certainly the most influential, in terms of being most widely used and adapted, is the model of family group conferences developed in New Zealand and taken up enthusiastically in Canada, the UK and the US (Barbour, 1991; Pennell and Burford, 1994; Marsh and Crow, 1998; Lupton and Nixon, 1999). The basic notion, which derived from Māori family practices, was to widen the circle of decision-making in child welfare by involving the wider family group and other people who are significant in a child's life. This process is undertaken through a self-directed staged model of discussion, decision making and planning, in which professionals take only a minor role in facilitating the process and its outcomes, rather than directing it as they might typically do. The flexibility of family group conferencing, particularly in regard to participants, venue, timing and duration, allows practitioners to modify the approach to suit different cultural contexts. For example, one suggestion aimed at increasing the cultural responsiveness of the approach arose from the observation that regardless of whether a meeting was intended to be held indoors or outdoors, Cherokee men were more likely to be outside. This led to the idea of having a 'cook out', a meal that would bring men and women family members together to improve communication (Waites et al, 2004). Family group conferences provide an excellent example of how 'Western' social work practice can learn new ways of helping from other cultures (Midgley, 1981; Lynn, 2001).

The question of how social services for indigenous peoples should be best organised, in terms of whether they are provided by separate agencies or are developed within existing mainstream provision, has been a contentious one (Briskman, 2007). For instance, Leonard (1997) contends that 'segregated' organisations may be necessary to overcome deep-rooted prejudices and discrimination. However, we doubt that a simple rule can be applied because of the diversity and variability of the circumstances of different people, and different contexts. At the heart of this question lie complex issues of power and capacity, and, as we indicate in regard to community-oriented practice in Chapter 7, decisions about the 'best' strategies for change may not be confined solely to narrow perceptions of effectiveness. The International Federation of Social Workers (IFSW, 2005) leaves the question open, but is forthright in supporting moves to self-determination, and is quite clear in stating that:

> As oppressed indigenous groups, they are to be given special consideration based upon an understanding of the conditions that have led to their displacement and economic upheaval, as well as the loss of their political and social rights and human dignity. (IFSW, 2005, p 1)

There appears to be no widely accepted view on this question (Briskman, 2007), but it is worth noting that many politicians who resist indigenous rights are opposed to separate service provision, which they typically characterise as 'special treatment' that stokes the resentment of disaffected white constituents. The underpinning arguments about welfare principles have been the subject of considerable debate in the literature on citizenship and welfare rights, where a key question has been whether the provision of differentiated services undermines support for universal entitlements (Offe, 1993; Pugh and Thompson, 1999).

The increasing political independence and autonomy available to some indigenous peoples is also permitting the development of different strategies for social helping and improvement. These will be further reviewed in Chapter 7, but worthy of note here is that while these strategies include the provision of personal social services, they are more likely to focus upon community development and link different agencies and domains of social and economic life. For example, this might involve recognition of the fact that improvements in the circumstances of individual women may well be best achieved through the emancipation of all women through literacy schemes, or through community banks offering small loans for economic start-up activity (Martinez-Brawley, 2006). The experiences of developing countries in Asia and Africa may also provide models for action as they share some similar difficulties in emerging from colonisation and its legacies. For instance, in a review of the lessons to be learned from survival strategies in sub-Saharan Africa, Laird notes the importance of 'reciprocal exchanges of resources within communities, the pooling of community resources ... domestic and economic collaboration within intergenerational households and diversification of livelihoods' (2008, p 147).

Conclusion

Examination of the histories and contemporary experiences of many indigenous peoples reveals a grim and lethal picture of abuse, exploitation, expropriation, marginalisation, displacement, deculturation and discrimination, which needs to be recognised. However, there is a risk in acknowledging this 'big picture', in that it may overshadow or discount more positive experiences and possibilities. For instance, if outsiders simply see indigenous peoples solely as the victims of colonisation, it can lead to an undervaluing of the strengths and positive capacities that do exist. In the Introduction we made the point that idealisations and stereotypes frequently distort external perceptions of rural people and places, and this also applies to understandings and expectations of indigenous peoples. For example, holistic belief systems may be rejected by some people, respected by others or even romanticised by still others. The very existence of differences in ethnicity and culture may, as we shall see in the following chapter, be ignored or exoticised. Moreover, any simple assumption that there is always a traditional culture to be reinvigorated, or that all indigenous people wish to do this, ignores the diversity of individual and group social locations and the complexity of cultures and how they change and become modified. Indeed, for many indigenous peoples the challenge is not so much how to resurrect and re-establish traditions, but how to live as indigenous people within societies where they may wish to use modern technologies and conveniences, but at the same time wish to resist or reject those aspects of Westernisation and colonisation that have been most damaging to their communities. Consequently, we urge readers not to make assumptions, but, instead, to base their understandings of particular individuals, groups and communities upon careful appraisal and first-hand knowledge.

The experience gained in work with indigenous peoples from a range of countries suggests seven key implications for social work practice. They are:

• the importance of working with local cultures and key local organisations and people such as Elders to avoid ethnocentric and stereotypical presumptions and irrelevant and damaging interventions;
• the need to promote self-determination for individuals and communities;
• the need to recognise the importance of interdependence rather than simply reifying notions of independence;

- the necessity of working with broader groupings of families and communities;
- the relevance of developmental models to promote community strengths and, in turn, community welfare;
- the importance of advocacy and political action;
- the importance of a commitment to change.

This last point is crucial for it underpins all those that precede it. A question repeatedly asked of social work audiences by Cindy Blackstock, the Executive Director of the First Nations Child and Family Caring Society of Canada, is 'Now you know the dismal state of indigenous child welfare in Canada, what are you going to do about it?' (cited in Green and Thomas, 2009, p 12). In Australia, Ban, commenting upon a literature review by McMahon (2002) that demonstrated the lack of published material on social work with Indigeneous Australians, noted that most of what did exist 'tended to reflect social policies rather than challenge them' (2005, p 384).

While the movement to self-governance continues to gain momentum in many countries, it is not without its own problems. In Canada, Dickson-Gilmore and La Prairie (2005) have pointed out how the push to get indigenous communities to 'take responsibility' for their own affairs and problems diverts attention away from the fundamental social injustice that prevails in terms of such things as poverty and unemployment, and, consequently, ignores the structural factors that hinder or obstruct progress. Shewell (2004) has also demonstrated how government policies that created dependence in the first place, as they became modified in Canada to an apparently more enlightened perspective of self-governance, still embodied the underlying presumption, that is, that First Nations were always responsible for their own problems. Furthermore, Davis (2007) in the US has noted that a legacy of poor funding continues to hinder the development of satisfactory indigenous services, and that there are also difficulties in coordinating services with external bodies, for example, in deciding who has authority in particular situations, and subsequent difficulties in meeting the needs of community members across regulatory boundaries. Moreover, such developments cannot take place in political isolation as external perceptions will play a significant role in the willingness of national governments to support independence and autonomy. As Davis has noted:

> The public's perception of tribes wrongly stereotypes an already marginalized population of American Indian people

and their governments. Tribal governments are seen as either unfit to address the modern needs of their people, or as groups that have an unfair advantage over other segments of society. (Davis, 2007, p 23)

Davis's observation is also applicable to other countries, such as Australia where erroneous perceptions of leadership incompetence by non-Indigenous Australians seemed to play a part in the abolition of ATSIC noted earlier in this chapter.

The situation of many indigenous peoples has some similarities with the situation in many developing countries, in that the need for political action or at least an explicit political dimension to social work is evident. Mmatli, writing in an African context, has argued that social work must embrace political activism because the 'majority of clients in Africa are affected by structural problems arising from political processes' (2008, p 297) and that unless social workers become more engaged, then the agendas for social work action will be set by other professional groups such as economists and bureaucrats. Mmatli, like other writers who argue for political engagement (Midgley, 1981; Mullaly, 1993; Reisch, 2000; Postle and Beresford, 2007), acknowledges that there are limitations to such action, but identifies four strategies – lobbying, participation in electoral politics, political education and diligent voting. The first three can be seen as part of the professional role, while the fourth one relates to personal choice in voting preferences. Similarly, in the US there have been significant non-partisan efforts to mobilise the indigenous vote to maximise influence in local, state and federal government. Davis (2007) has noted that this can be an effective way of educating non-native populations about native issues.

Approaches to practice need to be selected according to the particular circumstances of particular societies and communities (see www.IFSW. org). One difficulty is assuming that an initiative that has worked in one place within one indigenous group will necessarily work in another. For instance, in North America, ideas that originally arose from Lakota and other Plains peoples that have been widely adopted and welcomed in many other places are also thought by some to represent another form of colonisation. Nonetheless, it is clear from the material reviewed in this chapter that the circumstances of many indigenous people impel social work towards community-focused and developmental modes of intervention, and these are likely to be the most effective means of improving welfare in ways that accord with traditional cultural values and contemporary practices. Of course, this does not preclude the possibility of using some individually focused interventions if circumstances merit them. A politically informed and activist practice may also be justified if the targets for intervention require it (Midgley, 2001), for example, challenging organisations outside of the community such as regional and national governments, or big corporations. However, there are situations where the challenge may need to be undertaken from within the indigenous society, perhaps in challenging the abuse, exploitation or oppression of marginalised groups or individuals within it. For some writers this creates a tension between commitment to a culturally informed and culturally appropriate practice that more or less explicitly embraces some degree of cultural relativity and acceptance of local customs and practices, and a more general or universal conception of human rights, which might support a more selective or critical perception of them. Midgley, for example, notes that 'it is extremely difficult to reconcile these different positions' (2001, p 32). We would not wish to deny these difficulties, but we do think it possible to navigate them more or less successfully by recognising that both 'positions' are social constructions.

Cultural practices clearly arise from behaviour and beliefs in particular societies and communities at particular times, and so are quite obviously 'human-made', and the same is true of universal declarations of human rights. The latter, of course, embody notions of moral behaviour that are not actually universal but are stated as if they were 'fundamental' entitlements, whereas they may be more accurately perceived as wish statements or desired outcomes. These declarations, too, also emerge from socially and historically specific circumstances and embody particular discourses. Nonetheless, our view as 'weak relativists' (see Butler and Pugh, 2004) is that even if the idea of universal truth is not sustainable, it is still often possible to discern the relative accuracy and merits of different 'truth claims'. Thus, we are pragmatists who recognise and respect the knowledge and practices of different social groupings, and obviously understand that social work interventions are unlikely to succeed without doing so, but who still wish to retain some broader perspective for judgement. However, since we do not think it is possible to have a 'view from nowhere', this inevitably is a socially located position that carries attendant risks of partiality and ethnocentrism. Our view is that social workers:

> should be quite adamant in rejecting the kind of simplistic multiculturalism which leads to a sense of uncritical relativism – a position which effectively neutralises the possibility of intervention ... we should accept that [there]

is a moral choice, namely a fundamental commitment to the core value of human equality. (Pugh, 1997, pp 19–20)

For without such a commitment how would we justify our concerns about the historical maltreatment and the contemporary inequities that we think merit action? In the final analysis, we think that the judgement of the value of our actions should be derived from an examination of the consequences of human behaviour. For example, in Western societies it may be that it is our knowledge of the damaging consequences of child abuse that provides the most secure justification for intervention. This position means that we can never be entirely sure about the legitimacy of what we do until after we have done it, and perhaps sometimes not even then. However, we can learn from past mistakes and, as in many other aspects of social work practice, while it is not always clear what may be the most effective means of action, because of a lack of knowledge, evidence or complexity, we often have firmer knowledge of what does not work or what may carry unacceptable risks.

In conclusion, we agree and support the long history of calls for the 'indigenisation' of social work goals and methods to meet the challenges of particular places (Khinduka, 1971; Nagpaul, 1972; Walton and El Nasr, 1988; Midgley, 2001; Mmatli, 2008), but note that there is, nevertheless, a great deal of agreement at an international level both within social work, for instance in the International Federation of Social Workers' International Policy on Indigenous Peoples (IFSW, 2005), and in larger fora like the United Nations, as to what desired goals in terms of human rights might be. We also recognise that these are often stated in abstract and general terms that belie difficulties in their application because of variability in perceptions and judgements of actions and outcomes. Ultimately, we do not think that there is a 'solution' to this tension and so being mindful of the mistakes of the past, and especially in terms of cultural and professional imperialism, we think that we have to work in this contested territory with goodwill, some humility and a constant dialogue as to the worthiness of our objectives and actions.

FOUR

The experience of other minorities

Introduction

The term 'minorities' is used here in a political sense to indicate the position of individuals and groups who may lack effective representation and political power, and whose needs tend to be neglected or ignored. It is intended to describe the status and social and economic position of a group rather than provide any indication of their size. It was noted earlier that the most common experience of minorities in rural areas is of relative disadvantage compared to other groups, and that owing to their comparative social and political invisibility, they were much less likely to have their needs addressed by welfare services.

This chapter begins by reviewing how the processes of discrimination and differentiation may operate in rural communities and draws upon an earlier paper (Pugh, 2004a). It then identifies some of the minority groups who may be found in rural areas and provides some general indication of their circumstances. Although this chapter reviews some of the ways in which minorities may be discriminated against, these accounts are indicative of general experiences and should not be taken as inevitable occurrences in the life of any given individual. This is a crucial point, as the social dynamics of small communities, as well as 'exposing' individuals who are perceived as different to the risks of social isolation and marginalisation, may also paradoxically provide opportunities for individual acceptance. That is, individuals without necessarily feeling integrated into a community may nonetheless feel that they are able to establish a satisfactory way of life. The ways in which they are able to do this are varied, but a common factor may be the degree to which small communities provide opportunities for social contact in which individuals from minority backgrounds may be encountered and perceived in ways that free them from the stereotypical assumptions that might usually be made about people like them (Pugh, 2004a).

Difference and discrimination in rural communities

In the Introduction it was noted that social problems in rural areas generally are not always recognised and often seem to pass unnoticed (Cloke and Little, 1997; Pugh, 2003). The privileging of urban perspectives together with the comparative 'invisibility' of problems among dispersed and remote communities are obviously significant factors. Furthermore, given the higher social visibility of life within small communities, people with problems may try to keep them hidden, so that they are not seen as being problematic, dependent or deviant in any way. However, in regard to discrimination there is another factor, which is that the recognition of forms of discrimination such as racism and homophobia is much less likely when idealisations of rural communities ignore these forms of social difference in the first place (Sibley, 1997). One of the most pervasive assumptions underpinning discrimination is the marginalisation of minorities by the assumption of social homogeneity, that is, the assumption of similarity and commonality within communities. We also noted that the idealisation of rural communities may serve important political functions as dominant groups choose to represent themselves and their communities in particular ways. Typically these sorts of representations ignore or underplay the presence of difference in communities, with the result that the histories, the experience and the realities of minority group lives are rarely recognised. For example, it is widely assumed in the UK that the presence of black people and other visible minorities in the countryside is a comparatively recent phenomenon, largely dating from post-Second World War migration. However, there have been black people in Britain since Roman times at least, and in the 17th and 18th centuries there were numerous reports and records of freed black slaves living in rural places (Fryer, 1984; Dabydeen et al, 2007). This assumption also ignores the presence of minorities such as Roma and gypsies who have been in the UK and in many other countries in Western Europe for hundreds of years.

If diversity is overlooked or ignored, then not only are some people not perceived as being present in the countryside, they are also much less likely to be included within the conception of the 'community'. In the US, Hayden (1998) has made this point about black invisibility in regard to African-Americans living in the Appalachians, and this has also been noted of rural areas in the UK (de Lima, 2001; Chakraborti and Garland, 2004). For example, if people's erroneous perceptions are that there are no black or other ethnic minorities living locally, then it follows for many of them that racism cannot be a problem. This is not simply a problem of idealisation and oversight, but also a problem of understanding, because it assumes that discrimination arises solely from the presence of difference, that is, that discrimination is essentially a reaction to that 'presence'. Unsurprisingly, those who embrace such 'explanations' will often argue that problems of racism can be diminished simply by reducing the numbers of those who are perceived as different. Crucially, this localisation of the 'explanation' ignores the dynamics of oppression that originate in the wider society.

Research into discrimination in rural areas is rather patchy in coverage and limited in scale, with some groups being under-investigated or entirely ignored, and this is reflected in the variable coverage in the succeeding sections of this chapter. Even where there is relevant research, it typically focuses upon the direct experience of particular minorities, and there are relatively few studies that examine the performance of rural social services in regard to minorities generally. For instance, in the UK there have been some valuable studies into the experiences of women and ethnic minorities in the UK (Jay, 1992; Whatmore et al, 1994; Nizhar,1995; Little and Austin, 1996; Agg and Phillips, 1998; de Lima, 1999, 2006; Dhalech, 1999; Chakraborti and Garland, 2003, 2004), but many of these are quite small in scale, and less attention has been paid to the experiences of other minorities, such as gypsies, gay men and lesbians, although there is an increasing awareness of these 'neglected others' (Philo, 1992; Cloke et al, 1994; Bell and Valentine, 1995). In the US, with its stronger tradition of rural research, there is a larger body of work especially on the experiences of migrants, women, gay men and lesbians. What emerges from many of these studies is that discrimination through processes of stigmatisation, stereotyping, marginalisation and victim-blaming are commonplace and that many individuals and groups experience social exclusion, harassment and even violence. A key concept in many accounts is the notion of 'othering', which refers to the process by which social groups affirm their own identity by stigmatising or denigrating the identity of an inferior 'other' (Said, 1993).

Overall, the picture looks pretty bleak as rural areas seem to have the same sorts of problems with discrimination as urban areas. However, it might be a mistake to assume that the lives of all minorities in the countryside are constantly blighted by discrimination. While being different in the countryside can be a peculiarly exposed and often isolated experience, it is not inevitably a negative one (Oswald and Culton, 2003; Robinson and Gardner, 2006). We want to make it clear that we do not wish to challenge or refute the existence of discrimination, or minimise in any way the harsh experiences that have been reported, or argue that such studies are superfluous. But, we do want to question whether the findings so far are entirely representative of minority experiences. In particular, we want to consider the consequences of adopting exploratory perspectives that are predominantly geared to examining negative consequences.

Unsurprisingly given their starting point, studies that set out to explore negative experiences usually find evidence of discrimination. However, we question whether such studies adequately reflect the variations and subtleties of minority experiences in rural areas, as there are some indications that perhaps they do not. Many people from minorities, having been born and raised in rural areas and not having had any initial choice about where they live, have nonetheless chosen to remain or, in some instances, return to the area. Although there are obviously social and economic obstacles to leaving, these are unlikely to have deterred all of those who have stayed in the area. What seems to be missing in many accounts is any recognition of personal agency, for instance, the possibility that individuals may have made considered decisions about what they want for themselves and their families, and have on balance concluded that the merits of rural life outweigh the disadvantages.

In Australia, the US and the UK, there is evidence of members of minority groups choosing to move into rural areas (ONS, 2002; Avant, 2004; Falk et al, 2004; Lichter and Johnson, 2006). Many of them are likely to have had some experience of racism or other forms of discrimination in urban areas, and while they may also have uncritically absorbed some of the idealised notions of rural communities, they are likely to realise that they are moving into areas where their 'difference' may possibly become even more evident to others in the community, and perhaps be risky for them. Yet they have still chosen to settle in rural areas, and, according to census data, their numbers are increasing. The point is that a broader examination of the experience of existing minorities in rural areas may allow a better appreciation of the variability of their lives and so undermine overly deterministic assumptions about negative experiences. Although discriminatory attitudes fuelled by homophobia, racism and sexism appear to be commonplace, negative outcomes such as exclusion and marginalisation are not inevitable consequences of social difference. There are grounds for thinking that the prevalence and experience of discrimination in rural communities is much more variable than most studies so far indicate (Oswald and Culton, 2003; Green, 2006; Robinson and Gardner, 2006). Our own observations suggest that there can be considerable variation from one locality to another, as well as between the experiences of different individuals and groups. For example, some small communities have a tendency to 'support their own', especially in the face of external threats, and so local identification as a community member may take precedence over minority status.

In Chapter 2 we noted that the problem with trying to make a simple distinction between insiders and outsiders is that it reduces the complexity of social location to a simple dichotomy of 'in' or 'out', despite the fact that this may not be how most people experience their social situation in rural communities, where their personal experience may be of a much more fluid and contingent set of possibilities. In earlier work (Pugh, 1998), we noted that although people may hold derogatory and damaging stereotypical ideas about particular groups, they may at a personal level operate with a degree of courtesy and respect towards individual members of such 'devalued' categories. One possible explanation for this might be found in Billig's contention that while humans have a tendency towards cognitive categorisation – generalisation – they also have a countervailing capacity to individualise and make exceptions – particularisation (Billig, 1976). This raises a key question: 'Do the social dynamics of small communities provide greater opportunities for this to happen?'

Local responses to difference are rarely as unified and homogeneous as is often thought, and there may be some tacit or covert acceptance that can be extremely supportive for individuals who are otherwise apparently isolated. Such 'freeing up' of expectations may only result in a conditional acceptance, but this may create the space in which a person can live their life more positively than might otherwise be expected. However, the awareness that one's identity is always potentially a point of issue, either for oneself in resisting and responding to the marginalising tendencies of the wider society, or for others who may use it in myriad ways to attack, scapegoat or otherwise discriminate, can create a condition of continuing uncertainty. Indeed, this feeling of contingency is experienced by many who are perceived as different who move into and apparently settle successfully in rural areas (Burnett, 1996).

Exceptionally, those who are different may find some acceptance through the exoticisation of their difference, that is, their difference may be celebrated or made special in some way, it can be seen in expressions of local pride in the fact that such a person lives in the area. Thus, the difference may be 'showcased' and used in a self-congratulatory way to indicate tolerance or sophistication (Grewal, 2000). It may be ritualised, as can be seen in the acceptance of the annual arrival of gypsies and travellers for horse fairs or seasonal work in some areas of the UK. Exoticisation is of course subject to broader cultural trends, but it seems to be more common when there is relatively limited social contact between those who are perceived as different and other members of the local community. Nevertheless, acceptance as an exotic is a peculiar status, because it is based upon the continuing presumption of the person's difference. Thus, it is likely to preclude any broader acceptance. Chakraborti and Garland (2004) consider that it is a complicit 'playing along' with othering that continues to confirm a person's inferior minority status.

Settled black and other minority ethnic groups

This section addresses the situation of minority ethnic groups who are settled inhabitants in rural communities, but who have originated from elsewhere or have found themselves isolated by political division and the redrawing of national boundaries. Perhaps the best-known, and certainly one of the largest, groups are the descendants of African slaves in the US, many of whom, especially in the southern states, continue to live in rural areas. Over 6 million African-Americans live in rural areas, with just over half (53%) of them living in the south (US Bureau of the Census, 2000, cited in Avant, 2004). They are disadvantaged compared to other ethnic groups, and disadvantaged even in comparison with other African-Americans living in urban areas (Snipp, 1996; Hayden, 1998; Avant, 2004). An analysis of race, ethnicity and underemployment (which included unemployment and low income) in rural areas in the US used population survey data from 1968 to 1998 and found large and persistent inequalities that were only partly explained by other variables such as education and marital status. It concluded that 'color remained a substantial barrier to adequate employment' (Slack and Jensen, 2002, p 221).

Nevertheless, in recent years there has also been an increase in the number of African-Americans moving to live in the south, partly because of the expanding economies of the southern states, partly because of perceptions of deterioration in many northern cities and partly because of a desire to re-establish older roots or to seek a better life (Avant, 2004). An analysis by Falk and his colleagues (2004) showed that there were some distinctive groupings within this internal migration, for instance, some people had been born in the south and were returning home, while others had been born elsewhere. Those who had been born in the south were more likely to be returning to rural places and were less well educated than those who had been born in the north. Overall though, this migration is comprised of individuals who are generally of higher socio-economic status compared to people in the places they came from and compared to people in their new home areas in the south, being both better educated and more skilled. Although their destinations include urban areas and cities, there is a trend towards smaller places, including residence in rural areas.

While most readers will be aware of the large numbers of Mexican migrant workers in the US, it is often not understood that people of Mexican descent have been settled in Arizona, Colorado, New Mexico, Southern California and Texas since long before the Mexican War of 1846–8 (Martinez-Brawley and Zorita, 2001). So, while large numbers of Mexicans in the US are often perceived as short-stay workers, in some areas many are permanent residents with their numbers increasing as more recent arrivals settle. However, as Chavez (2005) has documented within a small rural town in California, while they remain a group with diverse experiences according to where they live and whether they expect to remain, local long-term white residents may nonetheless marginalise and stereotype them in negative ways, for example, in seeing them as lacking interest in traditional community activities, or perceiving their youngsters to be responsible for drug misuse and other crime. Chavez contends that while 'Mexicans were embraced as cheap transnational laborers necessary for agricultural production ... white residents have ambivalent feelings about [their] social integration' (2005, p 328). Lichter and Johnson, in a study of settlement patterns among immigrants, noted that although America's immigrant populations are increasingly spread over the country, they still remain more concentrated than the native-born population (2006). Cultural differences, such as displaying Mexican flags or speaking Spanish, may be things that crystallise local resentments particularly in places that have not had much ethnic diversity (Chavez, 2005; Lichter and Johnson, 2006).

In many countries there may be small 'residual' populations remaining in particular areas. In the UK there are pockets of people, some former prisoners of war and others former soldiers in the free forces, who have remained living in the localities around former camps and bases, especially where they were employed in agriculture. Similarly, in Australia, some of the descendants of Chinese miners remain in the former Gold Rush areas, although today few are employed in mining.

Roma and travelling peoples

The term 'travelling peoples' is an umbrella heading that covers a wide range of groups. Perhaps the best-known, certainly in Europe, are the Roma who are not a homogeneous grouping and are also present in Canada and the US (Weyrauch, 2001). There are also other distinctive groups, such as the Sinti in Germany and Irish travellers and tinkers within Great Britain. It is important to recognise that 'The terms "Gypsy" and "Traveller" (and "Roma") are not neutral and are heavily contested, both within and outside communities' (Cemlyn and Clark, 2005, p 146). Within the literature there is a continuing debate about how best to describe and characterise these groups, some of whom share common cultures and language, but others sharing only, perhaps, a propensity for frequent movement and relocation (Belton, 2004, 2005). A common feature that is noted is the importance of an oral tradition of history and close family and kinships ties. Okely (1997) makes the point that the differences between travelling and non-travelling people are often exaggerated especially when groups are exoticised as 'proper' gypsies. Although not all travelling people do actually move around from place to place or live in caravans and trailers, this feature of their culture remains commonplace for many. While many travelling people live permanently in urban areas, those who do move around are often found in country areas or on the rural outskirts of larger towns. Historically, travelling peoples have been an important part of the rural workforce undertaking seasonal employment, especially at harvest time.

Travelling peoples have endured a long history of social antipathy, discrimination and violence, and they are often viewed as an undesirable and troublesome presence (Hawes and Perez, 1996; Lucassen et al, 1998; Barany, 2001; Petrova, 2003; CRE, 2006). In recent years the social policy response to travelling peoples has either been to ignore them or, alternatively, to 'encourage' or force them to settle in one place and assimilate into the dominant culture. Negative attitudes towards gypsies in Europe and America have resulted in many of them adopting a survival strategy of invisibility to avoid unwanted attention (Harris, 2001; Csepeli and Simon, 2004). In recent years there has been much concern about the treatment of Roma in some of the former Soviet bloc countries (Barany, 2001). One woman cited by Clark said:

> My family has always tried to appear Romanian. Especially during the war it was much better not to be a Gypsy. Actually, it has always been better not to be a Gypsy. (Clark, 1998, p 7)

Clark notes that this strategy, together with the sometimes hostile or ambivalent attitudes of governments who do not always identify travelling peoples in census data, makes it difficult to ascertain their numbers and often results in their needs being ignored or underestimated, as 'If they don't "exist" then their needs can be denied, they do not require grants, services or "special needs" funding because they are "invisible" or "look after their own"' (Clark, 1998, p 10).

A more recent phenomenon in Western Europe has been the emergence of new groups of travellers who have been described by a number of names, including new travellers and new-age travellers. Some of these groups emerged from the free festival movement while others are explicitly aligned with particular political movements, such as green politics, and groups with anti-globalisation and anti-capitalist agendas. While some groups have an explicit counterculture, others may be more idiosyncratic with the common base for membership being simply the rejection of a settled lifestyle. Some travellers may have a permanent base to which they return from time to time, while others spend their lives moving from place to place, perhaps seeking casual employment, better weather or joining up with others for social gatherings. While these groups may have little in common, the singular feature of their behaviour that tends to arouse resentment and antipathy is the rejection of a conventional lifestyle. In many cases they are commonly perceived as 'work-shy scroungers' (Webster and Millar, 2001) whose behaviour, at best, is a nuisance and, at worst, is criminal.

The available evidence on welfare indicates that travelling peoples generally do worse than the non-travelling populations (Walsh et al, 2006). Those who do move around often have difficulty in finding healthy and safe sites to park up in, and their children typically have difficulties in accessing education and when they do so are more likely to be excluded. Their health chances are poor, and even when welfare services are available, travellers may be reluctant to engage with them, fearing an insensitive, overbearing intrusive experience with officialdom (Brearley, 1996; Liégeois, 1998; Cemlyn, 2000; van Cleemput, 2000; National Assembly for Wales, 2003; Parry et al, 2004; Cemlyn and Clark, 2005). Within travelling groups that have a strong and well-established culture it can be very difficult for members who transgress group norms in some way, or are subject to violence and abuse, to seek help from outside of the community. In some instances, efforts to turn to the outside world may lead to sanctions and even expulsion from the travelling community (Boushel, 1994; Weyrauch, 2001).

Migrant workers

The presence of migrant workers in urban areas around the world is commonplace. However, with a few exceptions, such as Mexican fruit pickers in California, their presence in rural areas often goes unnoticed and unrecorded. Nonetheless, in many Westernised economies migrant workers have moved in to replace local workers in labour-intensive and traditionally low-wage enterprises in rural areas, such as agriculture and food processing. In many instances, migrants are filling vacancies for jobs that local people do not want. Mexican migrant workers can now be found in rural areas in the northern states of the US. In Italy and Spain, African workers are replacing local people who have either secured better jobs, or have moved to jobs in urban areas. While in Greece, Albanians have become an important resource to farmers in the northern mainland areas and have also become a significant feature of the informal care workforce (Kasimis et al, 2003). Of course, in many Westernised economies, the arrival of migrant workers into rural areas is not a new phenomenon as there is a long history of Irish and gypsy seasonal workers in the UK, Mexican workers coming into southern California to work as fruit pickers in the US and itinerant workers in the vineyards in France.

More recently, the expansion of the European Union to include former Soviet bloc countries has led to massive population movements into employment in the wealthier member states. In the UK, it is estimated that nearly a million Polish workers and their families entered after the accession treaty in 2004, and migrant workers comprise 12.5% of the working-age population (Home Office, 2007), although there are signs that economic recession and unfavourable exchange rates have diminished their numbers. While these workers have mostly settled in urban areas, increasingly they are moving into rural areas, finding work on farms, in food processing factories, and in catering and hotel work (TUC, 2004). In Ireland, in the small rural town of Gort in Galway, for example, one third of the population of 3,500 have come from Brazil, drawn by employment in the local meat processing industry. Some migrants may have a preference for working in rural areas, as one man said, 'I am from a country area at home in Latvia. I would be too frightened to live in a big city such as London or Manchester – too big, too noisy' (Hold et al, 2007, p 37).

There are concerns about the exploitation of these workers, in terms of wage rates that sometimes fall below the minimum wage level, illegal deductions from pay and, of course, given the risky nature of some of these industries, workplace safety (TUC, 2004; McKay et al, 2006).

Other areas of concern that have been noted include poor-quality housing, exploitation by unscrupulous landlords, limited access to public services, patchy access to advice, language services and opportunities to learn English, and potential exposure to discrimination and crime (de Lima et al, 2005; Wales Rural Observatory, 2006a; CAB, 2007; Institute for Public Policy Research, 2007; MIF, 2007). Migrant workers usually have limited entitlement to benefits and may quickly become homeless or destitute if they become unemployed (Audit Commission, 2007). While many migrant workers are young single adults, those who do have families may have difficulty with child care especially when they have early or late work shifts. In the UK, efforts to improve accessible advice and information on workers' rights and housing law for migrant workers are commonplace, although the development of other services, such as interpretation and translation facilities, is patchy.

These changes in location towards more rural employment have brought migrant workers into areas that have little experience of inward migration of foreign workers or asylum seekers and refugees. Their presence can add to existing problems such as local shortage of affordable rented accommodation, and create new challenges. Although many migrant workers do not initially intend to settle in their new workplaces, as Norman (1985) has documented in relation to post-war migration into the UK from the Caribbean, these intentions can be eroded by new family ties, limited income and limited opportunities. Within social work, concern about migration issues has taken a number of forms. Valtonen (2001) writing in a Finnish context sees welfare as being best maintained through support for employment. In Spain, Hernández-Plaza and her colleagues (2006) note that immigrants might prefer to seek help within their own informal social networks rather than use public services. In the UK, Humphries (2004) has pointed out the potential for social workers to be drawn into illiberal and oppressive measures aimed at monitoring and controlling immigrants, while Sakamoto (2007) contends that an uncritical assumption of conformist assimilation often underpins official notions of successful integration. However, the problem as Balgopal has noted, is that 'new immigrants, especially those who belong to ethnic minorities of colour, are expected to assimilate behaviorally without being given opportunities to assimilate structurally' (2000, p 231, cited in Sakamoto, 2007, p 519).

Migrant workers may be welcomed if they help to keep local services viable by registering for medical services and sending their children to local schools, or if they contribute directly to local welfare through their own employment or the employment of others. Simard (2009) researched a Canadian programme that provided medical services to rural communities in which many of the doctors originated from Asia, the Middle East, South America and the West Indies. They found that there was a complex interaction between professional, financial, geographical, social and community factors. Doctors were more likely to stay in the rural areas when they had a good level of social integration that included satisfying social relations with other members of the community, respect and social recognition, and feelings of belonging.

Gay and lesbian groups

The situation of gay men and lesbian women in rural areas is complex. Unlike other immediately visible minorities, whose difference may be recognised or signalled by their skin colour, mode of dress or cultural and religious behaviours, sexual differentiation, because it arises from the intimate sphere of sexual preference and behaviour, is not intrinsically evident to other people, unless, of course, individuals signal that they are 'out'. Moreover, because homosexuality has historically in most Westernised societies been seen as an aberrant phenomenon often subject to negative social perceptions, many young gay men and lesbian women have struggled to establish a satisfactory sense of personal identity in the context of an overwhelming heterosexual norm. Typically, a choice has to be made as to how to manage one's sexual preference or sexual identity and whether to reveal or signal this to the wider community. An audience may hold reductionist views and assumptions about homosexuality, believing that it is only about sex, whereas heterosexuality is seen to encompass a wider range of possibilities, including affection, attachment, commitment and romantic love. Furthermore, there may be considerable variability from place to place in how individuals are perceived and treated. In the US, for example, numerous rural lesbian communities have been established, yet there have also been attacks and murders of isolated individuals, such as Mathew Shepard in Wyoming in 1998 (Loffreda, 2000).

Being gay, lesbian or bisexual regardless of where one lives appears to carry greater risks of bullying, harassment, violence, drug and alcohol abuse, self-harm and suicide (Bridget, 1996; D'Augelli et al, 2001a, 2001b; Beard and Hissam, 2002; Breitenbach, 2004). However, while it may be possible in urban centres to commit wholly to a lifestyle organised around one's sexual identity, or, alternatively, to compartmentalise one's behaviour and social life in ways that minimise the risks of social disapprobation, and the attendant risks of exploitation or violence, in rural areas these choices are largely absent. Consequently, life in a small community may be marked by social isolation, and the lack of support networks may contribute greatly to the marginalisation and stress suffered by individuals living in rural areas (Smith and Mancoske, 1997; Oswald and Culton, 2003). Indeed, given the general assumption that rural communities are illiberal and intolerant of minorities, these depressing possibilities might not be unexpected, as it is often assumed that many gay men and lesbians move to urban areas to escape these pressures. Once again, the reality may be somewhat more complex than this over-simplistic set of assumptions, and Bell (2003) warns against simplistically viewing rural space as one 'big closet', suggesting that it is a more variable place with a mixture of both opportunity and constraint.

One of the main problems has been that many rural studies have collected information from professionals providing health and social services to known individuals, rather than from the wider population of gay men and lesbians who live in the countryside (Oswald and Culton, 2003). It is likely that there are unmet needs among this wider population, but there is also evidence that suggests that being gay or lesbian in rural areas is not always a negative and oppressive experience (Crwydren, 1994; Smith and Mancoske, 1997; Green, 2006; Edwards and Cheers, 2007; De Warren, 2008). Oswald and Culton (2003) speculate that perhaps those who go to cities do so partly because of a lack of family support in their home areas, and that, correspondingly, those who stay do so because of the support they do receive. Two studies into the experiences of gay men who lived in the bush in Australia found that many noted and valued this support, which could be emotional, practical and even physical if need be (Green, 2006; De Warren, 2008). For instance, in Green's study one man when asked about the risk of homophobic violence answered: 'My father is here and my two brothers are here and I know that if anything happens to me that they … wouldn't hesitate to step in and do something for me' (Green, 2006, p 139).

Moreover, in every instance the men in Green's study had not resorted to a rural lifestyle because of pressures elsewhere, but instead expressed a positive preference for rural life. They cited many of the same reasons that other people do for their choice such as space, clean air, comparative freedom and the quality of life. Nonetheless, the relative solitude and privacy of life on a farm was also an important factor in the sense that they could be themselves at home, free from critical gaze. As Loffreda (2000) succinctly notes, 'Elective isolation and self sufficiency permits the pleasures of country life without the hassles of homophobia' (cited in Bell, 2003, p 186). Both Cody and Welch (1997) and De Warren

(2008) also noted that some people preferred rural life because they found the urban gay and lesbian scene off-putting.

Clearly, those who provide social services in rural areas need to be aware of some of the complexities of identity and social context for gay men and lesbians in rural areas. While it is evident that their daily experience may not always be an oppressive one, there is little doubt that like other minorities they are aware that their position is a contingent one that can be disrupted by 'misbehaviour' on their part, or by the unanticipated actions of others. Green (2006), like Oswald and Culton (2003), found that even when gay men or lesbians were 'out' and known in their local communities, most of them recognised that they still had to manage their presence when in public settings, for example, by not showing public displays of affection, appearing too different or doing things that might direct attention to their sexual orientation. Furthermore, in places that are less tolerant or where individuals are reluctant to expose themselves to the risks of being 'out', some very different dynamics may operate.

In regard to welfare, the problems facing gay men and lesbians in small communities include: a greater risk of loneliness when a partner dies because of the greater level of interdependence (Bridget, 1996); fears of being excluded from decision making (Oswald and Culton, 2003); the risk of unconscious prejudices held by social workers and volunteers influencing service delivery (Foster, 1997; Rounds, 1988; Bell, 2003); the difficulty in gaining access to rural gay and lesbian networks for both new settlers seeking support and social workers offering help (Oswald and Culton, 2003); and, of course, being deterred from seeking help because of fears of being exposed or unwittingly 'outed' through contact with welfare agencies.

Linguistic minorities

Linguistic minorities in rural areas are likely to be of two types. The first consists of what might be considered 'old languages', that is, languages that have been spoken for many years, and in some cases even pre-date the dominant or majority language. These languages include the older languages of the British Isles, such as Gaelic, Irish and Welsh, languages such as Breton and Occitan in France, Spanish in the south-western states of the US and, of course, the various tribal languages spoken by indigenous peoples. The second category of linguistic minorities includes the languages spoken by more recent arrivals into rural areas. These might include the languages of new migrant workers, such as Polish, Lithuanian and Slovak in the UK, and Spanish in other states of the US. Minority languages may be defined as those whose existence is threatened because they are spoken by small numbers of people, or whose status is weak because of a lack of formal recognition, resulting in those who speak them being disadvantaged or marginalised (see European Bureau of Lesser Used Languages at www.eblul.org).

Excluding the languages of migrants, within the European Union alone there are some 40 million people who speak a different language to the majority language in their country. Languages vary also in the formal status accorded to them, and this may have important consequences for speakers of minority languages. In countries where more than one language is formally recognised there are a range of different policies as to when and where the minority languages can be used and what rights speakers of them are entitled to. Where the choice of language is nominally left to the individual, this is termed a 'personality' approach to language choice (Mackey, 1977). Some countries, such as Switzerland, have a 'territorial' policy, where the decision about language is predetermined according to the relative dominance of languages spoken in the region. Thus, welfare services are only made available in the official language of the region. This territorial form of linguistic policy can also be seen in Belgium, where the division between Flemish and French majorities in different areas of the country is the basis of separate welfare systems.

Overlaying the legislation and policy adopted within individual countries are a number of international declarations. The 1992 United Nations Declaration on the Rights of Persons Belonging to National or Ethnic or Religious Minorities states that linguistic minorities have the right to use their own language in both private and public life. However, this declaration is not binding upon countries. Similarly, while the 1996 Universal Declaration of Linguistic Rights goes further in explicitly recognising 'The age-old unifying tendency of the majority of states to reduce diversity and foster attitudes opposed to cultural plurality and linguistic pluralism' (UNESCO, 1996, p 1) this document has not been universally ratified.

Our view is that it should not matter to us as social work professionals whether a language is an older or newer one, or whether its status is formally approved or not, although we need to be aware of the consequences of these things. Fundamentally, we think that the basis of professional practice and, therefore, the rationale for requiring linguistic responsiveness from service agencies, should be a pragmatic recognition of the social reality of linguistic variation (Pugh, 2003). Unfortunately, in the UK there is little evidence of progress in language services as the findings of earlier studies are frequently replicated in later studies

(Sanders, 2003; Pugh and Williams, 2006). For example, research into the provision of interpretation and translation services in five local authorities by Turton et al (2003) found some familiar points, such as the inappropriate use of family and friends, and complex and often ad hoc arrangements funding interpretation and translation services. In the US, the often bitter political debates about whether English should be formally declared the national language have sometimes obstructed efforts to establish effective provision. In contrast, in Quebec the dual language system ensures that speakers of French or English can access services in their preferred tongue.

Asylum seekers and refugees

In many countries the context into which asylum seekers and refugees come is one where they are often portrayed negatively as 'invaders' or as economic migrants entering under false pretences. Most asylum seekers and refugees quickly come to realise that there are ambivalent and sometimes hostile attitudes towards them, and in some countries such as Australia and the UK, their situation is made worse by harsh and stigmatising government policies (Cemlyn and Briskman, 2003). In most cases, asylum seekers and refugees gravitate towards existing populations of people of similar background, and these are nearly always in urban centres. Consequently, the presence of asylum seekers and refugees in rural areas is usually the result of dispersal and placement policies adopted by government agencies. Such policies are highly contentious, typically arousing strong local resistance to the inward relocation of such people, which may foster hostile and aggressive reactions to their presence (FPC, 2002). Dispersal reduces the opportunities for informal support and welfare among such groups, and may add to their problems by moving them to places that provide further difficulties to people who are already under pressure. A particularly crass example of this was evident during the 1970s in the UK, when Vietnamese 'boat people' were relocated to predominantly rural areas of Wales, in some instances to communities where Welsh was the predominant language. The use of detention centres in rural and sometimes remote areas has also been a feature of policy, most notoriously in Australia, where the Woomera detention centre was the subject of much criticism and reports of suspected abuse (Goddard and Liddell, 2002). The deleterious effects of these policies upon children have been widely noted and both Australia and the UK have failed to meet their obligations under international conventions (Save the Children, 2002, cited in Cemlyn and Briskman, 2003). The Independent Asylum Commission's inquiry into the treatment of asylum seekers within the UK confirmed that children are not receiving the same level of legal protection as other children and that the needs of the most vulnerable asylum seekers and refugees, such as those with disabilities, sexual minorities and victims of torture, are being poorly met (IAC, 2008).

The problems facing asylum seekers and refugees in rural areas are broadly the same as those documented for their counterparts in urban areas. The reasons that led to their leaving their home countries in the first place may have enduring effects in terms of high levels of stress, insecurity and poor health (Cemlyn and Briskman, 2003; Kohli and Mather, 2003). Because of their often uncertain official status as residents, they may not have full or any entitlement to social security and sometimes may have only limited access to health care and other welfare services. Like travelling peoples and other linguistic minorities they may find themselves subject to discriminatory stereotyping, hostility, harassment and violence. For example, a small study of Roma refugees in Canada (Walsh et al, 2006) found that the comments of workers in service agencies often reflected myths and stereotypes. Correspondingly, the strategies to encourage and inform potential clients from other minorities may also be appropriate for these groups, that is, to develop information and advice services, especially in regard to housing, health and social security systems, and to provide access to interpretation and translation services. Of particular concern to asylum seekers and refugees is the difficulty in getting satisfactory information about the progress of their applications for residence or leave to remain in the country (IAC, 2008). Dispersal policies may hinder the development of specialist resources and services by reducing opportunities for specialisation and any economies of scale. However, asylum seekers and refugees may be suspicious of government bodies and authorities, and being unfamiliar with the systems of social welfare that operate in most Westernised industrial societies, they are likely to need some reassurance as to the implications of engaging with such services. Social workers may also need to be alert to the possibility that official bodies may cast them in roles that could have profoundly illiberal consequences for asylum seekers and refugees (Humphries, 2004).

Understanding local context and local factors

The experience of minorities in rural areas and the reactions to their presence are likely to be the result of the wider social context of events and attitudes, and a range of more specific and localised factors. For example, the impact of homophobic bigotry by the 'religious right' in the US was noted by respondents in a large survey undertaken in rural Illinois by Oswald and Culton (2003), yet, as we have noted earlier, the individual experience of gay men and lesbians may be very much more variable. The crucial question is, what sorts of local factors might play a part in mitigating the impact of the wider social context or operate to enhance the prospects of tolerance at a local level?

It is clear from the research and the reported experience of rural workers that when there are opportunities for local people to engage with individuals who are perceived as different, perhaps from proximity of housing or from their children playing together, or from contact arising from work, the process of particularisation noted earlier may facilitate acceptance. For example, the presence of Asian shopkeepers in many British rural communities has kept open shops and post offices that would otherwise have closed, and has provided opportunities for people to see beyond the stereotypical expectations that they may hold of each other. These opportunities for closer contact with people who are different can have some unexpected consequences. For instance, in a rural area in the UK that was almost exclusively 'white', a local man driving past a neighbouring farmer's fields was startled to see two Bangladeshi men working on the potato harvest. Later when he enquired as to their presence it emerged that the farmer who frequently ordered takeaway food from their father's restaurant situated on the main road that passed through the area, knew that business was slow and had offered them casual work. These may not be typical instances, but they illustrate how overly deterministic assumptions about minority experiences may be mistaken, and it may be that these 'exceptions' are more prevalent in some areas and at some times than others.

Integration into community life by personal connection into established networks through friendship and association have long been noted as a significant feature of life in small communities (Frankenberg, 1957; Cohen, 1982; Crow and Allan, 1994). A quotation from a Barbadian woman living in an all-white community in rural Northamptonshire captures this sense of commonality very well, 'We had good neighbours…. Nothing was too difficult for them…. We were all thinking about earning a living, getting children into school and getting on' (Myers, 1995, p 5). Marriage into a community is probably one of the most likely ways in which a newcomer from a minority background might become tolerated or accepted into a community, as de Lima (2006) in her research found to be the case. Association extends of course to ideas and beliefs. For example, in informal conversations with social workers in Scotland, a number of them commented to us that the prospects of acceptance of newcomers into island communities were enhanced if they were Catholics coming into a predominantly Catholic community. One worker observed that, 'it doesn't matter what colour you are as long as you're Catholic'.

In earlier work we attempted to identify some of the key factors that might have a bearing upon the local response to the presence of perceived difference. These were:

- the influence of dominant individuals within the local community;
- individual opportunities for engagement with other people;
- perceptions of utility;
- kinship;
- other connections to established networks;
- personal behaviour of the individual;
- a sense of commonality in life stage or task;
- local perceptions of the nature of the local community;
- the degree of local economic and social security (Pugh, 2004a, p 263).

Clearly, this was not a complete listing of all possible factors, but was an attempt to show how a more sophisticated exploration of the experience of rural minorities might be developed. Since the publication of this list of possible factors, more recent reports into the experience and impact of immigrant workers seem to lend support to their potential utility.

Kasimis and Papadopoulos (2005), in research into the local response to migrant workers into Northern Greece, noted that they contributed greatly to the survival of farming in an area where local young workers were shunning agricultural work and moving into employment in the more populous southern areas. In addition, the influx of new workers from Albania has provided a workforce for private social care support for older people in the region. They note that attitudes varied according to age, with older people generally being welcoming because of the rejuvenating effect they perceived that migrants had upon the local area, while younger people who remained in the area were less tolerant as they feared increased competition for jobs. In contrast, research from Northern Ireland found that younger people were generally more relaxed about the presence of new migrants than older people (DEL, 2007). This age gradient or relative tolerance/intolerance is also more widely found throughout the UK.

The state of the local rural economy is likely to have a bearing upon how new migrants are treated, and this may be a factor even for existing settled minority groups as racism may be mobilised to scapegoat them. Typically, such racialised discourses focus upon the supposed displacement of local workers by migrants or other minorities. Research into urban areas has already shown that such resentments can be extended to perceptions about entitlement to welfare services (Dench et al, 2006). In the UK, a report from the Institute for Public Policy Research that looked at both urban and rural areas noted that 'conflict often arises when a new division, such as the arrival of new migrants, is overlaid on an already disadvantaged community' (2007, p 16). This report also noted that 'hostility towards new migrants frequently stemmed from a strong sense of procedural unfairness, and was prevalent among the economically most vulnerable groups' (p 19). This sensitivity to the potential impact of migrant workers upon welfare arrangements for existing local populations is also evident in Northern Ireland where research found a consistent response between urban and rural areas in some regards, as 63% of respondents felt that new workers were adding to the burden on local services (DEL, 2007).

While these sorts of local factors may well reflect the broader social context, the things that influence local responses can be extremely localised, as comparatively minor issues may lead to tension and resentment of migrant workers. These include noise and disruption as workers leave for work early in the morning, or incomers failing to understand or appreciate local expectations in regard to public behaviour, even in regard to such things as how to dispose of refuse and where to park (Audit Commission, 2007).

Conclusion

The overall picture is patchy; there is a shortage of research into both the experiences of minorities and into the responses of social services to them. Understandably, much of the existing research focuses narrowly upon the negative experience of minorities and in doing so tends to lead to overly deterministic assumptions about their lives, for example, the assumption that diverse incomers coming into rural communities will inevitably be met with indifference or hostility. Unfortunately, the tendency to focus largely upon negative experiences limits what we might be able to learn from this potentially more variable range of experience. Unless we report and research the otherwise unremarkable experiences of minorities who are comparatively well settled and who do not apparently report negative experiences, we are unlikely to understand how they manage their lives and any transitions they may have made, or identify what factors seem most pertinent in explaining their apparently exceptional experiences.

There are relatively few accounts of 'what works' best in particular situations, yet practitioners are undoubtedly trying to respond effectively to diverse local needs in rural areas. In many countries it is evident that local initiatives are often not reported or are under-reported and this impedes service development by making it difficult to learn from previous experience and build upon the work of others. Although we do not have as much evidence upon which to base specific recommendations for particular individuals and groups as we might like, it is possible to identify some clear themes and principles to guide practice.

Most notably, from the research that is available and from our own experience, we know that many people from disadvantaged minority groups in rural areas who would benefit from services are reluctant to seek help or 'make a fuss'. They fear that in drawing attention to their problems and needs, they may be blamed for their own situation, or, even worse, may become the subject of further discrimination and hostility. As de Lima (1999, p 37), writing in a Scottish context, observed, 'there is often a reluctance to become involved in any initiative which they feel would focus attention upon them as individuals, and they are often not keen to discuss their experiences of living in communities'. We should recognise how inhibiting this reluctance may be. While it may be a reasonably successful strategy for 'not being noticed', it represents the considerable anxiety and fear of exposure within the rural locality, and reminds us just how fragile and contingent the appearance of tolerance may be in any small community.

Social service organisations need to ensure that they:

* are knowledgeable about minority group culture and needs;
* understand the potential barriers that may deter individuals from seeking help, such as fear of drawing unwanted attention or other attendant risks;
* are able to build links to minority groups and communities through existing organisations, networks and known individuals;
* present a 'client-friendly' public face in the local media, their literature and on their premises;
* are capable of undertaking an educational role in regard to combating stigmatisation and prejudice;
* promote a committed agency position on equality of access and civil rights with explicit policies that cover the particular situations of local minorities;

- effectively engage with other welfare agencies to share knowledge appropriately, to develop access to services and to develop non-stigmatising joint provision where this is needed.

Unless agencies do these things and combine them with a clear system of management and review, they will have no effective way of evaluating and developing services for minorities. Well-intentioned, but ad hoc, approaches to minorities are vulnerable to changes of personnel and can be difficult to defend politically. If the agencies that are formally charged with providing social services do not openly advocate for minorities it is hardly surprising that the consequences are:

> that which is not demanded is not provided, that which is not recorded is not planned for, and that which is not planned for has no resources allocated to its provision. Then, when it is not available, no one thinks of asking for it. (Johnson, M., 1998, p 75)

The development of effective services for minority groups requires social work educators and service agencies to provide relevant education and training on equal opportunity issues and to develop cultural competence among staff where this is appropriate. Often the best way to do this is to ensure that the demographic profile of the staff reflects local populations, but the most important shift in practice is to ensure that professional discretion in assessment processes and decision making in regard to minorities is not undertaken from positions of ignorance and prejudice. Clearly, as many writers have noted (Dominelli, 1988; Davis and Proctor, 1989; Fook, 2002), the service response to minorities raises important questions about power and identity. It is a matter of great concern that differentiation in service provision for minorities is often resisted on the basis of arguments underpinned by assimilationist assumptions, that is, by ideas that individuals and groups who are different should 'fit in' with the dominant culture. Apart from the fact that such calls for conformity usually have little to say about the position of individuals and groups who are not allowed to 'fit in', this position rests upon a mistaken notion of social solidarity and an idealised notion of community against which the cultural differences of minorities are typically contrasted and found wanting. Finally, as Modood has noted:

> Equality is not having to hide or apologise for one's origins, family or community but expecting others to respect them and adapt public attitudes and arrangements so that

the heritage that they represent is encouraged rather than contemptuously expected to wither away. (Modood et al, 1997, p 358)

FIVE

Problems and possibilities in rural practice

Introduction

As the previous chapters have shown, the variability of rural contexts, the complex dynamics of rural societies and the continuing difficulties of indigenous peoples and other minorities provide a range of specific challenges for those who wish to develop and deliver good services in rural areas. In this chapter we turn to some more general issues that emerge from the experience and the literature on rural social services, the most commonly noted being the problem of poor access to services, which is compounded by a lack of alternative opportunities and other supportive provision. Problems of distance from the point of delivery of services may be exacerbated by local terrain, weather and the absence of public transport networks, and all these factors may add greatly to the costs for service users in accessing help, or, alternatively, result in higher costs for service providers.

Another area of difficulty in rural social work is the fact that there is often little service back-up available. This is most evident when workers operate in isolation without other colleagues available to provide support, or to step in at short notice. This can result in services being vulnerable to staff absence through illness, or the withering of any innovations that depend upon the initiative and drive of staff who leave. Rural social workers also often lack access to other services, especially more specialised ones, to which they can refer clients. From the perspective of service users, the absence of alternative sources of service results in a lack of choice, and while the merits of more personalised relationships with professionals may be preferred by many rural residents, this may be problematic for those who wish to maintain a higher level of privacy or separation from other domains of their life in the community. The generally weaker infrastructure of welfare services, perhaps lacking such things as independent advice centres, voluntary support and advocacy groups, may result in problems being presented to whatever service is available, simply because a more appropriate service is not available, or, perhaps, people simply not seeking help at all. The consequences of this relatively weaker service infrastructure include: a lack of support for individuals or causes whose problems are uncommon or unpopular or require more specialised assistance; poor take-up of even what little provision is available; and knock-on effects in terms of access to opportunities for employment and education. For instance, there is some evidence that the general take-up rates for welfare benefits in rural areas seem to be lower than in urban areas (Bramley et al, 2000), and Marson and Powell (2000) have noted that the lack of child care is a serious structural barrier to welfare recipients hoping to move into employment.

The first part of this chapter examines the question of access to service and then reviews some of the assumptions and issues that face some people in rural areas such as isolation and stigmatisation. The question of the higher costs of service and different approaches to the funding of rural services is discussed, and then the chapter turns to consideration of partnerships with service users, carers and other organisations. The sections on access to services, service cost, funding formulas and rural standards draw upon previously published work (Pugh, 2000, 2007; Pugh et al, 2007). Finally, the conclusion notes that although these difficulties might seem to produce a somewhat depressing picture of rural practice, paradoxically many of the features of small rural communities that arise from their location and their demographics also provide opportunities for innovative practice that can improve service provision and result in social workers gaining great satisfaction from their work.

Access to services

For many people living in rural areas access to services is impaired by difficulties in travelling to the point of service (Marson and Powell, 2000) and the paucity of public transport has a significant bearing upon people's health and welfare. One consequence of the general problem of travel in rural areas is that car ownership becomes a much more significant factor in everyday life. Poor people in rural areas are more likely to have a car than those in urban areas and consequently are likely to spend a higher proportion of their income on transport. Access also varies between different people, even when they live in the same household (RDC, 1996; Cloke et al, 1997; Denham and White, 1998; Moseley, 2000), for example, women may have little opportunity to use a car if it is used by their partner to get to work. Similarly, children, younger people, people with disabilities and older people without a licence, or who may be unable to drive longer distances and so have to rely upon other people or public transport, also face difficulties in getting to services. For people who are vulnerable, lengthy waiting times for sparse or erratic transport services, together with the potential risk of being stranded far from home, are likely to be barriers to service (Scharf and Bartlam, 2006). A study in North Carolina found that many elderly black women with impaired vision became increasingly isolated when they could no longer drive, as there was no effective public transport available (Carlton-LaNey, 1998). MacLean and Kelley (2001) in a review of palliative care in rural areas in Canada noted that geographic isolation and poor local transport systems could add greatly to the travel times required to access cancer care and resulted in an even greater reliance upon informal support from families. One UK study found that the excessive costs of using local taxi services, with fares of between £40 and £70, were a considerable barrier preventing people in rural areas getting to mental health services (MIND, 2008).

The transport infrastructure of an area comprises systems of bus, rail and air transport, the availability of alternative means of provision such as dial-a-ride schemes, post buses and lift sharing, as well as the quality and extent of the road network. In more remote places and in locations subject to severe weather, alternative modes of transport such as boats and snowmobiles may also be needed. While the effects of a harsh climate are generally to make travel more difficult and possibly more risky, this is not always the case. The necessity of using air travel, expensive as it is, may reduce journey times compared to the alternative of travel by road. In areas with long snowy winters, such as northern Canada and Finland, it may be possible to travel more speedily when there is a frozen base, as journey times may be much reduced when cars and snowmobiles are able to travel directly across lakes and along rivers. In many rural areas, and in most remote areas, public transport networks are often very limited, and where they do exist can be relatively expensive to use.

Public transport may run at inconvenient times, making return journeys to larger towns difficult or excessively time-consuming, for example, in rural mid-Wales, one sex offender on probation was required to attend a treatment programme in an urban centre that required over five hours of travel. Consequently, completion rates for programmes located in distant service centres are likely to be lower (Pugh, 2007b). Not only are the poorest offenders disadvantaged compared to urban offenders in terms of the time taken to comply with court orders, but also as they are less likely to complete their programmes, they may find their difficulties exacerbated. In Chapter 1 we noted the phenomenon of 'distance decay', where service uptake is linked to distance. Thus, the more remote an area is, the less likely its inhabitants are to receive or continue with services (Harrop and Palmer, 2002; DEFRA, 2004b; Mungall, 2005) resulting in negative consequences for their health and welfare (Deaville, 2001; Asthana et al, 2003).

An added problem for many people living in areas whose populations are declining is that existing services may also begin to withdraw. MacKenzie in a study of older people in rural Saskatchewan noted that the consolidation of rural health and social services and their relocation to other communities posed great problems for some residents, as 'without independent access to transportation ... the new network might as well be one hundred miles away' (2001, p 78). She made a number of useful suggestions for improving services including a plea for reconsidering the closure of small nursing homes in rural areas and noted that a partially subsidised or private transportation system could improve mobility and, thus, improve quality of life. In some rural areas in the UK this is exactly what has been developed in community transport schemes, sometimes called social car schemes, in which either paid or voluntary staff (who receive fuel costs) provide a bookable door-to-door rural car service. However, while such schemes are highly valued, many are limited to certain types of users and often exclude young people. This, for example, can result in further disadvantage to unsupported young carers (Moseley, 2000). One interesting finding from research undertaken by Bowden and Moseley (2006) was the potentially complex nature of people's preferences for service, in that people would trade off some factors against others depending upon the nature of the problem and the service concerned. For example, people were prepared to travel further for access to primary health care if it meant that they could have a full-time service rather than easier access to a local part-time service.

Stoicism, isolation and stigmatisation

In the Introduction to this book we noted that assumptions are often made about rural life that are not based upon sound evidence, or that do not reflect the variability of individual experience, which nevertheless influence how service providers respond to local needs. It is not that such assumptions are invariably wrong, but, rather, that they need to be considered more carefully. For instance, while it may be a mistake to assume that rural dwellers are necessarily more stoical about their circumstances, a small narrative study of isolated older women in rural Saskatchewan found that most had a positive world view that was based upon a lifelong habit of 'making the best of things' and 'being grateful for what one does have rather than complaining about what one does not have' (MacKenzie, 2001, p 78). Another study of older women's preferences and concerns with regard to health showed that many expected to encounter problems in health and mobility, but were less concerned with the question of accessibility of service than with maintaining their own independence and capacity for care-giving (DePoy and Butler, 1996).

The assumption that rural life is necessarily a more isolated experience than urban living is often made without any appreciation of the variability of individual experience. For instance, while problems arising from reduced mobility may be oppressive for some people, for others the enforced aloneness may not be problematic. As Wenger's research into older women in rural areas has shown, there is a significant difference between the facts of aloneness (lack of contact) and the subjective experience of loneliness (1994a, 1994b, 2001). One Irish study noted that there were important distinctions to be made between social, family and romantic loneliness. While living in a rural area was found to be a contributory factor to loneliness generally, other considerations such as gender, income, greater age, health status and losing a partner or never having had one were also influential. It contended that loneliness for older people is 'variable, multi-dimensional and experienced differently according to life events', and that the 'strategies that are used to address loneliness need to take account of the complexity and individuality of the experience' (Drennan et al, 2008, pp 1113, 1123). For example, even relatively strong family and social networks do not seem to protect individuals against romantic loneliness. This complexity can also be seen in the results of a study in the Netherlands of the effectiveness of a friendship enrichment programme (Martina and Stevens, 2006), which unfortunately did not distinguish whether the participants came from urban or rural areas. While noting some success, it found that the results were not as definitive as might have been expected. What is also often ignored is the fact that aloneness may for some people be a preference they have exercised by choosing to move to, or choosing to remain living in, relatively sparsely populated places. Although many rural people value their independence and take pride in their capacity for self-reliance, their possibly lower (or different) expectations of public services should not be understood as indicating stoicism. Lowered expectations may simply be a pragmatic acceptance of the facts of patchy or non-existent provision.

This sort of accommodation to the practical realities of welfare provision may also inform perceptions of satisfaction with services. Evidence for this comes from British studies comparing urban and rural dwellers' perceptions of social services that have generally found relatively high levels of satisfaction for both groups, with little difference between them. For instance, one survey that reviewed opinions about five services, including transport and health services, found few differences between urban and rural respondents with satisfaction rates of over 90% (DEFRA, 2004a). However, Bowden and Moseley (2006) have noted that while some studies have asked users what they thought about particular aspects of a service, others have enquired into users' overall satisfaction with a service, and that this may also stimulate different perceptions. Moreover, they suggest that the tendency to aggregate rural results collapses the views of the most disadvantaged rural dwellers with those who may have better access to personal transport and the internet and those who have higher incomes.

In Chapter 4 we suggested that the experience of minorities in rural areas was often more variable than might be expected and suggested that local factors played a large part in the range of possible responses to difference. Nevertheless, problems of stigmatisation, isolation and discrimination are widely reported in general studies of people with mental health problems (Read and Baker, 1996; NIMHE, 2004), in work with people who are HIV positive (Rounds, 1988) and in family violence (Wendt, 2005). Problems of shame and 'keeping face' would appear to be universal features regardless of the level of development or the sophistication of the network of welfare services available. In rural areas of South Africa, Schenck (2003) has noted that some clients prefer to call at social workers' homes after hours, because this makes it look like they are a friend visiting rather than someone who needs help. It is clear that perceptions of anticipated stigma can be a significant deterrent to seeking help (Thornicroft, 2006). One survey in Scotland found that a lack of anonymity made some people reluctant to seek services and that local culture could also result in people being reluctant to talk about emotional problems (Philo et al, 2003). It also found that a more tolerant attitude to heavy drinking meant that alcohol misuse was sometimes used as a cover for mental health problems. Limited local understanding of mental health problems further isolated people, as did the lack of 'drop-in' facilities or other places to talk. Carers also reported feeling isolated and unsupported, especially when they lacked private transport, though the social contact with service providers and other carers was helpful (Innes et al, 2006). Thornicroft (2006) cites a Greek study that found that less than half of the people with mental health problems had sought help, and the most common reason given for this was the avoidance of the risk of stigmatisation. There is also some evidence that problems are even more pressing for young people with mental health problems in rural areas where their behaviour may be labelled as 'bad', and where they may have little idea of how to access appropriate help (Big Lottery Fund Research, 2008).

Higher service costs

There are likely to be significant differences between the travel costs associated with service delivery in remote areas, where workers may need to travel for many hours simply to reach the point of service and may have to travel by air or boat to get there, and the costs associated with practice in other more accessible rural areas. Both situations are likely to result in higher costs in terms of staff time and transportation. While it is unwise to generalise inappropriately from one set of circumstances to another, evidence from the UK suggests that the additional staff time required to provide rural services, with the exception of the far north of Scotland and the islands, typically amounts to around 20% of staff time. An unpublished report of the time spent travelling in one mental health team in the Scottish Border region found that rural staff spent approximately 25 33% of their work time travelling compared to 7–10% by staff in more urban areas (Wilson, 2002). It also found that the lack of suitable facilities and poor public transport networks resulted in workers having to undertake more home visits. A review of service costs in rural areas in the UK concluded that there was a clear cost premium if services were provided to the same standard as those available in urban areas (Hindle et al, 2004).

Higher costs also arise from the less intensive use of facilities and buildings as well as the duplication of facilities in dispersed locations. This considerably increases the fixed costs of service provision, especially where a generally poorer infrastructure results in fewer alternative options such as sharing premises with other agencies (NPS, 2002). Low population densities together with a scattered distribution means that there are few opportunities for the economies of scale in services that are sometimes possible in urban areas. Unsurprisingly, this common problem in provision has sparked efforts to improve provision and restrain costs, some of which are discussed in the following chapter, although evidence of their merits is sometimes patchy.

Funding formulas

In some countries, such as the US, there appears to be little or no formal recognition of the higher costs of provision of rural services (Lohmann and Lohmann, 2005), so relative disadvantage would seem to be an institutionalised problem, particularly if local services are funded almost entirely from local revenues (Warner, 2007). In others, like the UK, where more funding comes from central government, these costs may be recognised but not systematically funded, as the uplifts in funding may not fully cover the actual costs of service. One English study found that in one local authority the uplift for rural domiciliary care was £51 per client, but the modelled costs were estimated to be around £460 (Hindle et al, 2004). Typically, when funding bodies begin to engage with rural issues, they try to establish some fixed urban–rural distinction, using indicators such as population size and density, or travel to service distances, as a proxy for actual costs. For instance, in the UK the probation service uses a sparsity indicator, based upon population density, which when reviewed in 2003 resulted in a 1.5% increase in funding to areas having less than 0.5 people per hectare. In one area, this more than doubled the amount received in recognition of higher rural costs from £315,000 to £733,000 in a year (Pugh, 2007b). However, there are a number of problems with these types of responses. The most obvious, and one that was reviewed in the Introduction to this book, is that they are often based upon a simple urban–rural dichotomy that fails to adequately reflect the social and geographical variability that exists between different communities. For example, the travel and time costs involved in delivering a service that involves visiting people in their homes are likely to be considerably different in a compact rural area close to a town with good road and transport networks than those incurred in a more remote rural area. The second area of difficulty is that such simple definitions take little account of other significant factors such as differences in the availability of public transport, differences in wealth and unemployment, or other forms of existing disadvantage that may affect the numbers of people needing help and services.

Funding regimes may offer a simple uplift for rural areas, or, alternatively, may develop more complex funding formulas that include a number of factors. In the UK, the funding of primary health care uses a complex algorithm (the Carr-Hill Resource Allocation Formula) to calculate the funding for general practitioner services that includes, among other things, the demographic profile of the area and travel costs. Such complex formulas would seem to offer a more responsive approach, but they can result in funding systems that are hard to understand and difficult to apply. They present the appearance of objectivity and rationality, but often there is considerable room for subjectivity and bias in deciding which factors to include and what weighting to give them. For example, the Carr-Hill formula includes the travel costs that doctors' practices submit for tax returns. Apart from the question of the reliability of such returns, this approach fails to consider the costs to patients. It is also intrinsically conservative in approach, as it reflects what is provided rather than what ought to be, and tends to fossilise existing inadequacies in service provision (Cheers, 1998). Although there is merit in at least recognising the problem of higher costs, ultimately most of these approaches tend to be inadequate responses to the question of rural funding because they institutionalise the notion of a simple dichotomy between urban and rural settings. Our view is that rural funding should be based upon specific calculations of the actual costs incurred in service provision and that such efforts should also consider the question of displaced costs, that is, those relating to service users and the impact upon them.

Rural standards and rural proofing

A different approach to the question of parity of provision between urban and rural areas is to establish some standard of service to either prospectively, or retrospectively (using performance indicators), assess proposed developments or measure the actual performance of service providers. In England and Wales this approach began in 2000 when the government established a Rural Services Standard to 'give people in the countryside a better understanding of access to services they could expect' (Countryside Agency, 2003, p 2). The government has subsequently tried to ensure that all developments in policy and provision are 'rural proofed', by getting policy makers and planners to:

> Think about whether there will be any significant differential impacts in rural areas; if there are such impacts to consider what these might be; consider what adjustments/ compensations might be made to fit rural circumstances. (Countryside Agency, 2004, p 1)

The Rural Standard applies to a wide range of public services and includes a number of activities and requirements, such as:

- collecting evidence to be used to develop rural standards and targets;
- efforts to improve access to information about available services, especially through the use of IT;
- efforts to improve access to services themselves;
- establishing clear lines of responsibility for rural issues across government departments.

Accordingly, government bodies, inspectorates and departments have, or are developing, performance indicators to measure progress, and the Department for Environment, Food and Rural Affairs provided a checklist of policy issues and information and guidance for the development of public services in rural areas (DEFRA, 2002). This drive to improve public services is explicitly linked to the government's social inclusion agenda and an early report noted that:

> There are a number of other less obvious issues which local authorities and other local agents should address in their rural proofing work. An example is supporting the needs of ethnic minority individuals and families. For ethnic minority citizens, families and communities living in rural areas particular issues include, comparative lack of sensitivity to their needs from public service providers; relative isolation from support services and from self-help and community groups; relative lack of information on services (including translation services); and additional costs in accessing services. (Moor and Whitworth, 2001, p 7)

One consequence of these developments has been a realisation that if 'one size does not fit all' then logically there needs to be increasing devolution and decentralisation of systems of service (Haskins, 2003). However, the reviews of the effectiveness of rural proofing so far undertaken indicate that most of the measures designed to reduce social exclusion have lacked a rural awareness (Community Development Foundation, 2006; Woods, 2006). They have concluded that the commitment to rural proofing was only partially fulfilled. One key issue in monitoring standards is the lack of data, such as the extent of intensive home care support for older people (Commission for Rural Communities, 2006a, 2006b).

Working with other agencies, organisations and service users

There are a number of reasons why social service providers might seek, or need, to work with service users, carers and other organisations including:

- it being a statutory requirement or policy directive;
- developing better information about existing problems, resources and provision;

- improving communications between service users and providers and shaping services to better meet local needs;
- cooperation in meeting complex needs;
- cooperation in meeting the multiple needs of a person, family or group;
- promoting the safety of individuals and the wider community;
- commitment to a project for which no agency alone bears sole responsibility;
- enlisting other people and other agencies to carry an existing initiative forward, or to extend its field of operation;
- legitimating an initiative that might otherwise be controversial or be resisted by a particular community.

This is not an exhaustive list of reasons, but clarity of purpose is an essential prerequisite for success when partnership is being considered. Partnership working is hard work and there are some common problems identified in the literature (Balloch and Taylor, 2001). Some of these arise from different perspectives on problems and issues, while others arise from mismatches in size, power, role and degree of commitment, between different organisations and participants. In rural areas, with scarce resources and limited funding, partnership is often driven by a common desire to maximise the effectiveness of existing resources and mobilise other potential resources.

Hague (1997, 2000), in her perceptive reviews of multi-agency initiatives in the UK, identified some common problems in relationships between organisations, some of which can probably be generalised to a wider range of countries. Specifically, these were:

- a tendency of some agencies to 'defend their own turf';
- a lack of clarity leading potentially to confusion about roles and responsibilities;
- a tendency to marginalise equality issues such as gender and ethnicity;
- the use of multi-agency initiatives as a face-saving strategy to avoid confronting shortages of resources;
- the consumption and wastage of scarce resources, especially of smaller agencies (such as small NGOs or users' and carers' organisations), in unproductive discussions;
- the futility of attempts to coordinate systems that are already inadequate or disorganised;
- difficulties in resolving differences of power, resources and philosophy between agencies;

- a tendency for larger agencies to marginalise smaller partners, sometimes even when they were the original initiators of the project;
- a tendency for larger agencies to leave too much of the work to smaller ones;
- a tendency to marginalise service users and prospective clients.

Of course, these are not intrinsic or inevitable problems, and it is prudent to regard them as potential risks that with foresight, commitment and clarity of aims and strategy can be avoided or mitigated. What should be avoided is any tendency to personalise or pathologise problems as being endemic within particular persons or agencies (Eaton, 1995).

Partnership with service users

In many countries, partnership is a key element in the further development of social services generally, as moves towards self-directed care, individual budgets and personalisation take place. So, the policy direction is largely favourable for those who work in small communities and wish to promote the engagement of clients and service users in service planning, development and delivery. But, as with notions such as empowerment and participation, local understandings and practices vary considerably and partnership may be used quite instrumentally without any strong commitment to enacting it. Goodwin (2000), for example, has suggested that many attempts to involve local communities in development are undertaken primarily to secure funding rather than from some deeper commitment to participation. However, even when participants' motivations may seem cynical or half-hearted, the actual process of working together can sometimes change perspectives and result in a more positive commitment to joint action. There are many good examples of rural partnership initiatives (see, for example, Taylor et al, 2008), especially in the field of mental health where service user groups and networks have an important role creating self-help and support networks and providing a constituency base for advocates and representatives involved in formal consultations with service providers. In both Scotland and Wales, user groups and alliances supported by and working with social services have shown how the views of dispersed people in sparsely populated rural areas can be mobilised (Pugh and Richards, 1996; Burns et al, 2002).

Given the difficulties of transport and the scarcity of services generally, opportunities for partnership working are likely to exist in, say, undertaking transport audits, surveying user preferences or evaluating existing provision. For instance, carers' respite services are unlikely to be effective if they are inappropriately scheduled and of insufficient duration, for example, if they do not allow carers time to travel for shopping, recreation or to other services for their own needs (Innes et al, 2005). In the UK, it appears that service users have little interest in who organises or provides their services. What seems to matter most is that services are available and effective (Brown et al, 2003), that service users have some opportunity to influence their development and that they have some control over what sorts of services they are offered (CSCI, 2006; Glendinning et al, 2006; Innes et al, 2006). What is clear is that service users and carers do not like support that is based upon urban models, such as a 15-minute support visit, a model that is particularly ill-suited to rural provision with its comparatively high transport costs (CSCI, 2006). The increasing interest in person-centred and outcomes-focused approaches (Glendinning et al, 2006; Innes et al, 2006), which hold out the prospect of more appropriate and individually tailored services, is welcome, as it is clear that some services like home care in the UK have become too narrowly targeted (CSCI, 2006). However, in the light of the policy shift to self-directed and self-funded home care in many countries, it is likely that some service users in rural areas may have difficulty in finding satisfactory service providers. One solution pioneered in some areas of the UK has been to organise home care service providers into geographically zoned areas; this reduces user choice but enhances access and reliability of service (Glendinning et al, 2006).

Partnership with informal care and support networks

It has long been recognised that most 'social work' is not undertaken by professionals but is instead provided informally by family members, friends and neighbours, most typically women. Consequently, most writers on rural practice have argued that professional workers should recognise, respect, facilitate and support informal systems of care, as not only do we share common aims with informal carers, but in many ways the notion of community itself is founded upon the networks of perceptions, obligations, choices and reciprocity that are represented in this caring work (Martinez-Brawley, 1982, 2000; Ginsburg, 1998; Lohmann and Lohmann, 2005; Scales and Streeter, 2004; Cheers et al, 2007). This view is supported by, for example, numerous studies of ageing in rural places in which respondents report positively about their perceptions of the quality of their lives (Wenger, 1994a; MacKenzie, 2001; Scharf and Bartlam, 2006). MacKenzie states that respondents 'participate in a range of activities, see their lives as relatively secure, feel respected and valued by their family and friends, and believe that others treat them well ... their experience of community is based upon a dense and overlapping set of relationships' (2001, p 78). Thus, it is well established that, as with their urban counterparts, the personal social, emotional, material and physical well-being of rural people is closely related to the accessibility, availability and strength of their informal social care networks (Lorenz et al, 1993; Ganguli et al, 1995; McCullough and Wilson, 1995; Cheers, 2001).

To link with informal supports, social workers need to know from where different kinds of people living in different communities prefer to seek help with different kinds of problems, and to learn what the outcomes are (Cheers, 2001). For instance, Farber and her colleagues, in a comparative study of low-income African-American and white women in South Carolina, noted that 'there is some evidence of greater exchange of support among rural than among urban kin members, suggesting stronger connection to kin networks', although the capacity to provide material support may be limited by similar circumstances (Farber et al, 2005, p 52). Previous studies tended to show that African-American women were more likely to live with their kin and to have more regular contact with larger kin networks, and less likely to receive help with child care or finance than their white counterparts (Heflin and Pattillo, 2002). These studies also found that poor white women in rural areas were more likely to have health, including mental health, problems and were more likely to have experienced family violence. Furthermore, Farber et al (2005), in their own study of low-income mothers, found that while both African-American and white women reported material hardships in the preceding year, such as electricity disconnections, evictions, lack of food, lack of medical care and poor housing, African-American women generally had higher incomes than the white women, even though their employment rates were similar at around 30%. Perhaps most surprising were the findings that showed that, on most measures, the white women were worse off. African-American women were more likely to receive emotional, financial and child care help than white women, who in turn were more likely to report asking for help in the previous year. However, one important factor that might have contributed to these differences was that many of the white women lived in more isolated locations in trailer homes, while many of the African-American women lived in public housing closer to other family and friends. The significance of these findings for social work practice is not simply that informal support matters greatly, but that:

in working with poor rural families, it is important to assess the structure and the functioning of kin networks. The mere presence of family and friends does not guarantee the availability of material and non-tangible resources to address the needs of families. (Farber et al, 2005, p 60)

There is some evidence that the support networks of rural residents tend to be larger and stronger than those of their urban counterparts, and that rural people generally prefer to seek help from close friends and relatives rather than more superficial acquaintances (Goodfellow, 1983; Kivett, 1983; Scott and Roberto, 1985, 1987; Mercier et al, 1988; Taylor et al, 1988; Romans et al, 1992), but who they turn to depends on a number of factors. For needs that are deeply personal, and/or potentially socially stigmatising problems, people generally prefer to seek help from only their closest friends and relatives, regardless of how far away they are (Fischer, 1982; Cheers, 2001). They also prefer these supports for help that typically involves a high level of reliance on the personal service provided, such as accommodation and child care. In contrast, for more minor needs and those where proximity is a factor, such as watching over the home during vacations or borrowing minor household items, people will settle for help from others who live nearby but with whom they may only have a more superficial relationship.

Informal support is a complex and individual phenomenon, with a long-established body of evidence suggesting that where rural people seek help and how effective it is depends on a combination of factors (Fischer, 1982; Kelley and Kelley, 1985; Patterson et al, 1988; Martinez-Brawley and Blundall, 1989; Williams and McHugh, 1993; Cheers, 2001). These include:

- the nature of the problem and the type of help being sought;
- characteristics of the help seeker and the support source, and the nature of their relationship;
- the relative accessibility and availability of various potential supports at the time;
- whether direct contact is important for the need in question;
- contextual factors such as availability of transportation, the cost of long-distance contact (for example, telephones, internet, fuel, public transport) and, in some places, geographic and climatic conditions.

Social workers can support personal social networks by encouraging clients to use them and also by providing resources to facilitate them.

For example, social workers could arrange access to telephone facilities at a local school or hospital for a depressed farmer to call his mate, or provide financial assistance for a relative to travel to help support a person recovering from illness. However, social workers need to be alert to the costs of participation in informal support and exchange, as well as the part that pride may play in inhibiting requests for help. The upshot of this research is, of course, that the rural social worker must assess each situation on its merits rather than make assumptions about people's informal supports.

There are two kinds of informal support relationships – those created by service organisations and those embedded in people's everyday social environments (Cheers, 1998). Created relationships include mutual aid networks of people in similar situations and clients' relationships with volunteers attached to organisations. Key helpers are local community members from whom many others seek help. They include role-related helpers, that is, those people who provide informal support outside of their formal position, such as nurses and schoolteachers. Research indicates that they are significant figures in stable communities with low population turnover, strong local kin networks and that share a common commitment to a religion, local language or culture. The corollary is that key helpers may not be present in all communities (Cheers, 1992, 2001). Where they do exist, formal organisations can support them by identifying who they are, and by providing advice, training, information and resources.

Partnership with volunteers and non-governmental organisations

There is a paradox in the fact that while the origins of many forms of social work practice lie in voluntary endeavours (Kendall, 2000), relationships between professional social workers, volunteers and voluntary bodies are sometimes difficult and strained. As Martinez-Brawley noted, 'professionals tend to be skeptical of the lack of educational credentials of nonprofessionals, who generally address problems in a very different and more emotional way' (2000, p 272), but, she argues, this is what is most valuable about volunteers. It allows them to act in ways that social workers could not or would not wish to, for example, the community engagement of a volunteer, and the subsequent lack of anonymity that accompanies it, may be a positive benefit when they refer someone for service, or decide to intervene directly themselves. Volunteers undertake a wide range of tasks for people who lack other supports such as providing company, transportation, meals and home maintenance, and in areas with scarce resources they may become the second most significant form of social support after personal and kinships networks.

It is widely assumed that there are fewer non-governmental organisations (NGOs) in rural areas than urban areas, and that, consequently, there are fewer alternative options for service and fewer bodies available to participate in community development, campaigning and advocacy. But this may not inevitably be the case. A study of a community development project in Western Australia found that one community had over 40 community groups, as well as a workers' club, a youth club and a family centre (Laing and Hepburn, 2006). Similarly, a survey in rural Illinois found that in relation to population size, NGOs were proportionately represented, although it noted that they lagged far behind in terms of resources, with rural spending per person typically being less than a third of the amount spent in urban areas (Hager et al, 2005).

In many countries, governments have explicitly identified partnership with NGOs as one of the key ways in which rural services might be improved, but there are some common problems that have been noted. Many of these derive from a failure of government funded organisations to understand how small voluntary bodies operate and the difficulties they can face in being drawn into partnership arrangements. In the UK, voluntary organisations have had difficulty in understanding the sometimes bewildering array of different government initiatives, and often find engagement with statutory services costly and time-consuming (Osborne et al, 2002; Blackburn et al, 2003). Funding remains a common problem for many voluntary organisations, and one study noted that the annual round of 'panic fund raising' made it 'chronically difficult to plan strategically' (Alcock et al, 1999, p 1). Moreover, an over-reliance upon a single funder can reduce the independence of NGOs and create vulnerability if funding priorities change. In addition to these sorts of problems, broader policy shifts, such as the increasing marketisation of services and the contracting out of services to make a separation between the purchasers and regulators of services on one hand, and the providers of them on the other, have created further difficulties in places where NGOs are less familiar with this role, or where they have not previously been encouraged or required to bid for local contracts. As Craig and Manthorpe (1999) have noted, this has been very disruptive of long-established local relationships, as existing contracts and grants have been terminated and new arrangements for competitive tendering introduced. Exploratory research into service provision for children and family violence in England (Stalford et al, 2003) found that unless children were in the child protection process, there were few supportive non-crisis services available, and that obtaining long-term funding for the voluntary sector was a major barrier to the development of such services. It is clear that if the voluntary sector is to be maintained and developed, then statutory services must provide support. This can take many forms including: start-up money, subsidised accommodation, administrative and legal support, and capacity building in terms of skill development and training, as well as civic recognition.

Edwards et al (1999), in a valuable review of partnership working in rural regeneration, identified four key features that contributed to success. They were:

- time, resources and training to facilitate and enhance community involvement;
- awareness of different partners' cultures and expectations;
- allowing sufficient time and providing resources to build trust;
- stable funding of programmes for adequate periods of time.

Another review that examined inter-agency initiatives in responding to family violence noted that committed volunteers and workers can become frustrated by the time statutory organisations take to make decisions, especially if it seems that they are 'taking over' projects, both marginalising them and the women who need their help (Hague, 1997). Briskman (2007) notes that the acceptance of government funding by indigenous organisations can be seen as a compromise that constrains its effectiveness. Workers in larger organisations should strive to develop a sophisticated understanding of power and be aware that social activists, particularly those from minority groups who have lengthy experience of marginalisation, are likely to be especially attuned to the nuances of interpersonal and organisational power in their dealings with more powerful agencies and individuals. Clumsy and thoughtless efforts may be perceived as insensitive or misplaced, or even as bullying and oppressive actions, which are likely to prove damaging and counter-productive in regard to the possibilities of a successful partnership.

Partnership with other service providers

There are a number of terms that are used to describe working in partnership with other service providers, but for the purposes of this discussion the term 'joint working' is used to avoid any potential confusions between different usages of the terms 'inter-agency' and 'multi-agency working'. Joint working may take many forms ranging from sharing of facilities, common assessment tools, joint provision of services, joint commissioning from other providers, shared planning and so on. It is widely assumed that joint working must be beneficial, but the evidence of positive outcomes is so far rather patchy. For instance, measures such as co-location are not sufficient in themselves to improve outcomes (Brown et al, 2003), and one small study of user involvement and multi-agency working to improve housing for older people found that 'multi-agency policy making ... [was] patchy at best, and at worst is virtually non-existent' (Midgely et al, 1997, p 1). A review of different approaches to partnership found that sharing premises was not always the best option, that mobile facilities were expensive to run and did not always reach the targets in remote areas, including the use of shared premises, and concluded that there was no 'first best solution' (Pickering, 2003). Pickering concluded that the most successful initiatives often involved linking outreach service provision to community transport initiatives. The sharing of facilities by agencies can be restricted by considerations of confidentiality, safety and security according to the nature of different service remits, and this may often be the case with services directed at offenders and victims. Furthermore, one UK study of partnerships between Youth Offending Teams and substance misuse projects found that where agencies had different remits, in these instances in regard to crime reduction and harm reduction, co-location was not a good predictor of the quality of the relationship between the two services (Minkes et al, 2005), that is, in some areas they had good relationships, while, in others, there were problems. A similar study also noted that while joint services were usually cheaper, this was not always the case and concluded that while joint provision 'is relatively well established at village level for voluntary and community sector services it has yet to be fully absorbed into mainstream public service planning and delivery' (Harrop and Palmer, 2000, p 1). Other UK research into joint provision (Moseley and Parker, 1998) found that the key success factors were:

- the support of dynamic/visionary individuals;
- getting potential partners involved early in planning;
- carefully assessing potential demand for proposed services;
- ensuring a real partnership among providers (sharing resources and responsibility);
- ensuring that facilities (buildings or vehicles) met the needs of different partners;
- a willingness (especially from large organisations) to seek local solutions.

Unfortunately, they found no firm information about any cost savings.

In many countries, the policy shifts towards community care have focused greater attention on the interaction of health and social care services, including, in the UK, moves towards the direct integration of local services. One way of doing this has been to link social workers with local general medical practices. However, these developments have sometimes been hindered by poor partnerships or poor relationships with providers, although there is evidence that continuing commitment and effort can overcome these difficulties (Parry-Jones and Soulsby, 2001; Glendinning et al, 2006). It has also been suggested that a narrow focus upon structural integration of health and care services is unlikely to succeed without integrated systems of goal setting, leadership and interdisciplinary delivery (Johnson et al, 2003). Indeed, this study found that barriers to effective cooperation arose from differences in organisational cultures and management styles, and discontinuities between agencies' service districts. Further problems arose when hard-pressed health agencies sought to reduce their costs by discharging patients into social care provision. Top-down approaches to joint working are unlikely to work unless there is a local commitment to change (Smale et al, 2000). Turbett (2002), in his action research initiative on joint working on the Scottish island of Arran, noted that modest gains could be made when there was support from front-line staff and engagement with a wider range of local representatives. Interestingly, a study of service coordination in South Australia (Munn et al, 2003) found that workers were more willing to coordinate their efforts when they focused directly upon service delivery and that they preferred to do this through informal networking.

Joint working or cooperation between agencies that share similar aims but have different geographical bases can lead to very different perceptions about how local developments should proceed. This was evident some years ago when a rural group seeking to develop ant-racism initiatives sought help from a national group based in an urban area:

> Black agencies come into the area wanting to undertake development work but they typically lack an understanding of rural issues.... An officer from a national agency offered support for developing a telephone help line modelled on a London borough. The several meetings between the officer and representatives of local Black agencies proved to be remarkably unconstructive because there was no recognition

of rural issues. As soon as the local agencies started discussing the idea between themselves an immediate consensus was reached and the ideas were developed. (Dhalech, 1999, p 29)

Cooperation can, of course, span a range of different types of partners, and this can be crucial in helping formal service agencies understand local contexts and respond more appropriately to them. One very successful example was reported by Tonna and her colleagues (in press) in New South Wales, where a coordinated effort was made to address mental health needs and problems in a drought-affected area. This included health and social services, farmers' organisations, rural financial counselling and farm finance organisations, health and safety agencies, community welfare services, and an academic mental health unit. They variously planned and delivered mental health workshops to some 800 participants, organised community mental health fora that were attended by over 1,900 people and established or improved 15 rural service networks. Briskman (2007) cites the work of Freedman and Stark (1993) in another example of service innovation. In this instance, an appreciation of the culture and concerns of the local Koorie community led to an extended family care system that overcame the deficits of the mainstream fostering system. Interestingly, Briskman comments that the fact that this took place some distance from the metropolitan area allowed some leeway for the workers and organisations to do this.

Conclusion

There is considerable variability in the provision and availability of services between different rural areas, and between different services and different social groups within them. Evidence from the UK, for example, indicates that older people in rural areas are less likely to receive supportive services such as domiciliary care and meals on wheels than those living in urban areas (Help the Aged/Rural Development Commission, 1996; Gilbert et al, 2006; Scharf and Bartlam, 2006). The relatively poorer levels of provision in the UK (White, 2001; Alston, 2005; Innes et al, 2005; Milbourne and Hughes, 2005; Bowden and Moseley, 2006; Wales Rural Observatory, 2006b) are also reflected in other rural places around the world. Problems of transportation, unsupported assumptions, higher service costs, lower rates of funding and weaker infrastructure of other supportive services all contribute to the relative disadvantage of rural residents. In some countries, such as the US, public service provision has traditionally been less extensive, and in countries like Australia and the UK, the marketisation of public services has led to the withdrawal of many local authorities from the direct provision of services. Private sector providers usually avoid the less profitable areas and services, and even the best efforts of NGOs may not be enough to establish and sustain viable alternative provision. Additionally, in some countries the changing governance of rural areas, with the formation and growth of a range of different organisations with responsibilities for different aspects of rural life, has resulted in the decline of local government power and led to fragmentation of responsibilities that may obstruct partnership (Shucksmith, 2003).

Readers may be forgiven, therefore, for supposing that the future of rural practice is all about problems and that the possibilities are limited or only negative. Our view tends to mirror the sentiment expressed in the French saying, 'plus ça change, plus c'est la même chose' ('the more things change, the more they stay the same'), that is, while the specifics of what is happening do indeed vary from time to time and place to place, the broad realities of social service provision in rural places remain surprisingly unchanged in many respects. Three continuing features have been the need for rural social workers to be creative in planning and intervention, for them to become actively engaged with their local contexts and for them to realise that the absence of extensive existing provision provides opportunities for influence and innovation. Indeed, this latter point is remarked upon in nearly every rural social work text. For example, Ginsberg (1998), in his discussion of some positive aspects of rural practice, notes that rural social workers often have much more autonomy over their work, may see much more tangible evidence of the impact of their work and may, consequently, be more likely to receive local recognition for their efforts. While Martinez-Brawley (2000) contends that rural practice typically involves working in circumstances where social workers have high-context knowledge about local circumstances, but have been tasked by low-context public policies. Thus, they need to become flexible and adaptive workers who can undertake a range of roles from direct help, service broker and resource manager, through to social activist and advocate, and do this with a sophisticated knowledge of how different forms of power and influence operate in communities.

Part Two
Developing rural practice

SIX

Models for practice 1: personal social services

Introduction

This chapter focuses upon the delivery of personal social services; approaches to practice designed to meet the particular needs of individuals, families and small groups. These are typically delivered through personal interaction in which the social worker directly provides the service or, alternatively, arranges it with other people or agencies. While personal social services have tended to use some form of casework theory or methods, other methods of intervention, such as advocacy, family group conferencing and group work, are also widely used. A new reader coming to the subject of rural social work might be forgiven for wondering if there was an intrinsic conflict between the personal social services and community social work. This is hardly surprising given the widespread use of the term 'community' to signify approaches to practice that are responsive to local context. For example:

> Community social work is a phrase coined to emphasize the need for social workers and social service deliverers to strive to make their services more relevant and effective with the population they serve. The aim is to move away from a service that is unintentionally bureaucratic and removed from the population, towards a greater dovetailing of informal help with the majority of care, support and control to be found in our society. (Smale and Bennett, 1989, p 11, cited in Martinez-Brawley, 1998, p 100)

Indeed, notions of partnership and localisation of service are hallmarks of what Martinez-Brawley more accurately refers to as 'community-oriented practice'. Unfortunately these imperatives are sometimes misunderstood as denying the possibility of personal social services. Although personal social services may be delivered in ways that do not accord with local needs by unresponsive agencies and practitioners who are remote from the communities they purport to serve, it does not follow that responsiveness to local context negates the possibility of personal social services. We prefer to use the terms 'community social work' or 'community-oriented practice' to describe forms of intervention that operate on a larger scale and seek to benefit a wider group of people than personal social services, rather than use them to refer to a particular orientation to service that we think all rural social services should adopt. Furthermore, while the models of service reviewed in this chapter, in contrast to the more community-focused approaches in Chapter 7, tend to be smaller in scale, being more personalised and more evidently problem-focused, this distinction is not absolute as there can be considerable overlap, as the discussion of community-embedded practice later in this chapter indicates. Instead, the distinction is a heuristic choice made for the purpose of identifying and highlighting particular features of different models of service provision, rather than one that necessarily signifies a particular service orientation.

The history of the recognition of rurality and localisation in the delivery of social services is one in which the significance of local community has until fairly recently been neglected, or viewed negatively as a barrier to efficient service delivery. Even when localisation has been recognised it has sometimes been eclipsed by shifts in public policy, or has been inadequately supported by subsequent funding and policy decisions. For instance, in the US the impact of Josephine Brown's pioneering text, *The Rural Community and Social Casework* (1933), together with much of the early interest in rural practice, had diminished by the 1940s and did not regain momentum until the 1970s (Locke and Winship, 2005). Moreover, as Martinez-Brawley noted, while 'The public language of politicians and influentials [*sic*] included "community ..." [it] seldom translated into the local level' (2000, p 218). Even the notional references to it that underpinned the shift towards deinstitutionalisation in many countries had little to say about the nature of communities, let alone rural communities, and too often relied instead upon uncritical assumptions about women's roles (Williams, 1989; Pascal, 1996). However, regardless of the policy context, many writers have emphasised that in small communities, 'a different form of practice has always been required, although this practice has not been systematically taught or recognised' (Martinez-Brawley, 2000, p 258). Indeed, while:

> Rural areas are often characterised by a lack of formal resources.... Social workers who serve rural areas ... are asked to deal with a wide range of problems and issues by

those seeking help. Within this context, especially valued are social workers possessing such traits as creativity, flexibility, knowledge about how to access both informal and formal helping services, and the ability to modify services as necessary to be more responsive to needs. (Locke and Winship, 2005, p 6)

Ginsberg observed that:

it appeared to us that the social worker in the rural community would have to know how to do a bit of everything, or at least know how to make a bit of everything available to clients in smaller communities … the rural social worker would have to provide direct counseling or casework services, community development skills, administrative ability and research competence. The rural social worker would also have to analyze, develop, and implement social policy of all kinds. (Ginsberg, 1998, p 9)

While these features do not necessarily determine a particular model for the organisation of service delivery, it has been widely accepted in rural social work literature that the rural practitioner is a generalist (Brown, 1933; Martinez-Brawley, 1982; Ginsberg, 1998; Lohmann and Lohmann, 2005). Our view is that while rural contexts and resource constraints have of necessity led many workers to become generalists, it does not follow that services necessarily have to be organised generically. Most texts on rural social work have tended to focus upon the knowledge and skills required by practitioners and have only indirectly addressed models of service delivery, although one exception can be found in an earlier text by Cheers (1998), which provides a classificatory scheme to identify, categorise and compare organisational models for the delivery of personal social services. This scheme is further elaborated in Cheers et al (2007). Essentially, it is organised around three key dimensions of service delivery that for the purposes of this chapter we term: service location and point of delivery; mode of delivery; and organisational independence and specialisation.

This chapter begins by identifying these three key dimensions of service delivery and then moves on to discuss different forms of practice in personal social services, that is, generalist/specialist, visiting, embedded and mandated/statutory forms of practice. It then turns to the question of local context and its implications for service delivery. This chapter does not review the application of particular theories and methods of intervention, as the general features of well-established models, such as task-centred casework, crisis intervention, cognitive behavioural approaches and so on, remain essentially the same regardless of the context (although these different approaches do of course differ in regard to the degree to which they have the potential to be responsive to different cultural contexts or have the potential for an empowering form of partnership). This chapter should be read with the material from Chapter 2 on the social dynamics of small communities very much in mind, in particular: the observations made about social visibility and confidentiality; the normative expectations of more personalised relationships in which reciprocity and continuity feature; the role of gossip; and the significance of different strategies for managing information, such as the practice of 'not knowing' used by some to maximise their own local knowledge.

Key dimensions of service delivery

The three dimensions identified – service location and point of delivery, mode of delivery, and organisational independence and degree of specialisation – are not an exhaustive list of possible dimensions, nor are they mutually exclusive dimensions, as some distinguishing features in regard to location and mode clearly overlap. However, they do provide a practical and easily used basis for identifying and comparing some of the important characteristics of the organisation of service delivery in rural areas.

Service location and point of service delivery

The most fundamental distinction is between centralised services that operate from a single geographic location and distributed services that are dispersed in several locations over a wider geographical area. Centralised services are typically characterised by their permanency, regular and extensive hours of access and close location to transport hubs. Distributed services vary considerably in the scale of dispersal, and the term 'satellite services' is sometimes used to indicate those located in smaller outlying settlements (Cheers, 1998; Cheers et al, 2007). Distributed services can be provided intermittently by visiting practitioners or more regularly by staff living in the local area, and, most importantly, can significantly reduce travel and time costs for prospective service users. Examples of distributed services can be found in a probation and after-care service operating through a satellite outpost, a child protection service provided one day a week from a local community hospital, or in The Royal Flying Doctor Service that regularly visits remote communities in outback Australia, and connects with remote area hospitals. Visiting staff are more likely to be used for smaller and more remote settlements where low demand can result in high per capita service costs. Research has shown that occasional satellite services are most effective when linked with an existing, ongoing front-line service that can provide support and can act as the point of initial contact (Blacksell et al, 1988).

The relationship of distributed services to any central service or management location that may exist is also extremely variable and a range of terms such as 'hub and spoke', 'regional', 'district' and 'local' have been used to indicate this. Distributed services include peripatetic or mobile services that do not have fixed service bases and may operate on a circuit of different locations perhaps using mobile premises such as a travelling bus, or temporary non-specialist locations such as health centres, community centres and village halls (Smith and Smith, 1987; Lifeline, 1992). For instance, a mobile child protection service was introduced for small remote Aboriginal settlements in the Northern Territory in Australia as part of the Northern Territory Emergency Response to the extreme disadvantages of these communities (Northern Territory Emergency Response Review Board, 2008). Circulating services are more likely to be perceived as locally relevant, and be well used by residents, when they are regularly scheduled and reasonably frequent. If necessary, circulating services can act as a point of referral for a wider range of services. This semi-localisation of service often results in practitioners accumulating a great deal of knowledge about local context that can be used to inform service responses, and which, if fed back to the organisational base, can be used to shape overall provision. However, circuit services require effective strategies for informing local communities of their availability, and must also have efficient contact systems for users that are sensitive to possible concerns about relevance, confidentiality and other risks. For example, research into Women's Aid services for family violence in one area of Scotland found that the use of an urban telephone contact number discouraged women from seeking help, as they felt that a city-based contact worker would not understand their local circumstances and concerns (MacKay, 2000).

A further distinction can be made between outreach and in-reach services. Outreach occurs when social workers and services go out to users by visiting them in their homes or using some other point of contact in the community to enhance access, such as a church, social group or another service's base, such as a school or health centre.

In-reach refers to services where clients themselves have to travel to the service centre itself. Outreach services reduce access costs and inconvenience for users as these are largely borne by the service, whereas in-reach services provide obvious cost savings for organisations as they transfer financial and other access costs to service users (Poole and Daley, 1985). The unpublished report of an intensive support service for people with substance abuse problems in the Border region of Scotland (Wilson, 2002), mentioned in the previous chapter, found that in the most rural areas workers could support only two or three clients compared to their urban counterparts who typically managed six or more. In-reach services are more appropriately used in larger towns or in more compact areas with higher population densities and well-developed transport options. Outreach approaches are likely to be more successful in extending services to smaller and more remote settlements and scattered populations, although they can also have limitations, such as slow response times, insufficient knowledge of local conditions and reduced community engagement in service provision and planning, and may require more specialised follow-up (Lifeline, 1992; Northern Territory Emergency Response Review Board, 2008).

Along with obvious cost savings for the service provider, in-reach services are more likely to provide opportunities for the development of multidisciplinary and joint working with other organisations based in the same locality. It may also be easier to attract appropriately qualified staff than more dispersed services. Because the burden of travel falls upon the prospective service user it might be assumed that users would not like them. However, user preferences are not always quite so easily predicted. One Australian study found that some people from remote settlements actually preferred to travel to services in regional rather than satellite centres, because they travelled to their regional centre every so often for other reasons anyway (Cheers, 1992). Thus, they perceived no extra costs and could often reduce these by staying with friends and relatives. Moreover, the additional hardships and costs involved in travelling the extra distance to the regional centre were minimal compared with those incurred getting to the satellite centre over long, rough roads or by infrequent long-distance public transport. In some instances, service users preferred to deal directly with the service decision makers rather than go through subordinate satellite staff, and other studies confirm that when questions of confidentiality and risk are concerned, the increased anonymity of service in a larger settlement is often preferred. Coorey (1988), for example, found this to be the case for women experiencing family violence in rural Australia, while Rounds (1988) noted that some men with HIV would travel to clinics some distance away from their home areas for medical treatment.

Distributed services are typically associated with higher service costs in terms of staff time spent travelling, increased travel costs and the costs of using multiple locations, especially where these are not continuously utilised (Pugh, 2007b). Furthermore, some forms of distributed service like circuit services cannot usually respond quickly to emergency situations unless staff are in the area at the time. Distributed services are vulnerable to disruption by adverse weather and unfavourable geographic conditions, especially in places like northern Canada, northern Scotland and tropical northern Australia. To summarise, given equivalent resources, progressively fewer clients can be served by a satellite service compared with a comparable centralised in-reach service, and fewer still can be served by a visiting service.

Mode of delivery

A distinction can be made between services delivered through direct personal contact using face-to-face meetings and those using indirect media, such as telephones, radio, video-conferencing, the internet and letter post. Whichever personal mode is used, the social worker is usually directly involved with the client in establishing and/or providing a service. However, a third-party worker or agency who may already have some contact with the person needing help, or who, because of their location, is able to quickly have direct personal contact, may undertake the initial referral, information gathering and assessment. As many of the advantages and disadvantages of these different modes of delivery are easily perceived, this section provides only a rudimentary discussion of some key features. A succinct overview can be found in Brownlee et al (2009), who note the need for further research into current usage and effectiveness. It should also be noted that the rapidity of development in some technologies means that the situation in some areas, particularly internet-based services, can change very quickly.

Telephone counselling services and crisis lines and helplines, such as ChildLine in the UK, which have general coverage, can provide a new service or extend a service that is not otherwise available in a rural area. Specific telephone services for rural areas have the advantage of being more readily identifiable as a service directed towards local needs, especially if they can link to other services and practical help, for example, at times of crisis the Farm Stress Line in Saskatchewan can also provide support with livestock care when required. The comparative anonymity of helplines may ease immediate concerns about confidentiality, but the frustrations that occur when people have to wait too long for connection, or have to wade through seemingly endless sub-directories to get help, can be a deterrent to their use. In addition, these modes of delivery may be used to justify the withholding or withdrawing of direct personal contact services. Moreover, although telephone counselling may help to avert some personal crises or may direct callers to other sources of assistance, there may be little possibility of immediate follow-up, especially where more specialised services are required.

Video-conferencing can extend some specialised services to rural people, such as counselling, psychological testing, psychiatric assessment and remedial education (Lundin and Arger, 1994; Lifeline Darling Downs and South West Queensland Ltd, 2005). It also provides more spontaneous, face-to-face interaction, with the visual and auditory cues that are important in establishing rapport, assessing behaviour and judging reactions. Video-conferencing can also be used to support dispersed practitioners and enable inter-professional collaboration. The main limitations of video-conferencing are its cost, the question of user access to the facilities and the frequent breaks in transmission that can occur with some technologies. However, costs may be reduced by sharing equipment among service organisations or by pooling funding for this purpose among several local organisations. In Australia, the national Centrelink programme has developed an extensive network of video-conferencing facilities that can be used by non-government organisations. Telecentres are also making the technology more available in some places but access is limited to people living nearby and who know how to use the equipment (Lawrence and Share, 1993). As these facilities become more widespread in other publicly funded services offices, such as schools, hospitals and local government offices, there will be further opportunities for widening access. In addition, as internet-based technology for video-conferencing becomes more commonplace and reliable, costs are likely to fall.

The internet provides inexpensive and speedy communication between social workers and clients and can be used to provide advice, information and some counselling support. The internet also assists communication between service users and other mutual support groups, such as web-based forums, as well as providing direct access to huge amounts of information. Embedding services within more general forums has advantages in enhancing awareness of the existence of a service and reducing fears of shame and stigma. Alternatively, more specialised sites, such as www.farminghelp.co.uk, signal their purpose more directly and can provide direct access to specific voluntary sector services directed towards stress, housing and other needs. Self-help groups can use the internet to create online communities that are not bound by geography or locality, and which can be extremely supportive for individuals and groups who are marginalised in some way within their communities (Graham et al, 1996). Similarly, advocacy organisations can use the internet to build wider networks, gather support, share information and exert political pressure very effectively indeed (Wasko, 2005).

In medicine and psychology the internet is increasingly being used to provide online diagnoses, intervention plans, consultation and advice to rural practitioners, although such usage is much less common in social work (McCarty and Clancy, 2002). In part, this probably arises from the nature of many social work interventions, but is also likely to be a result of lower levels of investment in technical services and support. However, in the US, internet-based counselling services are becoming more well-established and the National Association of Social Workers provides guidance on such practice (Coleman, 2000). In Australia, parenting training programmes using computers and telephone support have reported positive results (Sanders, 1999), and the Whyalla and Upper Eyre Pensinsula Parenting Project in remote South Australia substantially modified the standard, urban-based Triple P Positive Parenting Program (Sanders and Markie-Dadds, 1996) to make greater use of such technologies and rely less on face-to-face contact (Burgess et al, 2004). The main advantages of the internet are that users can access services without the costs and inconvenience of travel, and can do so at times convenient for them. The main limitations are its cost and the availability of internet provision and access to suitable technology.

Many rural areas have no access to dial-up or broadband provision, or have unreliable access through expensive long-distance telephone services. Satellite technology and access is also comparatively expensive. Regardless of which technology is used, service users and small local community organisations often bear the costs of equipment and access to internet services. Other technological developments may improve access or support for some people, such as the remote monitoring of isolated individuals (CSCI, 2006). However, it remains the case that the poorest and most marginalised groups are the least likely to have access to these technologies (Wasko, 2005; Bowden and Moseley, 2006). There are also concerns about the security and confidentiality of computer-based communications, and Wasko (2005), in noting the lack of uniform protocols, has identified the need for wider use of encryption in emails and clear lines of accountability for access to personal data. She also points out that evidence of the cost-effectiveness of new technologies is, thus far, limited.

Organisational independence and specialisation

With the exception of statutory or mandated services in child protection and mental health, and small independent sector organisations, stand-alone specialist services tend to be uncommon in rural areas, largely because of their comparatively high costs of provision and a lack of sufficient demand to justify them. However, statutory or mandated services that are directly accountable to legal systems and processes are often required to demonstrate independence. For example, the Guardian ad Litem service, the court-appointed social work service for children in England and Wales, is organisationally separated from local authority children's services. Specialist services in rural places often cover very large geographical areas with relatively sparse staffing levels. Consequently, service provision can be vulnerable to the ordinary contingencies of staffing, such as illness, staff leaving and lack of cover (Cheers et al, 2007). There are a number of organisational responses to these difficulties, such as the more extensive use of part-time staff to provide geographical coverage and avoid over-concentration of resources, although, as we shall see in Chapter 8, such arrangements can create other challenges in terms of supervision, continuing professional development and consistency of service.

A common response to the problem of providing personal social services in large areas with dispersed populations is for social service organisations to integrate their provision with the work of other local or regional organisations, perhaps the most common being the co-location of a number of different services in the same building or institution. This is aimed at reducing financial overheads and may facilitate inter-service coordination in referrals, interventions and service planning and development (Cheers et al, 2007, ch 5). Alternatively, smaller service hubs can be attached to other larger local service organisations such as a hospital, school or local council (Morton Consulting Services Pty Ltd, 1990). For instance, community health, counselling, disability, child protection and family violence services could be co-located in a country hospital. Attaching small service hubs to other well-established local institutions and services can enhance local responsiveness and relevance, and consequently, increase their use by local people (Morton Consulting Services Pty Ltd, 1990). Integration may include the integration of specialist workers within other service teams, such as a primary health team or a school welfare service, where immediate day-to-day supervision and personnel support may be provided by a senior worker from another profession, supplemented with visiting back-up specialists or remote access to such advice.

Social work roles and tasks may even extend to their integration into the remit of other workers. For example, a family violence worker might also provide youth counselling because no other local provision for this exists. Results from a study of social support in remote areas of Australia indicated that this extension of remit, whether formally recognised by the organisational hierarchy or simply informally done in response to local demand, was commonplace (Cheers, 1992, 2001). It also found that parents preferred to discuss child development problems with local schoolteachers and nurses, rather than with specialist social workers and psychologists in regional centres, and that, generally, the parents were satisfied with the outcomes. This extension of remit or diffusion of role boundaries may also occur informally as local practitioners respond to local expectations, or may be formalised as an existing service becomes funded to expand the range of its provision and provide integrated multi-purpose services according to local needs and priorities.

Integration in its various forms is usually assumed to reduce the fixed costs of provision, such as office accommodation or the costs of employing additional specialist staff, but the trade-off may be the reduction in the local availability of specialist knowledge and skills, which may not be adequately replaced by multi-tasking by other professionals or joint working with other services. Nonetheless, as noted in the preceding chapter, measures such as co-location and structural integration are not generally sufficient in themselves to improve outcomes (Brown et al, 2003; Johnson et al, 2003; Glendinning et al, 2006). A further problem, which was noted in Chapter 3, arises when different services span different geographical and political boundaries. This may lead to uncoordinated provision and uncertainty about responsibilities. Encouragingly, one small study found that over time many of these problems of multidisciplinary practice diminished as respondents later reported very positive experiences (Parry-Jones and Soulsby, 2001).

Forms of practice

This section distinguishes four dimensions or forms of practice – generalist/specialist, visiting, embedded and mandated or statutory practice – and reviews their implications for the provision of rural services. In reality, a particular service may embody more than one form of practice. For example, a statutory mandate may be carried out by a visiting or a community-embedded service, and so the merits and demerits of each approach to service organisation and delivery are likely to vary according to the nature of the statutory remit and the tasks allocated to the service, while all services may be perceived as varying along a continuum from generalist practice through to more specialist provision.

Generalist and specialist practice

A distinction is commonly made in North America (Martinez-Brawley, 2000) and Australia (Cheers, 1998; Cheers et al, 2007) between generalist practice, which refers to working across several fields of practice (for example, child protection, family violence), and generic practice, which spans several practice methods (for example, casework, community development). In contrast, in the UK the term 'generalist' is not widely used and the term 'generic' has been used to refer to social service organisations that span several fields of practice, as well as to individual practice that does likewise. To avoid confusion we use the term 'generic' to encompass both practice fields and practice methods. While research into what rural social workers actually do in practice is limited, what is available supports this generalisation of the term, as do other commentaries on rural social work (Collier, 1984; Cheers, 1998; Martinez-Brawley, 2000; Pugh, 2000; Cheers et al, 2007). Arguments for and against specialisation have a long history in social work and these will not be reviewed here except to acknowledge some tensions that may be more prominent in rural settings.

Specialist practice is distinguished by either a sole focus upon a field of practice, such as mental health or substance dependency, or, alternatively, by the use of a particular practice method, such as counselling or family therapy. Accordingly, a specialist counselling service with a defined methodology may target a particular group such as depressed youth, or be more generally available to everyone in a community. Conversely, a highly targeted service for youth might encompass a range of methods including counselling, group work, health education and casework. Access to specialised services is usually determined by an assessment of client characteristics or the type of problem faced and the type of intervention required. From an organisational perspective, specialisation facilitates efficient use of resources by selectively controlling access to service and filtering out unsuitable, irrelevant and inappropriate referrals. It allows social workers to develop specialist knowledge, skills and expertise in the practice field or method, and, historically, has permitted relatively high levels of professional discretion. In theory, specialisation in rural areas allows clients to have access to this expertise and, potentially, to a higher quality of service than might be received from a generic service or practitioner (Cheers et al, 2007), although there is little comparative evidence to support this assumption. Specialist expertise can be made more widely available by sharing it with local practitioners through training, consultation and case support (Cheers et al, 2007). For example, this was incorporated into the Whyalla and Upper Eyre Pensinsula Parenting Project where the specialist child development expert provided information and back-up support for practitioners from various backgrounds working in a variety of agencies such as kindergartens, preschools, primary schools, hospitals and local support groups (Burgess et al, 2004).

Research evidence from Australia (Lonne, 2002; Munn, 2002) indicates that Australian rural social work is highly generalist in terms of fields of practice. In Munn's study of rural human service workers (2002), 92% of respondents described at least part of their work as generalist, with 30% being entirely generalist and 62% combining specialist and generalist roles. In regard to the methods of practice, in Lonne's (2002) study of rural social workers, 43% of respondents reported their 'primary function' as generic casework and another 23% reported combining this with other methods such as community work, while 35% undertook specialist practice either exclusively (12%) or combined with other roles (23%). A comparative study of rural practice in the US and Australia (Saltman et al, 2004) did not find quite such widespread engagement with multiple fields of practice but also confirmed the generic nature of much of rural social work, as well as the predominance of casework in both countries. However, it is not clear whether this genericism is the result of considered assessment and decision making or simply a response to the lack of specialist services. What is clear, though, is that the more holistic appreciation of local context that is commonplace in rural practice encourages social workers to see the links between social and individual factors and problems, for instance, the closure of a local quarry resulting in a father's unemployment may well contribute to family stress and disruption and a child's subsequent truancy. These factors can be seen to be interrelated and so, potentially, may be responded to as such.

All specialists must establish boundaries to distinguish what they can and cannot do, but the lack of alternative services in rural areas may result in additional pressures that work against the maintenance of specialist services. Maintenance strategies include: social workers identifying role boundaries and intervention time limits with clients at the outset; acknowledging limits to expertise with clients; articulating role boundaries with other agencies and local stakeholders; and resisting pressure from employers and funding bodies to take on inappropriate cases and tasks. Social workers who are not able to satisfactorily establish these professional boundaries face the possibility of being rejected by the community for failing to respond to pressing local needs, or may become overwhelmed by their workload. As noted in Chapter 3, this may be a particular problem for indigenous workers working in their own communities. Social workers must be sensitive to client concerns and possible resistance to referral to other practitioners or agencies. When onward referrals are made, appropriate support should be provided, such as a more personalised introduction to the new worker and a willingness to help establish the client's position in helping negotiate the terms of service at the outset (Andersen and Darracott, 2004; Cheers et al, 2007).

Tensions may occur when a specialist service or practitioner cannot provide for people whose needs are ineligible or unsuited to the specialised service or when available funding fails to match local needs. In one Australian community a youth suicide prevention programme was provided in accordance with Australian government policy based upon national statistics, although it was local farmers who were especially at risk in this particular community and who could not access any other services (Cheers et al, 2007). In such situations, practitioners are presented with a dilemma. If they try to maintain the integrity of the funded programme while offering some response to the more pressing local needs, then apart from any organisational pressures for conformity with service objectives, there are likely to be serious questions about professional ethics and accountability. However, there are several strategies that specialists can use to increase responsiveness and access to services (Cheers et al, 2007), which include:

- broadening referral criteria relating to presenting issues or client characteristics such as age, gender and geographic location;
- widening the range of practice methods used, for example, incorporating community education into a child protection service;
- sharing specialised knowledge by providing training and supervision for other practitioners;
- advocating for additional or alternative services to meet community needs within their own and other organisations.

Visiting practice

Visiting practitioners should tailor the service to the characteristics, cultures and needs of a community and potential service users, rather than adopt a one-size-fits-all approach. Ideally, this should be underpinned by a good working knowledge of the place and its people, including some understanding of the dynamics, history, relationships and politics of each local community. While all personal social services should be contextualised, that is, tailored to the community's characteristics, concerns and preferences, this is especially important for visiting services. If this is not done, then the service may be seen as irrelevant or intrusive provision, rather than an integral part of local services. Contextualisation involves the practitioner and their organisation negotiating and finding common ground between what the community needs and what is possible within the procedural, policy and legislative constraints of the service organisation. For example, in Ceduna in South Australia a culturally embedded parenting support programme was developed through sensitive negotiation between a local Aboriginal women's organisation and the visiting service provided by a university in the region within the parameters of the government funding body's requirements. Rather than provide a Western-style, standardised Triple P Parenting Program (Sanders and Markie-Dadds, 1996; Sanders, 1999), the women's organisation was subcontracted to employ an Aboriginal Support Worker to provide support for local Aboriginal mothers and fathers to raise their young children in accordance with cultural and community customs. The early childhood coordinator for the university programme provided mentoring, support and materials in response to the needs and requests of the local Aboriginal community. Among the important questions relating to visiting practice that must be settled are decisions about the nature of the service, how and where it is delivered, and how potential clients will engage with it. For instance, will referral always be through other local services or will those who wish to keep the contact entirely outside their community for privacy reasons be able to access it directly? When new services are being developed, it may be necessary for social workers in the early stages to take a proactive stance in regard to their own agency's position, especially if they come to a negative view about the relevance and limits of what is proposed.

Meaningful participation in these decisions about service organisation requires the development of good links with communities and with existing service providers. Enabling effective local participation involves the identification of key people and organisations and networking with them to understand their perspectives on community dynamics, and their visions for the service and its users (Cheers, 1998; Cheers et al, 2007). It also requires broader publicity about the processes of consultation and representation throughout a community, and particular efforts should be made to ensure that minority groups have the opportunity to engage with these processes. Ad hoc and opportunistic informal discussions with local people can help to legitimate new developments and sometimes present surprising insights into local opinion and local politics. Although efforts to ensure wider participation may partly be achieved through existing local bodies, use should be made of other resources, such as local newspapers, radio stations and public libraries.

Local politics are especially hazardous for visiting practitioners because they will usually have significant gaps in their knowledge of the community and little opportunity to influence events when they are not there. The local and regional politics that surround visiting services, including, for example, territorial rivalries with other services, the threat they may pose to community-driven campaigns for more locally based services and the interactional dynamics between communities in the region, can facilitate or hinder practice. For instance, in situations where there are inter-community rivalries, strong alliances formed by a practitioner in one community might create barriers elsewhere. Similarly, the location of the service may be a crucial issue if residents of other communities object to using it. In divided communities, the practitioner should strive to maintain strong relationships with key members of all factions and avoid unnecessary or unhelpful participation in factional disputes. Conversely, strong ties between communities arising from kinship and friendship networks, or population shifts between them, can enhance the credibility and acceptance of a practitioner as information flows between them.

The establishment and maintenance of effective working relationships with other local services and practitioners will contribute to service coordination and effectiveness, most notably in facilitating client access to the visiting service (Manning and Cheers, 1995). A strong service network also provides the opportunity for visiting practitioners, especially specialists, to provide consultation, support and information to locally based colleagues, who may be more isolated from professional, organisational and common-interest networks. There may also be occasions when the visiting social worker can support local workers and activists in regard to contentious service issues around, say, child protection, family violence, juvenile justice and substance abuse. They can support local colleagues in debates, provide them with information and/or lend them their credibility, and having the 'outside expert' on board can sometimes get contentious issues onto local agendas. Indeed, several of the studies of small communities mentioned in Chapter 2 noted how 'outsiders' can perform useful roles in promoting change as they may take on positions or tasks that might be divisive if undertaken by a local person, or that are avoided by them because of the risk of being stigmatised by the possible failure of an initiative (Frankenberg, 1957; Emmett, 1964; Cohen, 1982; Jedrej and Nuttall, 1996). Incomers/ outsiders may articulate opinions that might be counterproductive in other respects if they were expressed by 'insiders'.

Community-embedded practice

Earlier in this book we noted that conceptions of rural community are often idealised and that notions of 'belonging' and 'insider' often oversimplify more complex realities of membership and status. Nevertheless, it remains a sociological fact that people subjectively perceive these terms as having meaning in their lives. Thus, community-embedded practice is a frame of reference not a theory. It is based on the practical experience of social workers living and working in rural communities and as reported and advocated for in a number of developed countries including Australia (Cheers, 1998), Canada (Collier, 1984), Spain (Martinez-Brawley, undated), the US (Martinez-Brawley, 1990, 2000) and the UK (Hadley and McGrath, 1980; Martinez-Brawley, 1986). Each of these writers has argued for the pragmatic acceptance of the fact that effective practice in small communities requires some degree of community engagement and involvement. Thus, attempts by workers to maintain social distance and a position of professional neutrality are rarely successful and may be counterproductive.

In Chapter 2 we reviewed some of the key ethical and professional issues associated with practitioners living and working in the same place and reviewed some of the literature on dual and multiple relationships in small communities. The point is that community-embedded practitioners accept that the demands of living and working in the same place will gradually tie them into networks of friendship, mutuality and reciprocity (Martinez-Brawley, 1990) and that while this can raise some challenging questions about their professional position, it can also make the experience of rural practice much more satisfying. This acceptance will occur spontaneously as they go about their private and working lives, but they may decide to enhance it by a proactive engagement with local professional and personal networks. Ideally, they will move from being an unknown 'foreigner' or outsider, perhaps treated with caution, to being a familiar and non-threatening person. Of course, such acceptance is never likely to be complete or comprehensive throughout a community; as with every other resident, it will remain conditional to some degree.

Community-embedded social workers, therefore, become more socially visible and as they work within local networks they learn of local needs, problems and emerging issues. Resource limitations and working in very small organisations and work groups mean that many rural practitioners often do not have administrative support or assistants to undertake supportive tasks for service users, such as taking a child to school, helping an older person with their shopping or arranging a teleconference for a support group. Undertaking such practical activities typically fits well with rural communities in which people are expected to 'muck in', and they help workers to establish credibility, to learn about the community and to gain access to local networks.

Being located at some distance from head offices and being away from the immediate presence of their supervisors, rural social workers generally have more freedom to respond to situations as they find them rather than being wholly driven by preordained procedures and processes. There is often space for innovation in devising new solutions to problems and situations that are not covered by existing organisational policies, or for which they have not been prepared by their professional training. Improvisation, making do with what is available, especially when other support or specialist expertise is unavailable, is also well regarded in rural communities (Collier, 1984). A sincere effort to help, even when the outcome may not be as successful as hoped, is still likely to be appreciated. Indeed, as the social workers in Lonne's (2002) study reported, these opportunities for innovation, improvisation and personalisation formed some of the main attractions of rural practice. However, probably the most attractive aspect of embedded practice for social workers, who are comfortable with the expectations of role integration noted by Zapf (1985) in Chapter 2, is the experience of social acceptance, that is, the feeling of being 'part of things' and being regarded as a valued member of the community. For some, the sense of greater social integration and social equality is enhanced in small communities when they live and work in the same place.

Martinez-Brawley (1990) contends that social workers in small communities, who have strong connections in both the local and external worlds, are well located at the intersection of vertical and horizontal ties. Being located at the intersection of horizontal ties between people and organisations in the community and also having vertical ties through their service organisation to the broader context of policy and decision making, community-embedded social workers are well placed to identify local needs and problems. They can relay information in both directions, from the community upwards and from political and organisational domains down to the local community. Moreover, embedded workers are well positioned to coordinate service provision from local and non-local organisations. The structural location of community-embedded practitioners means that they can make important connections between practice and its immediate social context and broader factors that interact with it. Even when their primary orientation is to working with individuals and families, there are indications that many rural social workers also focus on wider community issues (Lonne, 2002; Munn, 2002). This is most likely to occur when they are closely identified with a community or when the issues have evident structural causes (Marson and Powell, 2000), such as those frequently encountered in working with indigenous groups (Dixon and Scheurell, 1995; Briskman, 2007). Community-embedded practice offers greater opportunities for preventive approaches to practice as practitioners with good local knowledge and networks are well placed to anticipate and respond to personal and community issues before they become major problems. They may do this in various ways. For instance, from direct case experience they may decide to challenge local cultures that deny family violence and make it hard for victims to find support or leave (Wendt and Cheers, 2004; Wendt, 2005), or they may become involved in the promotion of minority language initiatives to enhance access and provide more culturally sensitive services to linguistic minorities (Kornbeck, 2003).

Being embedded in the community raises several boundary issues. First, as part of the community, the practitioner has multiple relationships with other people. For example, a client might also be the social worker's neighbour, their daughter's schoolteacher and netball coach, and an agency board member. Second, the boundary between personal and work time can be blurred, as clients sometimes want to talk to the social worker after hours and outside the office. Being too readily available can contribute to work stress and burnout, which are associated with higher rates of staff turnover in rural places. Third, as we shall see in the next section, some practitioners, especially those with mandated social control responsibilities in child protection or juvenile justice and probation work, may be at risk of abuse or threats. Fourth, boundaries are often blurred within and between social care organisations and workers' roles.

There are also tensions in embedded practice, especially when there may be a conflict between the social worker's professional commitment to equity and social justice and the attitudes and behaviours of some local people. For example, social workers may find it difficult to help girls and women in settings where they encounter some of the strongly conservative ideas about gender roles noted in Chapter 2. Often they may wish to avoid overt conflict and will need to work skilfully to provide effective help and support. Nevertheless, there may be a conflict between being embedded within a community and effectively carrying out one's professional duties. Rawsthorne, in her study of sexual violence in rural communities in New South Wales, reported that:

> In deciding to act on an allegation of violence ... workers had to weigh up the risk to their standing in the community and their friendships, and on many occasions decided to disbelieve or not support the victims. Criticism of their town (implicit in an allegation of sexual violence) is simply not accepted, with rural communities being very skilled at closing ranks around the locals and excluding anyone that challenges the community's views of itself. (Rawsthorne, 2003, p 8)

Rawsthorne argues that the assumption that community problems can always be solved from strong ties of engagement is mistaken when the problems are deeply embedded in its structure. She contends that strong ties may render 'invisible the divisions of power, privilege, disempowerment and deprivation that enables acts of sexual violence' (2003, p 10) and suggests that workers might need to 'maintain a degree of separateness', perhaps by living outside of the community in which they work.

Mandated and statutory social work

Mandated work, that is, work undertaken with statutory authority and using legal powers within practice, may be challenging in any context, but in small communities it problematises assumptions about the nature of the relationship between social workers and the community. While the perceptions of the immediate people involved and those of the wider community are bound to be dependent to some degree upon their view of the worker's competence and credibility, these perceptions will also be framed by the nature of the role and the statutory responsibilities being undertaken. For instance, statutory responsibilities that are primarily supportive and are regarded positively are less likely to attract negative comment or hostile reaction. In contrast, the compulsory detention under mental health legislation of a person whose behaviour is regarded as odd or eccentric but is not perceived as being dangerous, or investigations into allegations of child abuse made against a well-known member of the community are much more likely to meet with antipathy and resistance. Indeed, in a study in rural Australia, Clapton et al (1999) noted that children's allegations of abuse by a prominent person had been regarded as not credible, and consequently were ignored, for many years because the abuser was highly respected and liked throughout the community. Social workers are faced with decisions about how best to comport themselves within a community when at times they are required to make decisions that are not widely understood or supported, and undertake interventions that may be contested. The point is that the higher social visibility of both workers and clients in small communities that was noted in Chapter 2 means that there is often a wider audience to an intervention, an audience that may wish to be convinced about the appropriateness of the decisions being made, and this can create some dilemmas in regard to confidentiality and also raise concerns about client and worker safety.

Lonne (2002) in his survey found that around 44% of rural social workers exercised mandated authority, and 71% of them had multiple mandated responsibilities. Generic workers are likely to encounter more difficulty when their responsibilities necessitate a wide range of work that requires different kinds of personal presentation. For instance, they might undertake work ranging from statutory responsibilities through to advice, counselling and personal support. In contrast, a specialist worker from outside of a community who is undertaking statutory work may find it relatively easy to present a professional persona that preserves a greater degree of social distance, and so avoid any perception of being compromised or of betraying local social expectations. Similarly, a specialist worker living within a community may adopt a more reserved professional persona and maintain this consistently while at work. It is not uncommon for communities to tolerate a disjunction between public and private personae providing that the behaviour adopted in the public role is justified and that the distinctions in behaviour and presentation are maintained consistently.

The challenging nature of these multiple responsibilities in rural social work is rarely acknowledged, although a report into child protection arrangements in Eilean Siar (the Western Isles of Scotland) did note that:

> We recognise the different environment of small communities. Workers can be much closer to the people they serve ... [but] [s]ustaining professional distance, and taking unpopular decisions with intimidating adults can be challenging. (SWIA, 2005, p 126)

Furthermore, relatively isolated practitioners operating with little immediate support or back-up may feel particularly vulnerable to threats made against them or their families. In small communities, a worker's home address is more likely to be widely known, and the increased risks of violence for children and women clients arising from comparative isolation may also be a factor for social workers. Women's Aid workers report taking additional steps to secure their safety, particularly when they are involved in contentious and fractious casework, such as staying at friends' houses, checking to see if they are being followed and avoiding some public places.

Understanding and responding to local context

All practice takes place within the context of organisational cultures and policies that shape the possibilities for practice. Policies specify target populations, referral sources and pathways, practice methods, and geographic service areas. The processes of practice are often formalised, as in much child protection work, case management and managed care, although typically some discretion is permitted as to how they are implemented. An organisation's culture also influences how strictly policies, procedures, job descriptions and funding guidelines are followed. Consequently, all workers have to make some assessment about the degree of flexibility permitted or expected in their own practice and align this with their own understanding of their professional obligations. However, their practice should also be responsive to the local context and local needs, problems and aspirations, for, as Martinez–Brawley has noted:

> The raison d'etre of social work has been the attempt to make the best sense of people's lives and situations, the attempt to improve their condition based on their own historical, cultural and geographical realities. The practice of social work has always required unique responses because individuals live under unique, local conditions and communities are all different. (Martinez–Brawley, 2003, p 293)

A responsive practitioner needs to develop what Martinez-Brawley (2003) calls 'integrative thinking', in which the specific histories and environments of local communities, the perspectives of local people and some of the possible local consequences are properly considered. That is, practitioners should attempt to integrate 'the various elements of the human encounter' (2003, p 296), including the broader cultural, social, physical, political, economic and spiritual context, so that innovative and practical responses can be devised. This, as was noted in Chapter 3, may mean adapting methods to better 'fit' the cultural preferences and accepted styles of interaction of particular communities. For example, one of the authors was surprised, when making an initial visit to a family about reported concerns about child protection, to find that what had been expected to be a meeting involving just the child's parents turned out to be a houseful of relatives. These included adult siblings, aunts and uncles, as well as two grandparents, who all expected to be able to hear what the concerns were, and to offer their views if minded to do so. Thus, social workers must develop some understanding of the community's expectations of the service and its employees and adapt accordingly. As a palliative care worker noted in her 'work with First Nation's peoples': 'A lot of times … what role I will take comes from the family and what it is they request' (MacLean and Kelley, 2001, p 71).

In the conclusion to Chapter 3, seven key points for working with indigenous peoples were noted, two of which pointed up the importance of working with broader groupings of families and communities, and the relevance of developmental models to promote welfare. This might seem to suggest that there is no place for personal working or casework with indigenous peoples, but of course, the reality is that not only are many services formally tasked to deliver services in such ways, there might also be an appropriate need for them. However, casework approaches to practice are particularly vulnerable to the risks of decontextualisation simply because of the narrower focus of action, which has allowed 'white' workers and agencies to operate without challenge to any ethnocentric presumptions they may have had. Accordingly, this has led to concerted efforts in some countries to ensure that past mistakes are not replicated through the introduction of new procedures, rules and principles to guide practice. For example, The Aboriginal Child Placement Principle in Australia, noted in Chapter 3, and similar protocols in Canada and the US, set out desired standards for practice and specify a hierarchy of preferred placements for aboriginal and indigenous children when their welfare cannot be assured within their immediate family. Typically, these protocols begin by addressing the formal identity or status of a child to ascertain which agency has jurisdiction in regard to their welfare. Washington State has a detailed Indian Child Welfare Manual (www.dshs.wa.gov) and in Canada, a new Casework Practice Model (see www.child.alberta. ca for an outline) was introduced after the passing of the 2004 Child, Youth and Family Enhancement Act. The underpinning principle in all of these developments is to ensure that decisions about indigenous children's welfare are informed by accurate knowledge of their culture and ethnicity. This is to be done either by the direct involvement of an indigenous agency or, where mainstream services are providing service, by the involvement of people from the child's tribe or band.

In an earlier paper, Cheers et al (2005a) used the notion of the 'practice domain' to help social workers identify these different sources of influence that might bear upon a situation. Rural practitioners work in a number of practice domains, each of which is a constellation of elements and narratives about how they should understand and respond to particular practice situations, and which factors they should take account of in their decision making. The eight domains identified thus far are:

- personal – the practitioner's personal, social and cultural background;
- geography – the geographic, demographic, built and natural environmental elements of the space of practice, such as local settlement patterns, distance from larger population centres and transportation systems;
- community – community narratives, characteristics and dynamics;
- society – narratives, characteristics and dominant values and beliefs of the wider society;
- practice wisdom – practice wisdom gained from the practitioner's previous experience;
- structural – policy, legislation and organisational structures and policies;
- professional – professional knowledge, skills, ethics, training and values;
- practice field – the narratives and characteristics of discrete fields of practice such as disability, child protection and community development (Cheers et al, 2005a, p 236).

The extent to which different domains influence practice depends in part on the relative domain alignment of social workers. That is, the extent to which their own personal/social/professional position aligns with the dominant narratives in the different domains. Some practitioners, such as recent recruits from outside the community, may be more comfortable strictly following organisational policies, while others who are more integrated into local life may be more attuned to community expectations. However, while rural practitioners should strive to understand their own position and the relative influence of different domains, they cannot simply react to the most dominant narratives in their practice environment, as to do so might lead implicitly or unwittingly into a collusion of sorts with discriminatory and inequitable standpoints, or run counter to other professional obligations and legal imperatives.

Many rural practice issues, such as conflicts between a practitioner's dual roles as professional and community member, can be seen as discontinuities between narratives in different domains, and may remain a continuing source of tension, as, for example, when societal and community demands to punish offenders conflict with professional requirements to help them. Although such conflicts may be resolvable through education, discussion and negotiation, some differences of opinion may not be amenable to these strategies. For instance, while an organisation would be expected to direct practitioners to investigate a situation where children may be at risk and in need of protection, the community, or at least some powerful members of it, might implore them to refrain from doing so.

Conclusion

The next chapter examines broader-based forms of intervention that focus upon larger groups and communities, which typically operate with different paradigms of problem analysis. Unfortunately, some supporters of community-focused or community-oriented approaches to practice have been dismissive of individual or family-focused personal social services as being residualist or 'casualty' models of practice. While, of course, the shortcomings and deficiencies of narrowly focused forms of casework have been much debated, we think that all approaches to practice have attendant risks and that the apparent antipathy to personalised casework approaches is mistaken. Our position, which echoes that made in earlier work by other writers like Bailey and Brake (1980) and Fook (1993), is that it is not the methods as such that are problematic, but the situational analysis upon which they are based, and the purposes to which they are then put, that matter most.

Given the wide range of responsibilities and interventions covered by the term 'social work', a mutually exclusive choice of one theoretical approach or other seems inappropriate and unrealistic. In our view, models of service delivery and methods of intervention should primarily be selected after:

- consideration of statutory responsibilities (if any);
- realistic appraisal of available skills and resources;
- analysis of the problem or situation, including an informed appreciation of the cultural, social and political context;
- consideration of the preferences of those needing help or service;
- an assessment of the potential risks of the methods adopted and potential outcomes of intervention.

There is a tendency to counterpose the drawbacks of traditional approaches to somewhat idealised notions of community and localisation, whereas, as Martinez-Brawley has pointed out:

> There are no ideal communities comprising only supportive people, or open minded people, or generous people, or benevolent people. Real communities will exhibit both positive and negative characteristics. It is how workers deal with these characteristics that matters. (Martinez-Brawley, 2000, p 242)

Furthermore, she notes that 'no one level of organization, whether central or local, has a monopoly on positive or negative attributes' (Martinez-Brawley, 2000, p 250). Although traditional approaches using centralised structures may well lead to a proliferation of bureaucratic processes that restrict professional autonomy, and thus reduce responsiveness to local circumstances, decisions about models of delivery can to some degree be separated from decisions about methods of service. Thus, a personal social services approach to helping can be operated in ways that enhance 'local fit', acceptance and credibility, while a naive approach to localisation may ignore important questions about 'which community' or 'communities' are being engaged with. For instance, localisation can be vulnerable to corruption of service by locally powerful individuals or groups who may sanction nepotism, ignore bullying and harassment, or institutionalise intolerant and unfair treatment of particular minorities. Thus, the mere recognition of attendant risks should not be taken as sufficient reasons for invalidating one approach over another. Instead, a more sophisticated assessment should be made of the likely pros and cons of alternative approaches.

Finally, it should be noted that the available literature on different forms of practice in rural areas is patchy, and so some parts of this chapter have relied rather more upon our personal experiences and the practice wisdom of colleagues than we would wish. The corollary of course, is that there are considerable opportunities for primary research into many aspects of rural practice.

SEVEN

Models for practice 2: community social work

Introduction

The dominant paradigms for social work over the last few decades in most Western countries have been personal in scale, with the history of social or community intervention in social work being overlooked. There are enduring arguments about what social workers should do, sometimes presented as a contest between two early positions, embodied, on the one hand, by Charles Loch, Mary Richmond and the Charity Organisation Societies in the UK and the US, who adopted a largely individualistic focus upon particular cases (individuals or families), and, on the other, by the settlement movement and social interventionists like Jane Addams in the US and Beatrice and Sydney Webb in the UK, who thought that social problems had social causes and therefore required social solutions (Soydan, 1999; Kendall, 2000). However, what is often not recognised is that both sides came to acknowledge the importance of a dual focus for intervention. Both understood the need for individual casework to ameliorate the immediate difficulties that people faced, and the role of social reform and social action aimed at the wider causes of social problems such as poverty, unemployment and poor health. Consequently, in many countries casework and community work (along with group work) came to be seen as complementary modes of intervention.

The valuable material in Martinez-Brawley's (1980) anthology of the historical development of rural social welfare in the US shows that many of the pioneering rural workers, like their urban counterparts (Lindeman, 1921; Steiner, 1925), took a broad-based community perspective on social issues and were strongly committed to democratic principles of participation and engagement. Accordingly, they adopted activist positions towards the problems and challenges they identified, particularly in the New Deal era in the 1930s. The communal perspective is evident in this quotation, 'Social action depends upon social feeling. We cannot work together without common bonds of sympathy and understanding' (Morse, 1919, cited in Martinez-Brawley,

1980, p 114). These pioneers thought that effective community interventions had to be based upon accurate information about rural communities and understood that many social institutions depended upon secure economic foundations. In Europe, although there were activist traditions of social pedagogy in Germany and animateurs in France, remedies for the problems of rural (and urban) areas were more often framed in terms of improved national arrangements for social welfare, education and health services (Hering and Waaldijk, 2006; Schulte, 2006). The experience of the settlement movement had shown how inextricably linked economic and social conditions were, but it remained largely an urban phenomenon, and consequently community approaches to social work in rural areas in Europe appear to have been much less well established.

An influential definition of community organisation was provided by Ross, who stated that it is:

> a process by which a community identifies its needs or objectives, orders (or ranks) these needs or objectives, develops the confidence and the will to work at these needs or objectives, finds the resources (internal and/or external) to deal with these needs or objectives, takes action in respect to them, and in doing so extends and develops co-operative and collaborative attitudes and practices in the community. (Ross, 1955, p 39)

Subsequently, other writers distinguished different strategies or processes of intervention (Smalley, 1967; Brager and Specht, 1973; Rothman, 1974; Jacobsen, 1980; Kenny, 1994; Tropman et al, 1995). For example, Rothman (1968) distinguished three forms of community intervention – locality development, social planning and social action. More radical theorists like Alinsky (1971) and later Kahn (1994) proposed a more robust and potentially confrontational approach to community organisation. Writers differed in:

- their conceptualisation of the role of the professional worker (for example, initiator, facilitator, negotiator, leader and so on);
- the emphasis placed upon the processes of development in relation to the outcomes;
- their desire to avoid pessimistic problem- or deficit-focused analyses (for example, a positive perspective may be signalled by the use of terms like 'assets' and 'strengths');
- their commitment to a more ambitious social/political project.

This variability is also mirrored to some degree by writers within rural social work (Collier, 1984; Cheers, 1998; Ginsberg, 1998; Martinez-Brawley, 2000; Scales and Streeter, 2004; Poole, 2005). However, they share a common perception that social workers have an important role in attempting to 'mobilize collective resources for positive collective ends' (Poole, 2005, p 125).

Martinez-Brawley (2000), in her discussion of the terminology that has developed in different countries, notes that 'community-oriented' practice as it developed in the UK was mirrored in the US by 'community-based' practice, with both approaches stressing the importance of respect for the capacity of communities to identify issues and mobilise resources. Indeed, she approvingly cites Johnson's definition of community-based practice as 'a direct service strategy implemented in the context of the local community…. It is the integration of direct services with skills traditionally associated with community organisation and community development' (Johnson, A., 1998, cited in Martinez-Brawley, 2000, p 257), while Poole states that 'Rural community building is the process of developing and sustaining partnerships between groups of citizens and practitioners to bring about planned change for the public good in communities' (Poole, 2005, p 125).

For the purposes of this chapter, the terms 'community-oriented practice', 'community social work', 'community work' and 'community intervention' are regarded as interchangeable, as our aim is to identify the common ground shared between different approaches. This commonality is evident in the value commitment to community participation and partnership, which includes the following principles:

- the routine involvement of local people in planning, developing and organising local services;
- the promotion of democracy and empowerment in decision-making and recognition of the strength and assets of local people and organisations;
- the advancement of common interests over private, organisational or professional interests;
- the promotion of social and economic justice (adapted from Poole, 2005, p 127).

Furthermore, most approaches recognise that rural social services, and the lives of the people who use them, as well as the lives of the staff who work in them, are interlinked with other sectors such as industry, health and education. They recognise that changes in one sector are likely to have implications in others. For example, the reopening of a mine in a small town in northern Australia without adequate consultation and planning resulted in education and health services staff becoming overwhelmed by increased demand for their services, which led to the subsequent departure of valued staff, some of whom were long-term residents. Social workers need to develop and contribute their expertise in planning for such impacts, secure services and the required resources, negotiate with funding bodies and advocate for disadvantaged individuals and groups. Above all, they need to facilitate participation in decision making, and help to build partnerships within and across sectors. As the example above indicates, they may need to know how to analyse actual and projected social impacts of rapid growth in local industry or extensive immigration into an area, especially upon those who may already be marginalised.

Community social work embraces a range of activities including:

- influencing and shaping the distribution of public services, such as education, health, social services and transport;
- developing a local project or innovation;
- stimulating and developing the local economy and the infrastructure that supports it;
- creating and sustaining social networks;
- seeking to change attitudes and public education;
- developing local capacity for social and political action and representation, such as self-advocacy;
- initiating policies aimed at promoting social justice.

For instance, Francis and Henderson (1992) report how the leadership of one local man helped to reinvigorate the village of Pentrefoelas and several others in North Wales. Through the economic development of tourist-related activities, he and others helped to strengthen the Welsh language and culture of the area. The core principles of partnership, equality and ownership make community approaches to social work valuable models for work with marginalised groups. Common problems of poor health, poverty or delinquency may have common origins arising from discrimination and wider social forces. Thus, in many situations, community-oriented practice may be the preferred form of practice with indigenous peoples. The emphasis upon collective forms of engagement and action may also be culturally more acceptable in communities where the importance of kinship networks and social ties take precedence over notions of individual autonomy and independence.

This chapter focuses on the ways in which rural social work can contribute to action at the community level aimed at assisting, sustaining, developing and, sometimes, helping to rebuild communities. Although different writers use different terminology for describing their ideas on community social work, and have developed different models to describe the processes of planning and development, there is considerable overlap between much of their work. Accordingly, this chapter draws upon earlier classifications developed by Cheers (1998) and Poole (2005) and reframes and adapts them to provide an accessible account for readers new to the field. It distinguishes three broad strategies for community intervention – social and community planning; community services development; and community development, which also includes community organisation.

Social and community planning

Social planning

The term 'social planning' originally referred to strategies of community intervention aimed at coordinating and developing social services, but is now applied to a wider range of services, including social care, health and other forms of welfare provision. Social planning is a goal-focused, data-driven process for identifying current social needs, anticipating future ones and developing and implementing plans to meet them (Rothenberg, 1961; Cheers et al, 2007). Originally, as Smith notes:

> Heavy reliance is placed on rational problem solving and the use of technical methods such as research and systems analysis. Expertise is the cherished value in this approach, although leadership is accorded importance as well. (Smith, 2005, p 7)

However, a more partnership-oriented tradition has also developed, in which expertise is valued, but only as one component among the many potential contributions that might be made (Chambers, 1994).

One specialised form of social planning is community service planning, and Participatory Rural Appraisal (PRA) is widely used. It has been defined as a 'family of methods that enables communities to assemble with formal service providers, identify and analyse critical elements of their life in their own idioms, and plan and carry through feasible changes' (Bar-On and Prinsen, 1999, p 277). With its overtly political stance, exponents of PRA contend that the underlying cause of underdevelopment and disadvantage for individuals and groups in rural communities is their exclusion from power and their marginalisation in decision-making processes (Bar-On and Prinsen, 1999). In PRA, a team of facilitators follows a six-step model in working with local people and local and non-local service organisations. The steps are:

1. Preparation (3–5 days) – facilitators sensitise potential participants to the process and study primary and secondary data about the community.
2. Data-gathering (4–6 days) – workshop participants 'picture' their community and how they want it to develop.
3. Synthesis (1–2 days) – facilitators and elected community representatives cluster the information into broad issue categories (for example, education, health and transport) and present it to the community for discussion, modification and verification.
4. Ranking (1–2 days) – participants prioritise concerns and their commitment to change increases as they see their concerns taken seriously.
5. Preparing and adopting a Community Action Plan (CAP) (3–4 days) – participants produce the plan as they devise strategies to tackle concerns and it is presented to the general community and service providers.
6. Implementation and monitoring – by government agencies, joint governmental and non-governmental committees, and local community workers (adapted from Bar-On and Prinsen, 1999, pp 282–3).

This process is informed by six principles that guide the intervention. First, active learning activities should be undertaken reflectively with stakeholder participation. Second, triangulation involves the involvement of participants from the widest possible range of groups and facilitators from a variety of disciplines and organisations. It also involves the gathering of information about as many aspects of community life as possible using a variety of methods, tools and activities, and then interpreting this information holistically. Third, goals and methodologies should be flexible in that they should be continually generated and revised as understanding of community needs increases. Fourth, there should be a focus upon strengths and assets rather than weaknesses and deficits. Fifth, the principle of 'sufficiency of knowledge' requires that information gathering should be action-oriented, thus, it may of necessity be fuzzy and proximate rather than exhaustive and precise. Finally, to promote learning by doing, all information should be analysed and used in 'on-the-spot' workshops (adapted from Bar-On and Prinsen, 1999, pp 282–3).

PRA is well structured, which enhances transferability from one community or issue to another, and it produces quick results, which helps unite insiders and outsiders in common action (Bar-On and Prinsen, 1999). A large-scale evaluation in Botswana (Prinsen et al, 1996) found that PRA had a number of advantages over other similar approaches, most notably in: generating new and more in-depth understandings of community realities among community members and service providers; increasing awareness of the capacity of local organisations to contribute to development; and increasing the confidence of local people and organisations in their dealings with non-local service providers. They also noted that through involvement in PRA, local people become more critical of how customary power structures disempowered some groups, such as women, young people, ethnic minorities and the poor, by excluding them from public decision making. Finally, the approach improved the quality of the work of service organisations because clients took greater responsibility for community and personal issues, and it also stimulated greater cooperation among workers. PRA has also been evaluated positively by the World Bank (1994).

Despite the strong structure of the model, in reality efforts at extending participation and community involvement and responding to a range of local concerns and positions typically result in a less tightly sequenced and orderly planning process. Indeed, Lea and Wolfe (1993), in a review of planning exercises undertaken with indigenous and non-indigenous communities in Northern Australia, observed that it required complex interlinkages between different participants and stages of development, as information needed to flow between different elements of the process. For example, the setting of goals and tasks is likely to be influenced by the initial structures that are established and then informed by the data collection, the identification of opportunities and constraints and, of course, the prioritisation of objectives. They found that communities did not follow a neat and orderly planning process, but instead started in different places, jumping forwards and backwards as they revisited stages, reappraising information and earlier deliberations.

An Australian example

In a small country town a range of people, including social workers, police, local government councillors and business leaders, had noticed that truancy, delinquency and homelessness had been increasing among local youth, and that many youngsters appeared to be socially disconnected from the community (Bone et al, 1993). Youth unemployment was high, local young people had little access to tertiary education and there were no youth-dedicated entertainment facilities or community-sanctioned places where they could gather. Discussions with other residents, including other young people as well as people with a particular interest, such as parents, teachers, health and social care practitioners, sports clubs, local government and police, stimulated interest in the problems. Subsequently, a youth planning committee was established comprising youth leaders and key local people and organisations, and the wider community was invited to participate in its deliberations.

After a series of meetings, conversations and written submissions, a vision was formulated. Early in the planning, information was compiled from community forums, workshops, surveys, interviews, case studies, reports and census data concerning perceptions of youth needs, and how best to meet them. An audit of services, resources and facilities was also conducted. Crucially, young people participated by identifying the questions to ask, by collecting and analysing data and by leading forums. After analysing this information, the planning committee, in consultation with youth and other key stakeholders, produced a youth needs profile and made recommendations for action. The most pressing needs were prioritised, opportunities and constraints were identified and alternative plans for responding to them were formulated.

The youth planning committee decided that the two main priorities were to increase youth participation in community governance, and to establish a community-sanctioned gathering place for them. Eventually, after considering a number of options, the committee chose to develop a youth council and a drop-in centre, both of which would be run by local youth. Implementation strategies were developed and tasks such as identifying funding sources, seeking funding and setting up management structures were decided, allocated and scheduled. The youth council, which was comprised entirely of youth, was established under the local council, with the chair reporting directly to the mayor. The drop-in centre management committee was a sub-committee of the youth council. Both organisations were supported administratively by local government and through mentoring by trusted community leaders. Monitoring by the youth council and local government found that they were achieving their objectives, for instance, increasing numbers of local youth used the drop-in centre and employers started to employ more local youth. Most importantly, through sound social planning, youth issues had gained widespread support and were firmly established in the community.

Community planning

Although one would expect social workers with a commitment to community participation and partnership to avoid technocratic exercises in planning, this is not always the case. In contrast, community planning, which extends the focus to the wider community and all its social fields, including social development, economic development and natural resource management, has a much stronger emphasis on participation and partnership (Walsh, 1993).

Community planning is often undertaken by local government and community development organisations, which can identify goals for the community and each of its sectors, and the strategies required to achieve them. Community plans that are underpinned by formal bodies and that have been legitimated through community participation in their production can be powerful instruments for change, having a major influence on development, investment, land use, infrastructure and service priorities. For a community plan to have local and external credibility, and the power to galvanise action by multiple stakeholders, it must be based on sound information and produced with the participation of local groups and interests. Unsurprisingly, then, community planning exercises may become battlegrounds for different constructions of community and the countryside, for example, middle-class incomers to a rural community may resist suggestions for economic development or low-cost social housing if these proposals threaten their sense of the rural idyll.

Typically, rural social workers have participated in community planning to represent the interests of marginalised and disadvantaged groups and to facilitate their contribution. Poole (2005) cites an example in the US from Molnar et al (2000), where social workers contributed to efforts to improve the distribution of private food aid in rural areas by linking with food distribution systems in urban areas and rationalising operating procedures and eligibility criteria. Social workers can also contribute their professional experience and expertise, by, for instance, providing leadership for planning in the social care sector, or helping to identify the implications of proposed developments through their input into a social impact assessment (ICGPSIA, 1993). One example of this occurred when a city council considered a proposal to redevelop a traditional working-class district, which was also the site of the city's port and rail terminal, to encourage investment and in-migration of middle- to high-income earners. The social impact assessment recommended special land zoning to provide for low-cost private and rental accommodation, the retention of existing industries and the preservation of existing 'social hubs' such as parks and shopping precincts (Harris et al, 1993a, 1993b).

As Table 7.1 below indicates, community plans usually incorporate a community profile, a vision for the whole community, prioritised goals and objectives, strategies to achieve them, performance indicators, time-frames and the identification of potentially useful resources.

There are a number of different approaches to producing community plans (see, for example, Franklin Harbour Community Development Group, 2002), and although PRA seems most effective, irrespective

Table 7.1: Community plan content

Component	Content
Executive summary	Concise summary of the plan, emphasising the vision for the community and key recommendations
Background	Why the plan was formulated; its history; who owns it; how it is legitimated and implemented; how it relates to other local, regional and central government plans
Community profile	Community history; present social, demographic, economic and infrastructural profile; significant dominant, secondary, subversive, latent and emergent narratives
Vision for the community	Future profile and character of the community
Priority goals and objectives	Short-term, medium-term and long-term goals and objectives for the community as a whole and for each sector
Strategies for each goal and objective	Preferred strategies; viable alternatives; comparative risk assessments
Performance indicators	Key performance indicators for each goal
Potential resources	• Funding – programmes, key contacts and strategies • Key organisations and people within and outside the community – skills; interests; potential partnerships; suggested lobbying strategies
Related reference material	• Local – research, consultancy and other reports; related plans and historical documents; statistical sources • External – for example, reports; national, state and regional plans; statistics

Source: Cheers et al (2007, p 52).

of how plans are developed they should normally fit with other legislatively binding decisions concerning resource allocations by central and local governments. It is counterproductive, for example, for a community to prioritise a new residential care home if government policy is prioritising home-based care. There may be circumstances, though, where the outcome of the planning process is a considered decision to challenge broader policy.

Some writers do not make a clear distinction between planning and implementation, and include both in their models for action, as, for instance, in this schema of the typical stages in community planning:

1. Create a vision.
2. Assess the current situation.
3. Set goals.
4. Establish objectives.
5. Develop action plans.
6. Implement action plans.
7. Evaluate progress and results (Frank and Smith, 1999, p 52).

Such schemas are not intended to be precise blueprints for action, but are typically intended as conceptual aids or signposts for practitioners. Community planning can inadvertently be taken over by government officials because they have the time and capacity to devote to it and they are unused to the messy business of participation. Community planning can also become rather narrow in its range of participants, as formal bodies are often happier working with those representatives of local organisations who are professional people, and are articulate and experienced in governance and structured action. Some communities, in particular some indigenous communities, may place great emphasis on process. For them, the process is what community planning is all about – and they may find it very difficult, if not impossible, to use or even relate to these schemas, which are highly goal focused, at the expense of involvement. Practitioners should generally avoid any tendency to the predetermined or mechanistic application of models and stages. In communities that adopt a more formal approach to planning, such processes risk being used by the powerful to exclude certain marginalised groups or further their own interests (Cheers and Luloff, 2001). In all communities, some groups have become accustomed to being excluded from community governance and planning, and so special efforts need to be made by social workers to include and empower them. Particular sensitivity needs to be shown to minority groups who fear the risks of possible 'exposure' by participation.

Community services development

Community services development goes further than social and community planning in seeking to actually develop provisions within a community (DFACS, 1995; Williams, 1996; Taylor, 1999a, 1999b; Taylor et al, 2008), thus, it attempts to identify needs, and design, fund, provide and monitor programmes to meet them. Typically, it involves a partnership of some kind between communities and government. Ideally, the partnerships are ongoing, mutually consultative and, on balance, more community than government driven. On the community side, organisations, community leaders and networks have to come together to identify needs and priorities, apply for funding, establish programmes and provide, manage and evaluate them, while government establishes the policy frameworks, programme parameters and funding guidelines within which community service developments take place.

Marson and Powell (2000) describe how staff at a church and community centre in North Carolina successfully gained funding for a transport service for families receiving TANF support (Temporary Assistance for Needy Families). Later they transferred the management of this scheme to a local Council of Governments who were able to provide more effective management and secure further grant funding to develop the scheme. The area, Robeson County, had a mixed population base comprising 49% Native Americans, 25% African-Americans and 36% white Americans, and a significant number of Hispanics who were moving into the area. Although Marson and Powell noted that the US areas with high levels of poverty and predominantly minority populations were more likely to succeed in getting grant funding for community projects, the changing political climate might threaten the continued availability of grant-based funding.

The extent of government involvement in community services development varies considerably, so while some government bodies may actively participate in helping communities to identify needs and priorities, and to develop, manage, monitor and evaluate programmes, others may be less proactive and confine their involvement to the planning stages and the subsequent monitoring and evaluation of initiatives. A more 'hands-off' approach has become common in many countries as governments have stepped back from the direct provision of services, adopting instead a dual role of funder and regulator.

In the mid-1990s, the Queensland Department of Family and Community Services in Australia placed regional managers in major regional population centres and resource officers in smaller local communities (DFACS, 1995; Williams, 1996; Taylor, 1999a, 1999b; Taylor et al, 2008). Resource officers developed a good understanding of communities within their region and established close working relationships with them. Regional managers supported resource officers and their communities, represented them in central decision making and mediated government policy frameworks and guidelines, on the one hand, and community needs, priorities and service designs, on the other. The regional managers met regularly to determine funding allocations, review existing programmes, develop policy and initiate new programme initiatives. They believed that local communities were best placed to decide what provisions were required, but recognised that local residents sometimes lacked the necessary skills and knowledge. Consequently, resource officers often acted as catalysts and consultants for local communities. In response to the wishes of remote indigenous communities in the northern mainland and islands to provide a safe and nurturing environment for their children, the Department helped them to form an advisory structure to support each other, to generate ideas, to advise government and to assist in allocating funds (Department of Families, Youth and Community Care, 1997; Cheers and Taylor, 2005; Taylor et al, 2008). From this came the Remote Area Aboriginal and Torres Strait Islander Child Care Program that demonstrated the benefits of community involvement and control. Community members participated in and owned the process of service development, and, with support, in the first two years of the programme developed 48 diverse childcare services throughout the region.

Community development

Community development involves people and their organisations engaging with each other and their community's social infrastructure for the betterment of the community. It focuses on both project outcomes and the processes involved in achieving them (Wilkinson, 1991; Cheers and Luloff, 2001). Whereas the preceding approaches focus on developing and implementing plans, programmes and provisions, community development is a broader concept that focuses more on strengthening (or developing) the community as a whole. Furthermore, while the other approaches tend to focus on social care in communities, community development spans all sectors such as the economy, the environment, health and education (Wilkinson, 1991; Luloff, 1998; Cheers and Luloff, 2001).

Community development can occur spontaneously in communities but may also be facilitated or led by a significant community member or paid professional. Community development is founded on the belief that people have the right to determine their own collective aspirations and how to achieve them. It incorporates the common principles noted earlier in this chapter and lays particular emphasis upon community ownership, control and participation. It is widely accepted that the social aspects of communities, including community ownership and control, are crucial to economic and social development and natural resource management, and asset-based community development is increasingly recognised as more useful than deficit-based approaches (Wilkinson, 1991; Flora et al, 1997; Flora, 1998; Luloff, 1998; Claude et al, 1999; Scales and Streeter, 2004). Successful community development relies upon participants having a sound understanding of the local community and there are a number of schemas for the analysis of local social infrastructure (Wilkinson, 1991; Cheers, 1998; Flora, 1998; Cheers and Luloff, 2001; McClure and Cock, 2003). Community development has become the preferred approach in many non-urbanised countries, and its popularity in other underdeveloped areas has been noted by Pozzuto et al (2004). In Lithuania, they found that over 300 community development organisations in rural villages have had a significant impact in achieving change. Interestingly, most of these organisations arose from existing social networks within the villages, which also accords with experience in Poland (Bienkowska, 1999), where women comprised some 90% of the membership.

A distinction is usually made between community development and community capacity building. Community development can be directed to any aspect of a community's physical, social, cultural, economic and political environment, and the development sought may be small or large in scale. Community capacity building refers to the capabilities and resources needed to achieve change. It includes skills, knowledge, commitment and motivation, effective communication, social organisation and, usually, money and time. Frank and Smith concede that there is a relationship between development and capacity building, and accept that you probably 'can't have one without the other' (1999, p 11). They make the crucial point that neither of these things necessarily flows from the other, for example, community capacity could be built, but it might not be directly supportive of the development that is planned. Similarly, a community development project in which professionals and 'experts' took the lead might well achieve the sought objectives, but leave little legacy of enhanced community capacity behind. Laing and Hepburn (2006) have described a project in Western Australia where changes in forestry quotas restricted logging activity and led to major changes in employment patterns. They describe how the project responded in different ways to different issues, such as providing assistance with welfare benefit claims, training in new skills, especially in using information technology, and establishing resource centres that provided information, IT equipment and internet access. The resource centres became meeting places for unemployed workers where they could discuss action and provide mutual self-help. Laing and Hepburn also noted that the needs of communities in the affected area differed, and so the project responded to these variations. One town had been unable to access earlier funding for a telecentre, so it became imperative to try to maintain low-cost access to computing facilities there. In another town that was suffering from retrenchment in local dairy farming, with many people being angry that they had been forced out of work, the focus became community cohesion and morale building.

Project-focused community development

In project-focused community development people build, strengthen and coordinate local structures and processes at the same time as they plan, execute and complete concrete tasks in response to particular issues. Following Wilkinson (1991), Cheers and Luloff (2001) describe these two spheres of activity as structure building and task accomplishment and suggest that they typically occur through five stages: initiation and spread of interest; organisation of sponsorship; goal setting and strategy formulation; recruitment; and implementation.

An example of this approach is the Far West Aboriginal Enterprise Network (FWAEN) in Australia, which was established by Aboriginal people and a team of community developers who had access to potential start-up funding with the aim of using Indigenous and Western knowledge about local native plants to generate products to benefit local communities (Cheers et al, 2006b; McAllister et al, 2008). An Aboriginal woman provided initial leadership and was well positioned to do so due to her prominent roles in other social fields, including business development and education. Early local interest was spread through conversations and meetings with other organisations and individuals, including Aboriginal enterprises. A steering committee was established chaired by a male Aboriginal Elder, and a local Aboriginal woman was appointed project coordinator. The coordinator and the steering committee found an organisational base for the project in a key local organisation, Weena Mooga Gu Gudba Inc, a women's group. A number of sub-projects and associated Aboriginal businesses were developed, such as a plant nursery and a commercial horticulture plot. Eventually, the products included bush foods, various 'light' health products such as soaps, a native plant tourist trail and educational materials. However, it is the purposes for which these were produced and the social interactions involved that made this a community development project, not the products. The project strengthened social engagement within and between different communities. The benefits have so far included: individual skill development; improved livelihoods and health outcomes for participants; and enhanced respect for traditional knowledge and the Aboriginal Elders who carry this. Over time the project helped to strengthen the community's capacity to tackle other issues, such as poverty, unemployment and family violence.

Table 7.2: Stages of project-focused community development

Stage	Task-accomplishment activities	Structure-building activities
Initiation and spread of interest	Identifying an issue as a potential focus for group action and generating cross-field awareness of the issue as a problem or opportunity	Generating widespread consciousness of linkages among various fields of interest
Organisation of sponsorship	Identifying an existing structure, such as a committee or organisation, or establishing a new one, to run with the issue	Coordinating actions within, and across, fields by creating multi-interest networks and inter-organisational linkages
Goal setting and strategy formulation	Setting goals and determining strategies for the task at hand	Developing long-range goals and strategies that go beyond the special interests of particular social fields
Recruitment	Mobilising resources, such as facilities, finance, participation, goodwill and organisational legitimacy	Legitimising coordinating groups, building cohesion across specific interests, developing leaders and leadership skills, and encouraging broad participation in community development and planning
Implementation	Implementing these strategies	Using particular projects to harness and strengthen community agency

Source: Cheers et al (2007, p 68, adapted from Wilkinson, 1991, pp 96–7).

Assessing community capacity

Community development is premised upon an appraisal of community capacity, that is, some identification of what social, economic and political resources are available for the purposes of change. These may include financial assets, physical infrastructure (for example, facilities and equipment), the knowledge and skills of individuals, relations among people and organisations, access to services and community attitudes. Building upon earlier work by Cavaye (2000), Black and Hughes (2001) and McKnight and Kretzman (2004), and earlier developmental work by McClure and Cock (undated, 2003) and Cheers et al (2005a, 2005b, 2006a, 2006b), a computer-based Community Capacity Assessment Tool™ has been developed that measures 17 capacities in each of eight sectors or social fields (Taylor et al, 2008). The sectors are social organisation (or the community field), health and human services, education, natural resources, business, primary industry, arts and entertainment, and sport and recreation. The capacities include the mass (i.e. the number and range of programmes, services, activities and goods available in the sector); access to these things, information about them and their suitability for the particular community context; marketing of the sector; financial and human resources, facilities and equipment; management and leadership in the sector/community; networks and relationships (within the sector, with other sectors and outside of the community); advocacy and government support for the sector; ethics (the principles, values and beliefs of people in the sector); and social capital, inclusiveness and community spirit in the sector. The Tool measures four variables relating to each capacity:

- strength – how strong it is, using indicators provided on the template;
- importance – how important participants in community assessment think it is to total community capacity;
- contribution – its contribution to total community capacity for the purpose at hand (a composite of capacity strength and capacity importance);
- confidence – the confidence that the participants in community assessment have in their assessment of each capacity in each sector.

The Tool is used to collect and analyse information as part of a seven-stage community capacity-building process: preparing to conduct the assessment; conducting it; profiling the community's capacity; developing a targeted, strategic plan to strengthen it; implementing the plan; monitoring implementation through further assessments; and adjusting the plan accordingly. Participants in the assessment should be representative of all sectors and groups in the community, including marginalised people such as youth, ethnic and cultural minorities, and older people. Because community capacity is a generic concept, the instrument can be adapted to measure a community's capacity to support a variety of purposes such as primary industry development, natural resource management, health care and establishing a youth drop-in centre. The Community Capacity Assessment Tool™ is owned by Primary Industries and Resources SA (© 2008 Government of South Australia, PIRSA), a South Australian Government department, and was developed in collaboration with the Centre for Rural Health and Community Development at the University of South Australia and Rural Solutions SA (another SA Government department). As Frank and Smith (1999) note, capacity building typically involves training workshops, mentoring and coaching schemes, self-directed learning, as well as learning from experience.

Community organisation

Community organisation, as Poole (2005) notes, embraces a range of activities including grassroots organisation, social action and policy action. It is most commonly encountered in defensive resistance to proposals or changes that threaten rural services, such as the closure of schools, post offices and health facilities (Taylor, 2002; Halhead, 2007). While different exponents have taken rather different views on the level of political involvement, and the degree of confrontation and commitment required (Lindeman, 1921; Ross, 1955; Alinsky, 1971; Piven and Cloward, 1982; Bilken, 1983; Kahn, 1991; Ife and Tesoriero, 2006), there is a common appreciation of the role that a community organiser can play in promoting change in communities, as well as a recognition of the significance of power in efforts to promote change. Thus, the community organiser may variously be a supporter of autonomous self-action and advocacy groups, a facilitator in the development of new networks or even become a figurehead or leader of a campaign to ensure improved policies and practices or secure social justice for relatively powerless groups. For instance, a social worker in rural mid-Wales employed by a voluntary sector mental health alliance helped initiate a successful project to link isolated people with mental health problems, who had little influence on local mental health services, to develop skills in self-advocacy and present their own agenda for change (Pugh and Richards, 1996). MacPherson contends that:

> Community organisation can be ... crucial in the
> emergence of movements for radical change. Even the
> smallest, seemingly most insignificant local programme
> which involves the people in controlling their own
> development may increase the solidarity and self-confidence
> of the mass of people, and contribute to the emergence of
> those pressures which will achieve development from below.
> (MacPherson, 1994, p 181)

However community organisation is conceptualised, it nevertheless
represents a shift towards a more proactive position for rural social
workers, which brings attendant risks. The most obvious being the
potential for conflicts of interest between personal and professional
activities and the possibility that it may lead to conflict with agency
expectations of its employees.

Community members' participation in social activism can have a
range of different impacts upon them and their families. For instance,
Soliman (2005), in a study on the impact of environmental poisoning
on the communities along the Pigeon River in East Tennessee, noted
that extensive engagement could lead to difficulties in fulfilling normal
roles. As one man reported:

> I'm not here when she really needs me for things and I
> hear about it when I get home. Sure, she complains about
> having too much to do. I hate to put all my energy into
> the river but some days I do, and I'm zapped when I get
> home. (Soliman, 2005, p 26)

And one woman who was anxious about the reactions to her husband's
activism said:

> I tried to let him know that his work may be dangerous to
> the safety of our family. But I also knew that he will not
> give it up under any circumstance. I respect the fact that
> he is strong willed and out-spoken, but sometimes I worry
> about him not being around. (Soliman, 2005, p 27)

Despite these pressures, Soliman noted that activist families tended to
'maintain strong family ties and effective patterns of communication'.
No resolutions to these stresses were found, although many families
tended to use avoidance as a coping strategy.

Personal skills, capacities and characteristics

Some of the characteristics and skills necessary for effective casework, such as personal credibility, vision and belief in the capacity of others, energy and stamina, openness to learning, and the capacity to energise and motivate others, will also be required if workers seek to become catalysts for development. From their training and experience, most social workers should have many of the capacities required for effective planning and development, such as good communication skills, record keeping and information gathering. However, they may need to use these skills in rather different ways than when working with smaller groups, families and individuals. For instance, personal contacts through letter or telephone may simply be impractical for some aspects of the work, so use will have to be made of newsletters, the internet and other cascading communication strategies. Frank and Smith note that problem-solving and conflict-resolution skills are required to:

> identify the issue; look at options and alternatives; help individuals understand the views of others; break the impasse if discussions get bogged down; manage conflict when it occurs; help find common ground; assist members to recognize agreement when it happens, and; ensure that everyone understands the agreement. (Frank and Smith, 1999, Section 4)

Constraints and problems

Clearly there are likely to be limits to what might be achieved at a local level in social planning and community development activities, the most obvious being that some social forces are simply too powerful and pervasive for local initiatives to have much effect. For example, climatic changes affecting agriculture and employment in an area may not be susceptible to local action, although, of course, more modest goals, including ameliorative responses and moves to stimulate the development of alternative forms of employment, may be effective. Community development can be obstructed by a range of factors, such as government social, economic, infrastructure and land use policy; local power structures, conflicts, inter-ethnic group rivalry; marginalisation and social exclusion; lack of information; poor networks within and outside the community; and insufficient community capacity (Cheers and Luloff, 2001; Lemos and Crane, 2004). Frank and Smith note that in marginalised communities:

community development may not occur (or at least right away).… Some are in social and economic paralysis and are dependent upon outside expertise and assistance. Sometimes communities remain damaged and unhealthy for a very long time. They need to heal, become safe and build personal and community wellness. Opportunities may be present, but the community is unable to identify or take advantage of them. Leadership is required, long-range thinking and strategic plans are needed, skills must be developed, attitudes often have to change and resources must be acquired … capacity must be built before community development can take place. (Frank and Smith, 1999, p 11)

However, in many instances the limits to action arise from the distribution of power in communities, and the role of the state in terms of its agencies and assemblies is often crucial in determining successful outcomes. Midgley et al (1986) have characterised the response of states and governments to community development in four ways. The state can be strongly resistant to it (anti-participative mode), it can exploit it to get preferred outcomes (manipulative mode), it can nominally support participation but not properly support local involvement (incremental mode), or it can resource and support local engagement satisfactorily (participative mode). Similarly, Abrams (1980, cited in Martinez-Brawley, 2000) pointed out the risks of appropriation and incorporation, while Poole (2005) has also noted that community development can be cynically manipulated by government bodies to create the appearance of participation to sanction their own plans. He also notes two other criticisms that have been made of community development:

- used incompetently it can do damage to communities;
- it has traditionally focused upon community needs rather than assets, and so fuels negative perceptions of deficiencies in rural communities.

Similar points have also been made in regard to the use of some forms of community work in indigenous communities, and Humpage (2004) notes that some approaches are value-laden in the ways in which they assume the desirability of progress and modernisation, and in their formal rationality. Nevertheless, Poole notes that exponents of community development, like Kretzman and McKnight (1993) and Rubin and Rubin (1986), are aware of potential problems and have subsequently emphasised 'empowerment, assets, strengths and local ownership' (2005, p 131). Certainly, recent exponents in social work have strongly emphasised the importance of a positive perspective, as Scales and Streeter contend in regard to Kretzman and McKnight's (1993) metaphorical challenge as to whether one sees a glass as half-empty or half-full:

> It has been said that perception is reality. What we believe to be true often becomes the center of our thoughts so much that it really becomes true.... By viewing the glass as half-full, we begin to see the depth of human spirit and the richness of the creative potential that exists in rural communities. (Scales and Streeter, 2004, p 1)

There are other potential barriers to effective community development that, as the extensive literature indicates, are not simply a question of perspective and motivation. Many of these are reviewed at greater length in Cheers (1998), the most significant of these potential drawbacks being:

- a lack of reliable information and data on local circumstances;
- the over-reliance and excessive dependency of a community upon external agencies for support, or upon a monolithic local employer whose interests may be threatened by community action;
- difficulties in establishing common interests and goals for action because of ineffective negotiations, or social divisions and factional conflict within communities;
- economic interests dominating all other aspects of social planning
- the possibility of resentment and obstruction from local politicians who may feel threatened by emerging movements and grassroots leaders;
- an uncoordinated approach to social issues from government departments that makes it difficult to establish a comprehensive response to local needs and problems.

Tensions and boundary difficulties may arise from the allegiances of professionals and local people working on a project. Martinez–Brawley (2000) points out that while a professional is accountable to the agency and professional standards, the community member is answerable only to community norms and expectations. This tension can become very apparent if the project becomes seen as being overtly political, or if the issues become politicised through local political debate. An example of this occurred in one community, when workers helped local youth establish a community newspaper that, among other things, became critical of their employing organisation. The perception that community working can lead to workers 'biting the hand that feeds' can become a very powerful constraint upon their activity. One notable example of this occurred in community-based development in the UK in the 1970s when funding for Community Development Projects in urban areas was ended prematurely (Loney, 1983):

> Workers in many of the projects came to reject the analysis and strategies of the original project proposals. They sought to organise and research around larger questions of inequality and deindustrialisation rather than more localized concerns around community organization. (Smith, 2006, p 6)

These potential barriers are not insurmountable, although they can be formidable obstacles to social development. Most exponents of community development have stressed the importance of making an accurate assessment of likely problems, and of the resources and capacities that can be mobilised to meet them. Some key points can be summarised from their work:

- establish realistic goals, and ensure that they are reviewed and reframed if necessary;
- never assume consensus or agreement, and work hard to establish common ground;
- keep dialogue and communication going and ensure that knowledge is shared effectively;
- make sure evidence is clear and accurate;
- use and develop the capacities of local people and organisations;
- make links, and establish goodwill and alliances with key people and organisations;
- make roles clear, review and amend them when necessary, and accept that they may change as a project progresses;
- do not alienate possible supporters, or unnecessarily antagonise likely opponents;
- use multiple strategies where there are multiple targets of influence
- as far as possible, work collaboratively with existing structures of power and political representation;
- anticipate likely problems and conflicts of interest;
- leave room for negotiation and some compromise if possible;

• understand that change is more likely to be sustained when it is owned by local people and embedded in local organisations and structures (old or new).

Conclusion

Change is an ever-present reality for all communities, and many rural communities face considerable social, economic and political challenges that require the broader focus that community social work brings in terms of its basic principles, methods of analysis and processes of intervention. However, the theorisation of community social work should not obscure its most important characteristic, the values that underpin it. As Martinez-Brawley comments:

> Community-oriented social work emphasizes an egalitarian environment in which local people help plan and provide services. Such an environment inevitably opens professionals and agencies up to closer public scrutiny and to even criticism from citizens: yet it also opens them to the possibility of attaining support they never had before.... [Ultimately] [c]ommunity-oriented services are as much an attitude as a collection of techniques. (Martinez-Brawley, 2000, p 289)

In this chapter we have reviewed a range of approaches to promoting community well-being that provide conceptual models for community intervention, but life of course is rarely as predictable and tidy as these might suggest. Indeed, as Ife and Tesoriero (2006) have noted, there is always uncertainty about the eventual direction of a project and its outcomes. Different people, communities and circumstances can lead to very different outcomes. In practice it may not be desirable to maintain a separation of methods between casework, advocacy and community social work, as a multi-methods approach may be a preferred option, for instance, in providing individual support, or direct representation, for those who might need it during times of rapid change and development. Indeed, Johnson contends that rural workers should move away from any strict separation of 'macro and micro orientations towards an integration of these skills' (A. Johnson 1998, cited in Martinez-Brawley 2000, p 287). Unpredictability remains a significant feature of rural social work as Laing and Hepburn (2006) found in their study of the service response to severe cutbacks in timber logging in Western Australia. There, the assumption that counselling and community development projects would be of equal importance proved mistaken, as only 10% of those seeking help from the Worker Assistance Project actually opted for counselling. While any assessment of the merits of personal counselling for individuals vis-à-vis the wider benefits arising from the community projects is likely to be a contested and challenging question, there is little doubt that this potential variability must be recognised. In another place, at another time, the balance of provision might differ according to the prevailing circumstances. Unsurprisingly, most accounts of community-oriented interventions acknowledge the importance of the regular review of aims and objectives to maintain the relevance of development plans.

Unfortunately there are a number of barriers to the application of community social work models to practice. The predominance of casework models for practice in industrialised countries such as Australia, Canada, the UK and the US, and, especially, of narrowly focused deficit models of casework, has led to a neglect of the historical traditions of community social work that we noted in the introduction to this chapter. Neo-liberal social policies and the shift to what has been termed New Public Management (Walsh, 1995; Lane, 2000), with its emphasis upon outcomes that can be easily summarised in performance indicators, has exacerbated the individualistic and materialistic focus of service development and provision. Furthermore, in many countries, social work has become increasingly insular and is organisationally separated from other services such as health and education, and from other sectors such as economic development and natural resource management. As a result, many of those who may be marginalised, disempowered and disadvantaged are not represented in important areas of decision making, often because they and their potential advocates, including social workers, are not represented or, if present, are unable to have much impact because of their lack of organisation and understanding of how best to promote their interests and influence others. Sadly, it seems as if social work education, despite its rhetorical protestations of commitment to broader forms of intervention, has largely followed suit, although there are some significant exceptions noted in the next chapter. Consequently, it is likely that many social workers do not enter the profession with a good grounding in the perspectives and models reviewed in this chapter.

More optimistically, the political climate in some countries is changing as governments increasingly recognise the importance of community and social cohesion and the role of community development in combating poverty and disadvantage. In the European Community, funding is being provided for a range of initiatives aimed at both urban and rural areas to regenerate local enterprise and reskill and empower local people, one interesting example being the setting up of an online trading association called Kivo-Ebiz. This is managed and run by volunteers selling unwanted items for a commission through eBay on behalf of local people. In its first 18 months it raised over £50,000 for other community activities (Arradon and Wyler, 2008). Although much of this development is taking place in what might be termed 'mainstream' community work, these shifts in policies may provide opportunities for social workers to help communities to access resources and piggyback social development upon economic initiatives. However, it should not be assumed that the politics of community-oriented practice are necessarily liberal or radical. For, as Sheldon commented:

> It is not surprising that community-based approaches to social work evoke, albeit for different reasons, the approval of radicals and conservatives alike since the idea of community is … paradoxical because historically it has inspired some of the most paternalistic philosophies of social welfare and some of the most libertarian ones. (Sheldon, 1982, cited in Martinez-Brawley, 1984, p 82)

We think this cautionary note remains equally relevant today. The problem is one noted at the beginning of this book, the assumption that there is a homogeneous community in the first place, an assumption that problematises the position of any person or group not included in whatever conception of community is being used (Levitas, 1998). As Shucksmith and his colleagues have noted, 'In rural areas, much more than urban areas, the actions and choices of one group … may have profound effects upon others' (Shucksmith et al, 2007, p 106).

EIGHT

Workforce issues

Introduction

Social work in rural contexts presents some additional challenges with regard to issues such as recruitment, retention, education and training that if not tackled can exacerbate the service disadvantages apparent in many rural settlements. This chapter begins by reviewing what is known about rural social workers and the work they do, and discusses why they choose rural practice and how they adjust to it, job stress and staff retention issues. It then turns to the issue of professional education and preparation for rural practice. It concludes with recommendations for employers, educators, the profession, communities and practitioners concerning how to attract the right staff and prepare and support them so that once they come into rural areas, they remain in practice. We continue to use the term 'social worker' broadly, to encompass both qualified and unqualified social workers, and other social care and welfare workers.

Rural social workers and their work

Unfortunately, there are no national studies published that provide general profiles of the rural social work and social care workforce, and certainly no comprehensive data for international comparisons. Thus, the evidence base is patchy, with most of the available information coming from comparatively small surveys in Australia, Canada and the US, typically involving samples of between 50 and 350 respondents. This discussion draws primarily from a comparative study involving rural social workers in Australia and the US (Saltman et al, 2004), and three Australian studies (Lonne and Cheers, 1999, 2000; Munn, 2002), and a comparison of burnout and job satisfaction among rural and urban workers (Dollard et al, 1999).

Demographic profile

Around 75–80% of the respondents in these studies were women and each sample had an average age of between 35 and 40 years. In Lonne's

(2002) sample, around 37% of the respondents were between 21 and 29 years, another 35% were between 30 and 39 years, and 24% were between 40 and 49 years of age. Generally, these studies report an experienced workforce with 75% of the US and 47% of the Australian samples in Saltman et al's study (2004), and 41% of Munn's (2002) sample, having 10 years' or more social work experience. Lonne's respondents had less experience, only 17% had 10 years' or more experience, 69% had less than five years' experience, and around 20% had less than three months'. Many of the social workers in these studies were well accustomed to rural life, with 63% of the US and 49% of the Australian samples in the Saltman et al study (2004) having been raised in a rural setting. Many were also native to their current community, 28% and 25% of the US and Australian samples, respectively (Lonne, 2002; Saltman et al, 2004). In Lonne's study although 18% of his sample had lived in rural areas for less than a year, some 69% had lived in such areas for five years or more. Furthermore, most had not come to their jobs from cities, as around 62% had either changed positions within the same settlement or moved from other rural areas. Gibbs' (2001) Australian study of rural child protection workers also found that the majority either were local people or had grown up in the country. In these studies, then, the overall profile is of a sizeable pool of social workers who are well accustomed to rural life and committed to living and practising in rural places. However, the marked differences between the US and Australian profiles indicate that one should be wary of generalisations across international boundaries.

Organisations and roles

The available data confirm the observations and accounts of experienced rural practitioners and researchers that much of rural practice takes place in relative professional isolation. For example, Lonne (2002) found that about a quarter of workers worked alone, with just under a third having only one or two colleagues in the immediate organisational environment. In Chapter 6 it was noted that rural social work is highly generalist with most rural workers providing service in a range of fields, using a range of different methods. Unsurprisingly, lone workers and those in small work units were the most likely to be highly generalist. Comparisons between Australia and US (Lonne, 2002; Munn, 2002; Saltman et al, 2004) appear to show some differences in the emphasis of social work in different countries. US respondents worked primarily in family services (40%), mental health (23%) and children and youth services (23%), followed by medical and health care (12%), public assistance and welfare (11%) and services for older people (8%). In contrast, Australian respondents worked mostly in public assistance and welfare (43%) and medical and health care (32%), followed by non-developmental disabilities (17%) and family services (13%). However, it is possible that these differences are partly a reflection of the different research methodologies employed.

The importance of community-level intervention appears to be supported by Munn's (2002) finding that 68% of his respondents reported practising community development, with 36% also citing social planning. In contrast, less than 4% of Lonne's (2002) respondents identified community development as their primary practice method. The discrepancy almost certainly arises from the different research approaches, as Lonne's respondents were asked to identify their primary practice method only, while Munn's sample identified all the methods they used. This indicates that most Australian social workers undertake some community development and/or social planning, although not as the primary emphasis of their practice. Additionally, there were significant differences between the two samples, as Lonne studied qualified social workers only, whereas Munn's sample included a variety of human and health services practitioners. All of the studies indicate that rural workers are required to undertake a wide range of roles and responsibilities, including being an advocate, educator and trainer, manager or supervisor, programme developer, community developer, and social planner, as well as directly providing services to clients.

Motivations for rural practice

The reasons that inform individual practitioners' decisions to work in particular rural areas strongly influence their commitment to the job and the community, and also play an important part in their retention and resilience to the stresses involved in rural work. Lonne's study found that, for the most part, social workers were in rural communities because they preferred to be there. For instance, around three quarters had commenced their current employment with a strongly positive attitude and thought that living in a rural community had far more advantages than disadvantages for their lifestyles (2002). When asked their reasons for accepting their positions, 'professional interests' (that is, the particular practice field), the employing organisation and professional skill development were foremost, with around half citing the attractions of the rural environment and career advancement as also being significant. Just over a third cited personal reasons. From Lonne's study it would seem that social workers accept rural positions primarily because of professional interests, and once satisfied that the position matches their interests, they take other factors into account, especially the rural lifestyle and, for some, the particular community and location.

Preparation, training and supervision

Most rural social work texts contend that some specific education and training is necessary or, at least, desirable before beginning rural practice. However, the evidence for both pre-practice and in-service preparation is not encouraging. In the UK there are no specialised qualifying programmes in rural social work, no specialist post-qualifying training as there is for doctors and in most universities it is likely that there is little or no specific input on rural practice. Green's (2003b) study of 20 Australian Bachelor of Social Work and 20 approved welfare training programmes found that only 10 social work programmes and four of the welfare courses referred to rural issues at all, and then often only minimally. This appears to be broadly consistent with Lonne's (2002) study in which 54% of his sample of 194 qualified social workers reported having received no input on rural issues or practice over the four years of their course, with a further 18% reporting very minimal (less than 10 hours of) preparation, with only 9% of Lonne's sample having received more than 40 hours' preparation.

It is possible that pre-entry and induction as well as in-service training opportunities and appropriate supervision may help offset these deficits, although Lonne found that around 61% of his respondents had not received any relocation briefing or pre-entry preparation to rural employment, and that where this was provided, it was often rather brief. Access to other general in-service training was widely available but variable in quantity with 34% of respondents receiving up to one hour per month, 38% between one and four hours and 29% more than four hours. Lonne's findings in regard to administrative and professional supervision indicated that 29% of his respondents received up to one hour per month, and 23% received no administrative supervision at all. In contrast, 64% received professional supervision of up to one hour or less per month, and most thought it effective.

Adjustment to rural practice

Several authors have documented the difficulties and the processes involved in adjusting to remote, rural and indigenous contexts, positions and environments (Riggs and Kugel, 1976; Phillips, 1983; Zapf, 1985,

1993; Lonne, 1990) and have tried to offer conceptual frameworks or models for recognising them. These proposals typically describe some variant of the 'U-curve' of adjustment derived from studies of migration to new cultures, where the stages of adaptation include initial excitement and hope followed by disillusionment and declining well-being, then adjustment, accompanied by increasing well-being and realism about the new environment. These models have not been widely reported outside of the specialist literature and, while their evidence base is limited, they may provide valuable insights into the processes of adaptation and offer pointers for supporting new workers moving into rural areas.

Zapf (1993) tracked the adjustment of practitioners moving to the Yukon and documented a 12-month passage from cultural outsider to insider, especially for workers recruited from the more densely populated southern areas of Canada and the US and undertaking an urban to rural relocation. Well-being decreased during the initial impact stage, which he called 'culture shock', because most practitioners moved into new environments in remote communities with significant indigenous populations. Zapf contends that initially:

> The community is considered [by the new worker] theoretically according to systems of attributes rather than as a place of immediate experience.... The newly located worker attempts to understand the community using frameworks from his or her own familiar culture and profession. Applying metaphors from the South leads to a limited view of the northern community as a pathological variation of the southern experience. (Zapf, 1993, pp 701–2)

This initial framework gradually disintegrates as the worker experiences life in the community. At first, this disjunction causes confusion and anxiety but most practitioners eventually enter into local systems of meaning and priorities, and he notes that:

> This shift will probably be accompanied by a stressful period of frustration and disorientation, giving way eventually to regained confidence and a sense of well being as the worker learns to operate within the new system of meanings. (Zapf, 1993, p 702)

Zapf also found that organisational variables, including job characteristics and the social work role, were also associated with the intensity of the culture shock experienced, while individual factors such as demographic characteristics, background and attitudes were more associated with recovery.

Lonne (1990), in his earlier work, proposed a five-phase rural adjustment framework with a more detailed 12–18-month process of adjustment, and the data from his later study (2002) largely supported this model of adaptation. He contends that initially there is a disorientation period, typically lasting up to six weeks as the worker settles into both their job and the community. This is characterised by confusion, uncertainty and mild anxiety, mixed with novelty, excitement and satisfaction with the new life. Work stresses are high and productivity is generally low, although early work satisfaction comes from the stimulation of learning a new job. This is followed by a honeymoon period, typically lasting from six weeks to three months, and characterised by optimism, excitement, high energy, moderate to low stress and achievement as the worker gains an appreciation of the community and undertakes job planning. Work performance and productivity steadily improve, and job satisfaction tends to be high. General well-being and coping levels are also high as workers and their families settle into the new community. A third phase of 'grief and loss', typically commencing between three and six months after arrival, continues for up to six months. This is characterised by diminished enthusiasm for the job, a flattening or decrease in work performance, reduced satisfaction with life, feelings of loss of the previous lifestyle, awareness of distance from friends and family, and moderate anxiety. At this stage, workers typically feel that they are coping satisfactorily, but not as well as they were earlier in the process. Following this, a period of withdrawal and depression ensues, typically beginning at between seven and 12 months and enduring for six to eight weeks, although it can last several months. This stage is characterised by reduced satisfaction with life and work, decreased work performance and coping ability, increased stress and anxiety levels, feelings of inadequacy, and sometimes sadness and social withdrawal. The final phase, reorganisation and adjustment, involves the worker deciding to either leave or make changes to their lifestyle and/or job. Those who stay usually experience increased work performance and satisfaction with their job and life, improved well-being, feeling more settled, having a renewed appreciation for their job, and feeling more of a connection with their community. Their feelings of coping, competence and confidence at work increase, their credibility in the community increases and stress levels either plateau or decline.

To summarise, there is evidence that many rural workers appear to go through some common stages of adaptation to their new employment, but as with all stage models of human adaptation, one should be wary of assuming their inevitability in every instance, and be alert to the possibility of pathologisation of what seem to be typical sorts of responses to change and resettlement.

Work stress

It is well established that excessive stress decreases job performance and satisfaction and increases turnover and absenteeism in the workforce generally, and that human services work shares much the same stressors as other occupations (Jayaratne and Chess, 1984). These stressors are more related to organisational than client, personal or other non-work factors (Sundet and Cowger, 1990). They include high workloads and job demands, poor supervision, poor resources, disempowering cultures and structures, work role issues (such as role ambiguity and conflict), unrealistic societal expectations of social workers, low worker autonomy, lack of efficacy and success in one's work, lack of collegial and personal support, and racism within the organisation (Balloch et al, 1995; Collings and Murray, 1996; Markiewicz, 1996; Dollard et al, 1999; Lonne and Cheers, 2000a, 2000b; Lloyd et al, 2002). Despite conjecture that rural social workers may be more vulnerable to stress than urban workers there is little comparative research (Brummell, 1985; Lonne, 1990; Munn, 1990), although the study by Dollard et al (1999) found no differences. Nevertheless, even though no rural–urban differences were evident in this Australian study, stress remains a key issue in rural practice (Green and Mason, 2002, Green, 2003a; Green et al, 2003; Lonne and Cheers, 2004a, 2004b; Green and Lonne, 2005).

Lonne (2002) found that a quarter of the rural workers suffered high levels of emotional exhaustion, and also noted that carrying statutory and mandated responsibilities was associated with these higher stress levels. Gibbs' (2001) study of child protection work had also noted that living and working in the same small community were strongly associated with job stress. Green's (2003a) qualitative study illustrated some of the high levels of stress. Poor administrative (but not professional) supervision, weak links between practitioners and their communities, and being young and professionally inexperienced have also been noted as contributory factors to higher levels of stress (Green and Lonne, 2005). Factors specifically associated with emotional exhaustion were increased by the amount of after-hours work, high social visibility and greater physical distance from the supervisor (Green and Lonne, 2005). Other stressors include: threats to personal and family safety; difficulties involved in delivering ethical and professional services in the community; and conflicts between workers' professional training and what is perceived as good practice in their community, especially around issues of dual and multiple relationships, confidentiality and maintaining professional boundaries (Green et al, 2003; Green and Lonne, 2005).

The significant buffers to stress, as one might expect, are good supervision, individual resiliency and pre-existing psychological well-being, high personal and professional commitment to the job, absence of tension between work and home life, and support from a partner and other social supports (Lonne and Cheers, 1999, 2004a, 2004b; Green and Mason, 2002; Green, 2003a; Green et al, 2003; Green and Lonne, 2005). Despite the stresses involved, rural social workers are generally satisfied with and prefer their rural lifestyles. Green and Lonne (2005) offer two explanations for this apparent incongruence. First, although rural practitioners are stressed by some aspects of their work, they also derive considerable satisfaction from other aspects, such as role affirmation by local colleagues and residents and making a difference in the community. Second, for many practitioners, low job satisfaction and high stress are strongly mitigated by other factors including their professional maturity and confidence, the benefits provided by their working lives, such as time for family and recreation, and the flexibility and professional opportunities provided by their jobs.

Retention

Staff retention among human services professionals has long been considered a major issue (Dollard et al, 1999; Lonne, 2002; Lonne and Cheers, 2004a; Kyonne, 2007). High staff turnover can lead to reduced levels of service and quality, lack of continuity, higher workloads and resulting stress and job dissatisfaction among remaining staff, and overuse of temporary and contract positions (Lonne and Cheers, 2004a; Schmidt and Klein, 2004). However, Lonne and Cheers (1999) suggest that employers have not seriously investigated the issue because they tend to assume that community and personal variables explain retention problems, rather than workplace factors that are within their control. There is surprisingly little research on the causes of high staff turnover in rural areas, but much of what there is comes from Australia and indicates that it is a significant problem there. Lonne (2002) found 34% of social workers stayed in post for less than 12 months, 33% between 12 and 24 months, and the remaining 33% for more than two years. He distinguished between 'stayers' (31%) who were in the same position at the end of the two-year data-collection period, 'retained leavers' (29%) who had moved to another position within the same organisation but not necessarily in the same settlement, and 'non-retained leavers' (40%) who had left both their employer and the settlement. Clearly, replacing 40% of social workers every two years is costly for employers and likely to cause disruptions to services and to agency–community relationships. The comparative study by Saltman et al (2004) reported average four-year retention rates of 56% for US practitioners compared with 28% for Australians.

The Australian evidence suggests that turnover is related more to organisational and job-related factors than to disenchantment with rural life and practice. Lonne (2002) found that 67% of those who left their positions continued to work in rural communities, with 38% continuing in the same place. He also found that 64% of the variance in length of stay related to employer-related factors and noted that many practitioners had intended to stay longer than they did, which suggests that their hopes for their positions had not been realised. His respondents typically cited dissatisfaction with line management and supervision, inadequate support and preparation for rural practice, the temporary or contract nature of their appointments, poor salary levels, and a lack of professional development and training opportunities. Those with more autonomy, responsibility and control were more likely to stay. For those who left, continuing dissatisfactions with their employment were often brought to a head by a single trigger issue, such as a declined request to attend a training programme, which resulted in their decision to leave. Significantly, even a mere two-hour preparatory briefing when they commenced their job appeared to make a large difference to how long respondents stayed in their positions and communities. With regard to personal reasons for leaving, the most common was a negative initial predisposition to living and working in rural environments. Those most likely to stay tended to like living in smaller communities, thereby benefiting from rural lifestyles. They had a positive initial predisposition to rural practice, and had a balanced amount of community involvement, local friendships and contact with colleagues, all of which were associated with success and impact at work. Other personal factors were also similar to the factors that impact on or mitigate stress generally, and included a stable personal life, a positive disposition to rural living and the location, prior experience of rural life and practice, and having more social work experience.

Comparative studies of retention between urban and rural settings are also scarce, but again the available evidence suggests that turnover is higher in rural areas. Gibbs and Keating (1999) found that turnover in the same statutory child welfare programmes in Victoria was higher in rural than metropolitan regions, while Dollard et al (1999) reported that metropolitan workers in a large state government department had been in their current positions longer than those in rural areas.

Practical steps to improve recruitment and retention

For the most part, these are rather obvious being largely logical developments from existing research findings, but the potentially important role of rural communities themselves should be noted. Not only should communities have a role in shaping developments in service, they also have an important part to play in recruiting and retaining appropriate practitioners. For instance, they may be involved directly in all stages of recruitment from developing job descriptions and relocation briefings to the initial introduction and induction of new workers.

Improving recruitment strategies clearly increases retention. Vacancies should be filled quickly because leaving positions unfilled for long periods reduces service levels and increases the workloads and stress of existing staff, which in turn exacerbates retention problems and impairs the organisation's relationship with the community. Short-term and temporary contracts for workers may deter potential applicants and over time are likely to weaken commitment (Lonne and Cheers, 1999, 2004a). Accurate information should be provided to applicants about the position and the community and applicants should have opportunities to discuss this information. Short-listed applicants should also have the opportunity to visit the community in which the position is located (Lonne and Cheers, 2004a).

Employers should identify whom they are targeting for recruitment and consider the reasons why someone would apply for the position, focusing obviously upon their professional interests and career aspirations, but also recognising the potential attractions of living in the area. Above all, the existing pool of experienced and committed rural social workers should be specifically targeted (Gibbs, 2001; Hodgkin, 2002). Job advertisements should be placed in rural as well as urban media, and should include information about practice fields, required knowledge and skills, career advancement opportunities and the locale, which may heighten the appeal of the post to those being targeted. Recruitment packs should highlight this information and can present the job as an opportunity for a positive change of lifestyle and career development, for example, in emphasising the positive contribution that generic and generalist practice can make to career development. Where necessary, employers should institute financial and material incentives and supports specifically for rural positions, such as increased flexibility over work hours, leave entitlements, salary enhancement, relocation allowances and housing, training and promotion opportunities. Furthermore, non-government organisations should be funded to provide the same incentives and supports as government departments because their inability to do so results in substantially higher turnover (Lonne and Cheers, 1999, 2004a).

The most important step for employers to increase retention is to recognise that it is primarily an organisational issue. To increase retention they can provide adequate administrative supervision, provide or subsidise external professional supervision, keep workloads manageable, minimise after-hours work and travel, and ensure opportunities for promotion and career advancement. They can also encourage worker autonomy and responsibility, and minimise workplace conflict. Opportunities for professional development, including postgraduate qualifications and attendance at conferences, workshops and seminars, should be commensurate with those of urban workers (Dollard et al, 1999; Lonne and Cheers, 2004b). It is important that employers recognise that many new rural social workers will go through a reasonably predictable process of adjustment lasting from 12 to 18 months, especially those who are young, inexperienced and/or from urban backgrounds. Supervisors should brief recruits about this process when they commence work, and throughout the adjustment period. They can help them to assess their experiences and the issues they are encountering, and help develop strategies to address them (Gibbs, 2001; Lonne, 2002). Special attention should be given to how new workers are managing their relationship with the community, including their visibility, community involvement and personal–professional–community boundaries. Supervisors can also help by facilitating time out through non-local professional development and training opportunities (Lonne and Cheers, 1999, 2000, 2004b).

Education and training for rural practice

There are four key reasons why social workers need to receive some specific preparation for rural practice in both their initial and continuing professional education programmes (O'Sullivan et al, 1997; Green, 2003a; Lonne and Cheers, 2004a, 2004b). They are:

- Many of those who come to work in rural areas, having been raised and educated in urban environments, are unfamiliar with, and often uncomfortable in, rural contexts. Some of them, as both Zapf (1993) and Lonne (1990, 2002) have found, are likely to suffer from adjustment difficulties when they move into rural contexts.
- Poor preparation prior to rural practice can contribute to worker stress and burnout, both of which are related to high turnover (Lonne, 2002).
- Preparation for working with indigenous and minority ethnic and cultural groups living in rural communities is likely to have been neglected in previous education and training.
- Some practice methods that are especially useful in rural practice, such as networking, forming partnerships with communities and their organisations, community engagement and community capacity assessment, are often not included or may have received relatively little emphasis in previous education and training.

Rural practice content can be integrated into core courses, and also delivered through rural electives and rural field education opportunities and placements (Cheers, 1986, 1998). Based on the evidence that indicates that much of rural social work practice is generalist, generic and community-embedded (Lonne, 2002; Munn, 2002; Saltman et al, 2004), the curriculum content should encompass these approaches (Saltman et al, 2004, p 529). However, substantial numbers of rural social workers also engage in specialist and mandated practice, either exclusively or in combination with other kinds of practice, so it is important that students are introduced to frameworks and methods that address these practice modes in a contextualised way (see, for example, Cheers et al, 2007). Students should be helped to develop the skills and the knowledge needed to work in rural, remote, indigenous, ethnic and/or cultural communities that will enable them to establish and maintain credibility, and sustain a balanced personal/professional life under conditions of high social visibility.

Clearly rural people are an important potential source of the rural workforce, and they are more likely to understand rural contexts, to stay longer in their positions and to be personally committed to rural practice. However, rural residents experience disadvantages in their access to tertiary education, finding it difficult and expensive and often logistically impossible to attend programmes delivered only in urban and regional centres (Alston, 2007). Thus, they are less likely to enter social work if they do not have access to initial professional education, and even if they do qualify, are likely to have fewer opportunities for continuing professional development. Similarly, indigenous people and those from minority ethnic groups are also potentially the most appropriate and best suited to working within their own communities, but they may face additional barriers to gaining access to education. Whiteside and her colleagues (2006) have shown how empowerment perspectives can be used to frame workforce development, particularly in regard to building capacity and confidence among indigenous workers. As one of their participants commented, 'I learnt that we can step up to the challenge and we all have that leadership potential and it's not about having to be some huge person in the department' (Whiteside et al, 2006, p 428). Furthermore, as we noted in Chapter 3, there are some tensions and ties facing indigenous workers working in their own communities that educators need to be aware of (Bennet and Zubrzycki, 2003). Being aware of the past and having experienced some of the same forms of oppression may be extremely valuable, but there are some difficulties, as Green and Thomas have noted:

> One worker talked about always having to remember where she was from and why she was doing this work ... remembering that she was a social worker and a First Nations person.... When asked what advice these workers had for future First Nations social workers they shared the following views ... 'I would recommend that they really try to deal with their own issues first before going out there. I mean things are going to happen that will trigger things for them, that will happen to everybody'. (Green and Thomas, 2005, p 18)

It is vital that schools of social work develop flexible and culturally relevant professional programmes to develop the potential rural workforce. The most encouraging examples of efforts to address local contexts have been seen in programmes that have a special, though not always exclusive, focus upon working in indigenous communities, for instance in New Zealand at the Victoria University of Wellington (Cairns et al, 1998). In Canada there has been considerable development, and the work of Morrissette et al (1993) and Hart (2002), in critiquing existing provision and beginning to set out Aboriginal models of social work practice, has been influential. There have been significant developments at many Canadian universities, including the University of Calgary, the Grant MacEwan Community College in northern Alberta, the University of Regina and Yukon College, the University of Victoria, and also at the First Nations University of Canada, Laurentian

University, McGill University, University of Northern British Columbia, University of Manitoba and the Université du Québec en Abitbi-Témiscamingue (Pelech, 1993; Senkpiel, 1997; Bodor and Zapf, 2002; Thomas et al, 2008; Schmidt, 2009). Most of these developments have had two aims: to improve access for indigenous workers, and to make the educational curriculum relevant to work with indigenous peoples. Some have set up specialised and distinctive programmes, such as a postgraduate certificate in Aboriginal and Youth Mental Health at Northern British Columbia, and the Bachelor of Social Work for First Nations Université du Québec en Abitbi-Témiscamingue. Interest in international developments is becoming better served by a wider range of literature that documents issues and developments in different places; two valuable collections are those edited by Gray et al (2008) and Thompson-Cooper and Moore (2009).

The Bachelor of Social Work programme at the University of Calgary typifies many of these programmes as it was developed to increase the 'accessibility, responsiveness, and affordability of … accredited social work degrees' to rural, remote and aboriginal communities throughout Alberta (Rogers, 1998, p 1). It also set out to develop innovative culturally and geographically relevant course content, and to adapt and redesign existing curriculum content to be sensitive to First Nations and Métis peoples by aligning it with traditional philosophies and knowledge systems. The programme adopted flexible modes of course delivery that included home-community placements and distance education technology, as well as direct face-to-face teaching and learning. It was developed through a wide community consultation process that recommended and affirmed a new 'Learning Circle' model based on a 'Medicine Wheel' framework, which had a strong cultural relevance for aboriginal students and communities (Bodor and Zapf, 2002). Accordingly, rather than commencing at a fixed starting point and progressing from one year or semester to subsequent ones through a system of tiered prerequisite courses or modules, students can progress through the programme in whichever order suits their circumstances. They can undertake the programme at their own pace and in their own communities. The programme content is 'grouped into four major theme areas that are regarded as essential for social work in rural, remote, and Aboriginal communities: Generalist Practice in Context; Communication and Information; Diversity and Oppression; Social Work Methods' (Bodor and Zapf, 2002, p 8). Each of these consists of eight modules. There is at least one module in each theme course devoted to 'Local Applications', which 'allows for local healers, Elders, agency workers and other community resource persons to present information and lead discussion with students' in an attempt to connect course content with the history, current practices and policy issues in the local region (Bodor and Zapf, 2002, p 9). A Planning Circle with representatives from all stakeholders, including students, provides advice and a forum for identifying the important issues facing social workers and communities in northern Alberta, and makes recommendations concerning curriculum, delivery and connections with the community (Bodor and Zapf, 2002).

Conclusion

Obviously, we need to avoid unwarranted generalisations from one national context to another, or even from one place to another within a particular country, but some broad points can be made. At the very least, in countries where research is lacking, existing knowledge from other places can be considered in terms of its potential application as it may provide an important stimulus for research and development, for example, the important points made by Weaver (1999) and cited in Chapter 3, and the seven key points noted in the conclusion to that chapter. Social work students and practitioners need to have access to knowledge from other disciplines, such as rural and community sociology, and regional and community planning and development. Access to relevant journals such as *Rural Society* or *Rural Social Work and Community Practice*, will improve dissemination of the existing knowledge base and will promote a broader appreciation of rural practice and its challenges. Students need to become aware of the social dynamics of living and working in the same place, including dual and multiple relationships, and the complexities and demands inherent in their relationships as practitioners to local communities. They should also be introduced to issues concerning indigenous people and those from minority ethnic and other cultural backgrounds, focusing especially on the different ways of knowing and helping. Finally, schools of social work should develop rural postgraduate coursework, research and other continuing professional education options such as workshops and short courses that are delivered flexibly and provide easy access for remote and full-time practitioners.

The responsibilities of employers to their rural workforce are paramount and the following key points all reflect the research findings, which demonstrate that most problems in recruitment are amenable to sound human resource policies and practices. They are that:

- the local populace, and rural people more generally, are often neglected as a potential workforce;
- improvements in recruitment practices, particularly in providing information about the locality and the expectations and challenges of rural practice, will improve both recruitment and retention;
- social workers, once recruited, may need support through the initial stages of adaptation;
- retention is likely to be improved by ensuring that social workers have manageable workloads and are provided with satisfactory administrative and professional support, access to effective supervision and opportunities for continuing professional development;
- improvements in service delivery also aid retention, and stress among workers can be reduced by avoiding role ambiguity and conflicting organisational and community expectations;
- job satisfaction is directly linked to the wider experience and appreciation of living and working in a rural community.

Funding models, of course, should be sufficient not only to support forms of practice that are congruent with particular local contexts, but also to permit employers to provide adequate incentives for recruitment, to maintain satisfactory levels of staffing and support, and to ensure manageable workloads.

Professional bodies and validating organisations should require rural and, where relevant, indigenous content in initial qualifying and in continuing professional development programmes. They can support knowledge development and dissemination though publishing special rural issues of journals and including people with rural expertise on editorial boards, promoting relevant conferences and workshops, and developing or supporting national interest groups and organisations, such as the Rural Caucus of the National Association of Social Workers in the US and the Rural and Remote Special Interest Group of the Australian Association of Social Workers, as well as promoting other peer support networks (Dollard et al, 1999; Murty, 2005), including web forums and blogs.

Finally, rural practitioners can actively contribute to managing the issues that lead to stress, job dissatisfaction and early departure. From the outset, they need to recognise that rural social work is different from urban practice and develop the relevant expertise. They need to understand their immediate context and tailor their work to it, which means maintaining a balanced involvement in community life and consulting with key local people and groups. As with supervisors and community leaders, the practitioner is responsible for monitoring her or his own practice, working environment and adjustment issues, and taking the initiative with employers and community leaders in managing them (Lonne and Cheers, 2004a, 2004b).

Conclusion

The core themes of this book, identified in the Introduction, were the importance of recognising the diversity of rural contexts and rural lives, the necessity of an informed appreciation of local context and, following from these, a rejection of any homogenised approach to policy and practice. Accordingly, there is a tension throughout this book as we have tried to demonstrate the variability of rural contexts and at the same time draw the reader's attention to some common features in regard to the challenges facing rural communities and the social service agencies and workers attempting to respond to them. Some of the commonalities between Western developed countries are due to similarities in social welfare systems and the fact that these countries are relatively wealthy and, thus, have considerable expenditures allocated to 'professionalised' systems of social work. While others derive from similarities in the economic base of many rural communities that remain in many places, primarily an extractive (for example, mining, forestry, fishing) and agricultural base, subject to the vagaries of weather and climate and international commodity prices, as well as to broader shifts in the national economies of particular countries. There are other commonalities that derive from the social dynamics of small communities, in which higher social visibility and local cultures, and patterns of relationships, play a great part in how people view social difference and social problems and how these things are experienced. In some countries, similarities arise from the experience of colonisation, whose legacies have resulted in the marginalisation of indigenous populations whose health and welfare prospects are, typically, considerably worse than those of the overall population.

We have tried to show, despite the patchy evidence base in regard to many aspects of rural practice, that there is a sufficient literature to establish some broad features of rural context and rural practice. These features, while not inevitably occurring in every place, should nonetheless be part of the framework of knowledge and skills used to prepare social workers for rural practice. In this regard, the knowledge problem is rather like that around, say, racism or sexism, we know the general facts and processes of discrimination, and we know something of their frequency among populations, but we cannot assume that they pertain to every situation or individual that we encounter. Nor should the emphasis upon the importance of understanding local context be taken to imply that context does not matter in urban settings, we believe that it matters greatly. However, the distinctive feature of much of rural practice is that many practitioners come to realise very early on in their working lives that much of what they attempt to do is more evidently reliant upon particular knowledge of a community or place, whereas in many larger urban settings it may not be so easy to appreciate the significance of such knowledge. Nor is this fact widely recognised in accounts of urban practice. There are exceptions, of course, as can be seen in accounts of social work practice in socially encapsulated settings such as large housing estates or projects, or in districts where there have been long-established traditional forms of employment, like mining and steel works.

Rural practice, at least in the Western industrialised countries covered by this review, is largely generic and generalist, encompassing both personal and community-level interventions, and is mostly undertaken by practitioners living and working in the same communities, typically with a deep commitment to rural life and practice. What this body of knowledge now needs is further empirical validation and further theoretical and practical development in a variety of community, regional and national contexts. We hope that readers will have noted the many opportunities for research as well as the importance we attach to the incorporation of existing knowledge from the wider social sciences to develop a more comprehensive knowledge base and to better understand how to improve rural social work. Moreover, because rural social work has been ignored or marginalised in many countries we need to show that the approaches and adaptations to practice that are commonplace in rural work have relevance for social work practice more generally. As Murty (2005) has noted, this is likely to be the most effective strategy for mobilising professional support for rural practice. Consequently, we are not proposing some novel or radical approach to practice that we believe will provide 'the answers'. Indeed, we agree with Ginsberg's perceptive and somewhat rueful statement that:

> the issues in organizing and delivering social services to people in rural communities are not very new. They existed in similar ways and the solutions offered were similar to those that are offered now by some writers on social work in small communities. I discovered, for example, years after I had written about social work in rural communities, that others had said substantially the same things, decades before. (Ginsberg, 1980, Foreword)

Instead, we hope that readers can see how working in small communities in rural areas should remind social workers of some things that appear to be forgotten or not fully appreciated, namely that:

- there is a long history of rural practice that is rarely mentioned in mainstream texts;
- rural practice demands a sophisticated appreciation of local context and social dynamics;
- most education and training programmes simply ignore rural context and rural issues;
- most practitioners operating in this tradition have, sooner or later, become acutely aware of the interrelationship between economic and social well-being and welfare and have understood that social problems require social interventions, not simply personalised ones;
- social workers have an ethical responsibility to advocate for and engage with socially marginalised individuals and groups.

We hope that experienced rural practitioners will have found much to support and confirm their practice in this book, while newcomers to rural social work will discover that there is an existing tradition of description and theorisation that can inform their understanding of their work and the challenges they face. Above all, we hope that we have persuaded readers that while rural practice provides many challenges, it remains an absorbing and rewarding endeavour in which one's efforts are often clearly evident and directly appreciated within the small community.

A common theme throughout this book is the need for social workers to commit themselves to action in the interests and needs of those who are neglected, marginalised and oppressed. Social workers, in Goffman's (1968) memorable term, are often the 'wise', who have privileged access to the lives and problems of other people and who are often trusted with this information. Of course, we do not have complete access, but what we have is often enough to realise the disjunctions between policies and practices, and to appreciate what Uma Naryan (1989) called the epistemically privileged knowledge that people have of their own situation. Social workers, because of their interstitial occupational location between individuals, groups and the wider society, have responsibilities in both directions, as Kenneth Pray (1949) noted long ago. We are well placed to observe and understand the complex interactions between private and social problems and broader social forces and structures, but generally the extent to which we move beyond narrower forms of intervention is limited. There are many ways to 'act' of course, and, as well as the mainstream methods we outlined in Chapters 6 and 7, these can range from 'insider activism' or 'active resistance' within organisations (Briskman, 2007), through public education and media work (Brawley, 1995), to the various forms of advocacy (Schneider and Lester, 2002), and may also encompass support for the campaigning work of others. In all these possible actions we need to carefully consider what sort of role and relationship we will have with the individuals and groups that we work with, and to consider what might be the unintended consequences of our interventions. Within the literature on advocacy there are some long-standing questions about the relationship between 'helper and helped', which in their essence could be applied to any form of intervention – is our position untenable, is it disempowering for those whom we purport to represent, can we really advocate from an insider position, or, most fundamentally, can we ever truly speak for someone else? However, ethically and professionally, act we must.

Finally, while this book has focused upon predominantly 'Western' practice in advanced capitalist countries, we would like readers to note that in many countries, especially some of those in South Asia and Africa, distinctive forms of analysis, policy and practice are being developed, and these often contain an explicit appreciation of rural context and rural problems. In these approaches, important questions are being asked about the appropriate focus of social work, including the relative costs and benefits of interventions and the necessity of developing forms of intervention that build upon local capabilities, especially in circumstances where resources are scarce. These accounts typically reject narrow 'clinical' models of casework based upon inaccurate assumptions of universality in human and social development in favour of more emancipative programmes, involving such measures as community education, clean water and effective sanitation, and community safety initiatives. Although the local contexts for these approaches differ greatly from those in many Western countries, this clear focus upon aims and purposes should prompt reconsideration of the aims of social work practice in rural areas and, accordingly, a reconsideration of the ways in which we prepare new workers for practice (Midgley, 1990).

References

Abrams, P. (1980) 'Social change, social networks and neighborhood care', *Social Work Service*, 22, February, pp 12–23.

ABS (Australian Bureau of Statistics) (2002) *Yearbook Australia 2002*, Canberra: ABS, available online at: www.abs.gov.au

ABS (2008) *The Health and Welfare of Australia's Aboriginal and Torres Strait Islander Peoples 2008*, Canberra: ABS, available online at: www.abs.gov.au

ABS (2009) *Regional Population Growth, Australia, 2007–08*, Canberra: ABS, available online at: www.abs.gov.au

Adams, D.W. (1997) *Education for Extinction: American Indians and the Boarding School Experience, 1875–1928*, Lawrence, KS: University Press of Kansas.

AEC (Australian Electoral Commission) (2007) *Electoral Milestone / Timetable for Indigenous Australians*, Canberra: Australian Electoral Commission, available online at: www.aec.gov.au/Voting/indigenous_vote/indigenous.htm

Agg, J. and Phillips, M. (1998) 'Neglected gender dimensions of rural social restructuring', in P. Boyle and K. Halfacree (eds), *Migration into Rural Areas: Theories and Issues*, Chichester: John Wiley and Sons, pp 252–79.

Alcock, P., Harrow, J., Macmillan, R., Vincent, J. and Pearson, S. (1999) *Voluntary Sector Organisations' Experiences of Funding*, Rowntree Research Findings, 149, York: Joseph Rowntree Foundation, available online at: www.jrf.org.uk

Alinsky, S. (1971) *Rules for Radicals: A Pragmatic Primer for Realistic Radicals*, New York: Vintage.

Allinson, J. (2003) 'Counting the counterurbanisers (continuing metropolitan outmigration in the UK over the 1990s)', *Town and Country Planning*, 72, pp 58–9, cited in S. Hartwell, L. Kitchen, P. Milbourne and S. Morgan (2007) *Population Change in Rural Wales: Social and Cultural Impacts*, Wales Rural Observatory Research Report no 12, Cardiff, available online at: www.walesruralobservatory.org.uk

Alston, M. (1991) 'Women's place in the future of agriculture', in M. Alston (ed), *Family Farming: Australia and New Zealand*, Key papers No 2, Centre for Rural Social Research, School of Humanities and Social Sciences, Charles Sturt University, Riverina, Wagga Wagga, pp 97–104.

Alston, M. (2003) 'Women's representation in an Australian rural context', *Sociologia Ruralis*, 43, 4, pp 474–87.

Alston, M. (2005) 'Forging a new paradigm for Australian rural social work practice', *Rural Society*, 15, 2, pp 276–83.

Alston, M. (2007) 'Rural and regional developments in social work higher education', *Australian Social Work*, 60, 1, pp 107–21.

Altman, J. (2004) *Indigenous Social Policy and the New Mainstreaming*, CAEPR Seminar Series, Australian National University, Canberra, also available online at: www.anu.edu.au/caepr/Publications/topical/Altman_Mainstreaming.pdf

Andersen, K. and Darracott, R. (2004) 'Family therapy when you're part of the system – up to your eyeballs', Paper presented to the National Family Therapy Conference, Brisbane, Queensland.

Arradon, G. and Wyler, S. (2008) *What Role for Community Enterprises in Tackling Poverty?*, York: Joseph Rowntree Foundation, available online at: www.jrf.org.uk

Asthana, S., Gibson, A., Monn, G. and Brigham, P. (2003) 'Allocating resources for health and social care: the significance of rurality', *Health and Social Care in the Community*, 11, 6, pp 486–93.

Audit Commission (2007) *Crossing Borders: The Local Challenges of Migrant Workers*, London: Audit Commission.

Australian Government (2001) *Human Settlements Theme Report*, Canberra: Department of the Environment and Heritage, available online at: www.environment.gov.au

Avant, F. L. (2004) 'African Americans in rural areas', in T. L. Scales and C. L. Streeter (eds), *Rural Social Work: Building and Sustaining Community Assets*, Belmont, CA: Thomson Brooks/Cole, pp 77–93.

Bailey, R. and Brake, M. (1980) 'Contributions to radical practice in social work', in M. Brake and R. Bailey (eds), *Radical Social Work and Practice*, London: Edward Arnold, pp 7–25.

Baker, P., Hussain, Z. and Saunders, J. (1991) *Interpreters in Public Services*, Birmingham: Venture Press.

Balgopal, P.R. (2000) *Social Work with Immigrants and Refugees*, New York: Columbia University Press.

Balloch, S. and Taylor, M. (2001) *Partnership Working: Policy and Practice*, Bristol: The Policy Press.

Balloch, S., Andrew, T., Ginn, J., McLean, J., Pahl, J. and Williams, J. (1995) *Working in the Social Services*, London: National Institute of Social Work.

Ban, P. (2005) 'Aboriginal child placement principle and family group conferences', *Australian Social Work*, 58, 4, pp 384–94.

Barany, Z. (2001) *The East European Gypsies*, Cambridge: Cambridge University Press.

Barbopoulos, A. and Clark, J. M. (2003) 'Practicing psychology in rural settings: issues and guidelines', *Canadian Psychology*, 44, 4, pp 410–24.

Barbour, A. (1991) 'Family group conferences: context and consequence', *Social Work Review*, 3, 4, pp 16–21.

Bar-On, A.A. and Prinsen, G. (1999) 'Planning, communities and empowerment: an introduction to participatory rural appraisal', *International Social Work*, 42, 3, pp 277–94.

Baume, P. and Clinton, N. (1997) 'Social and cultural patterns of suicide in young people in rural Australia', *Australian Journal of Rural Health*, 5, 3, pp 115–20.

Beard, K.W. and Hissam, A. (2002) 'The use of Erikson's developmental theory with gay men from rural communities', *Journal of Rural Community Psychology*, E5, 2, pp 1–13, available online at: www.marshall.edu/jrcp/Archives.html

Bell, D. (2003) 'Homosexuals in the heartland: male same-sex desire in the rural United States', in P. Cloke (ed), *Country Visions*, Cambridge: Pearson, pp 178–91.

Bell, D. and Valentine, G. (1995) 'Queer country: rural lesbian and gay lives', *Journal of Rural Studies*, 11, 2, pp 113–22.

Bella, L. and Lyall, B. (2004) 'Collaborative methodologies: evaluating an Inuit social work initiative', *Rural Social Work*, 9, pp 60–8.

Belton, B. (2004) *Gypsy and Traveller Ethnicity: The Social Generation of an Ethnic Phenomenon*, London: Routledge.

Belton, B. (2005) *Questioning Gypsy Identity: Ethnic Narratives in Britain and America*, Walnut Creek, CA: Rowman Altamira.

Benediktsson, K., Manning, S., Moran, W. and Anderson, G. (1990) *Participation of Ragian County Farm Households in the Labour Force*, Occasional Publication 27, Auckland: Department of Geography, University of Auckland.

Bennet, B. and Zubrzycki, J. (2003) 'Hearing the stories of Australian and Aboriginal and Torres Strait Islander social workers: challenging and educating the system', *Australian Social Work*, 56, 1, pp 61–70.

Bennett, M. (2007) 'Kalahui Hawaii: Self-government Bill introduced', Speech by the Hawaii Attorney General originally reported in the *Hawaii Reporter*, available online at: www.unpo.org/content/view/6668/118/

Bevan, M., Cameron, S., Coombes, M., Merridew, T. and Raybould, S. (2001) *Social Housing in Rural Areas*, York: Joseph Rowntree Foundation.

Bienkowska, M. (1999) 'The activation of local communities in Poland as illustrated by the Small Homelands Program', *Eastern European Countryside*, 5, pp 75–81.

Big Lottery Fund Research (2008) *More Than a Number: A Study of Young People's Experiences of Mental Health Services in Rural Wales*, Cardiff: Big Lottery Fund.

Bilken, D. (1983) *Community Organizing*, Englewood Cliffs, NJ: Prentice-Hall.

Billig, M. (1976) *Social Psychology and Intergroup Relations*, London: Academic Press.

Black, A. and Hughes, P. (2001) *The Identification and Analysis of Indicators of Community Strength and Outcomes*, Occasional Paper No 3, Canberra: Department of Family and Community Services.

Blackburn, S., Skerratt, S., Warren, M. and Errington, A. (2003) *Rural Communities and the Voluntary Sector*, London: Department for Environment, Food and Rural Affairs, also available at: www.defra.gov.uk

Blacksell, M., Clark, A., Economides, K. and Watkins, C. (1988) 'Legal services in rural areas: problems of access and local need', *Progress in Human Geography*, 12, 1, pp 47–65.

Bodor, R. (2008) 'Nonsexual dual and multiple relationships; when urban worldviews define rural reality', *Rural Social Work and Community Practice*, 13, 1, pp 7–19.

Bodor, R. and Zapf, K. (2002) 'The learning circle: a new model of rural social work education from Canada', *Rural Social Work*, 7, 2, pp 4–15.

Bodor, R., Zapf, M.K., Bastien, B., Carriere, J., Pelech, W. and Kallsen, L. (2001) *A Canadian Model of Distance Social Work Education: The Learning Circle*, Paper presented at the Australian Association of Social Workers National Conference, Melbourne, Australia.

Bodor, R., Green, R., Lonne, B. and Zapf, K. (2004) '40 degrees above or below zero: rural social work and context in Australia and Canada', *Rural Social Work*, 9, pp 49–59.

Bone, R., Cheers, B. and Yip, K. (1993) *The Needs of Young People in the Hinchinbrook Shire*, Townsville: Welfare Research and Studies Centre, James Cook University of North Queensland.

Boonstra, W. J. (2006) 'Policies in the Polder: how institutions mediate between norms and practices of rural governance', *Sociologica Ruralis*, 46, 4, pp 299–317.

Borys, D. S. and Pope, K. (1989) 'Dual relationships between therapist and client: a national study of psychologists, psychiatrists and social workers', *Professional Psychology: Research and Practice*, 20, 5, pp 283–93.

Boushel, M. (1994) 'The protective environment of children: towards a framework for anti-oppressive, cross-cultural, and cross-national understanding', *British Journal of Social Work*, 28, 2, pp 173–90.

Bowden, C. and Moseley, M. (2006) *The Quality and Accessibility of Services in Rural England: A Survey of the Perspectives of Disadvantaged Residents*, Wolverhampton: ADAS, also available at: www.defra.gov.uk

Boyle, P. (1995) 'Rural in-migration in England and Wales 1980–1981', *Journal of Rural Studies*, 11, 1, pp 65–78, cited in S. Hartwell, L. Kitchen, P. Milbourne and S. Morgan (2007) *Population Change in Rural Wales: Social and Cultural Impacts*, Cardiff: Wales Rural Observatory Research Report No 12, available online at: www.walesruralobservatory.org.uk

Brager, G. and Specht, H. (1973) *Community Organizing*, New York: Columbia University Press.

Bramley, G., Lancaster, S. and Gordon, D. (2000) 'Benefit take-up and the geography of poverty in Scotland', *Regional Studies*, 34, 6, pp 507–20.

Brandth, B. (2002) 'Gender identity in European family farming: a literature review', *Sociologica Ruralis*, 42, 3, pp 181–201.

Brave Heart, M.Y.H. (1999) 'Gender differences in the historical trauma response among the Lakota', *Journal of Health and Social Policy*, 10, 4, pp 1–21.

Brawley, E.A. (1995) *Human Services and the Media: Developing Partnerships for Change*, Luxembourg: Harwood Academic Publishers.

Brearley, M. (1996) *The Roma/Gypsies of Europe: A Persecuted People*, London: Institute for Jewish Policy Research.

Breitenbach, E. (2004) 'Researching lesbian, gay, bisexual and transgender issues in Northern Ireland', Belfast: Office of First Minister and Deputy First Minister, Stormont, available online at: www.ofmdfmni.gov.uk/transgender.pdf

Bridger, J., Luloff, A.E., Ploch, L.A. and Steele, J. (2001) 'A fifty-year overview of persistence and change in an old order Amish community', *Journal of the Community Development Society*, 32, 1, pp 65–87.

Bridget, J. (1996) *Effects of Multi-Oppression on Lesbian and Gay Youth*, Todmorden, Lancashire, available online at: www.lesbianinformationservice.org

Briskman, L. (2007) *Social Work with Indigenous Communities*, Sydney: Federation Press.

Brown, H. and Smith, H. (1993) 'Women caring for people: the mismatch between rhetoric and women's reality', *Policy & Politics*, 21, 3, pp 185–93.

Brown, J.C. (1933) *The Rural Community and Social Casework*, New York: Little and Ives.

Brown, L., Tucker, C. and Domokos, T. (2003) 'Evaluating the impact of integrated health and social care teams on older people living in the community', *Health and Social Care in the Community*, 11, 2, pp 85–94.

Brownlee, K., Graham, J., Doucette, E., Hotson, N. and Halverson, G. (2009) 'Have communication technologies influenced rural social work practice?', *British Journal of Social Work*, advance access, 16 February, pp 1–16.

Brummell, V. (1985) 'Rural social work – the end of the line?', *Australian Social Work*, 38, 4, pp 50–72.

Bryant, L. (1991) 'Farm family displacement', in M. Alston (ed), *Family Farming: Australia and New Zealand*, Key papers No 2, Centre for Rural Social Research, School of Humanities and Social Sciences, Charles Sturt University, Riverina, Wagga Wagga, pp 81–96.

Buller, H., Morris, C. and Wright, E. (2003) *The Demography of Rural Areas: A Literature Review*, London: DEFRA.

Bulmer, M. (1987) *The Social Bases of Community Care*, London: Allen and Unwin.

Burgess, C., Cheers, B. and Fisher, D. (2004) 'Early intervention parenting assistance for rural and remote families in South Australia', *Rural Social Work*, 9, pp 69–77.

Burnett, K.A. (1996) 'Once an incomer, always an incomer?', in P. Chapman and S. Lloyd (eds), *Women and Access in Rural Areas*, Farnham, Surrey: Ashgate.

Burnley, I. (1995) 'Socio-economic and spatial differentials in mortality and means of committing suicide in New South Wales, Australia, 1985–91', *Social Science and Medicine*, 41, 5, pp 687–98.

Burns, N., Parr, H. and Philo, C. (2002) 'User networks: social geographies of rural mental health', Glasgow: University of Glasgow, ESRC Award R000 23 8453, available online at: www.esrcsocietytoday.ac.uk

Burton, M. (2006) 'The effective interventions initiatives and the high number of Maori in the criminal justice system', Presentation at the New Zealand Police Management Development Conference, Royal New Zealand Police College, Porirua.

Butler, I. and Pugh, R. (2004) 'The politics of social work research', in R. Lovelock, K. Lyons and J. Powell (eds), *Reflecting on Social Work*, Farnham, Surrey: Ashgate, pp 56–72.

CAB (Citizens Advice Bureau) (2007) *Supporting Migrant Workers in Rural Areas: A Guide to Citizens Advice Bureaux Initiatives*, London: CAB.

Cairns, T., Fulcher, L., Kereopa, H., NiaNia, P. and Tait-Rolleston, W. (1998) 'Nga pari karangaranga o puao-te-atu-tu: toward culturally responsive education and training for social workers in New Zealand', *Canadian Social Work Review*, 15, 2, pp 145–67.

Campbell, H., Bell, M.M. and Finney, M. (2006) *Country Boys: Masculinity and Rural Life*, Rural Studies Series of the Rural Sociological Society, College Station, PA: Penn State University Press.

Carlton-LaNey, I. (1998) 'Elderly black farm women: a population at risk', in L.H. Ginsberg (ed), *Social Work in Rural Communities*, Alexandria, VA: Council for Social Work Education, pp 199–212.

Castex, G.M. (1994) 'Providing services to Hispanic/Latino populations: profiles in diversity', *Social Work*, 39, 3, pp 288–96.

Castles, I. (1995) *Year Book Australia 1995*, Canberra: ABS.

Cavaye, J. (2000) *The Role of Government in Community Capacity Building*, Brisbane: Department of Primary Industries.

Cemlyn, S. (2000) 'Assimilation, control, mediation or advocacy? Social work dilemmas in providing anti-oppressive services for traveller children and families', *Child and Family Social Work*, 5, 4, pp 327–41.

Cemlyn, S. and Briskman, L. (2003) 'Asylum, children's rights and social work', *Child and Family Social Work*, 8, 3, pp 163–78.

Cemlyn, S. and Clark, C. (2005) 'The social exclusion of Gypsy and traveller children', in G. Preston (ed), *At Greater Risk: The Children Most Likely To Be Poor*, London: CPAG, pp 150–65.

Chakraborti, N. and Garland, J. (2003) 'An "invisible" problem? Uncovering the nature of racist victimisation in rural Suffolk', *International Review of Victimology*, 10, 1, pp 1-17.

Chakraborti, N. and Garland, J. (eds) (2004) *Rural Racism*, Cullompton, Devon: Willan Publishing.

Chamberlayne, P., Cooper, A., Freeman, R. and Rustin, M. (1999) *Welfare and Culture in Europe: Towards a New Paradigm in Social Policy*, London: Jessica Kingsley.

Chambers, R. (1994) 'The origins and practice of participatory rural appraisal', *World Development*, 22, 7, pp 953–69.

Champion, A. (1989) *Counterurbanisation*, London: Edward Arnold.

Champion, T. and Watkins, C. (1991) *People in the Countryside*, London: Paul Chapman Publishing.

Chapman, P., Phimister, E., Shucksmith, M., Upward, R. and Vera-Toscano, E. (1998) *Poverty and Exclusion in Rural Britain: The Dynamics of Low Income and Employment*, York: York Publishing Services.

Charles, N. and Davies, C.A. (2005) 'Studying the particular, illuminating the general: community studies and community in Wales', *The Sociological Review*, 53, 4, pp 672–90.

Chartrand, P. (1991) 'Terms of division: problems of outsider naming for Aboriginal people in Canada', *Journal of Indigenous Studies*, 2, 2, pp 1–22.

Chavez, S. (2005) 'Community, ethnicity and class in a changing rural California town', *Rural Sociology*, 70, 3, pp 314–35.

Cheers, B. (1986) 'Integrating a rural perspective into social work training', in R. Berreen, D. Grace and T. Vinson (eds), *Advances in Social Work Education 1986*, Kensington, NSW: University of New South Wales Press, pp 22–34.

Cheers, B. (1992) 'Social support in small remote towns in Far North and North-west Queensland, Australia: implications for human services', Unpublished PhD thesis, James Cook University of North Queensland, Townsville.

Cheers, B. (1998) *Welfare Bushed: Social Care in Rural Australia*, Aldershot: Ashgate.

Cheers, B. (2001) 'Social support in remote areas of Australia', *Rural Social Work*, 6, 2, pp 4–16.

Cheers, B. and Luloff, A. (2001) 'Rural community development', in S. Lockie and L. Bourke (eds), *Rurality Bites: The Social and Environmental Transformation of Rural Australia*, Annandale: Pluto Press, pp 129–42.

Cheers, B. and Taylor, J. (2005) 'Social work in rural and remote Australia', in M. Alston and J. McKinnon (eds), *Social Work Fields of Practice*, Oxford: Oxford University Press, pp 237–48.

Cheers, B. and Yip, K. (1994) *The Needs of Young People in the Hinchinbrook Shire*, Townsville: Welfare Research and Studies Centre, James Cook University of North Queensland.

Cheers, B., Edwards, J. and Graham, L. (2003) 'A better place to be – strengthening rural communities in Australia', in *Diversity and Inclusion: Putting the Principles to Work / Diversite et Inclusion: Mettre les Principes en Pratique, Proceedings of the Canadian Association of Schools of Social Work Conference / Association Canadienne des Ecoles de Service Social*, Halifax: Dalhousie University.

Cheers, B., Darracott, R. and Lonne, B. (2005a) 'Domains of rural social work practice', *Rural Society*, 15, 3, pp 234–51.

Cheers, B., Kruger, M. and Trigg, H. (2005b) *Community Capacity Audit Project Technical Report*, Whyalla: Centre for Rural Health and Community Development, University of South Australia, and PIRSA/Rural Solutions.

Cheers, B., Binell, M., Coleman, H., Gentle, I., Miller, G., Taylor, J. and Weetra, C. (2006a) 'Family violence: an Australian Indigenous community', *International Social Work*, 49, 1, pp 51–63.

Cheers, B., Fernando, D., Gentle, I., Gibbs, J., Miller, P., Semple, S. and Sparrow, S. (2006b) *Plants for People – South Australia, Final Project Report*, Alice Springs: Desert Knowledge Cooperative Research Centre.

Cheers, B., Darracott, R. and Lonne, B. (2007) *Social Care Practice in Rural Communities*, Leichhardt: Federation Press.

Clapton, S., Lonne, B. and Theunissen, C. (1999) 'Multi-victim sexual assault: a case study in rural Australia', *Child Abuse and Neglect*, 23, 4, pp 395–404.

Clark, C. (1998) 'Counting backwards: the Roma 'numbers game' in Central and Eastern Europe', *Radstats*, 69, Autumn.

Claude, L., Bridger, J.C. and Luloff, A.E. (1999) 'Community well-being and local activeness', in P. Schaeffer and S. Loveridge (eds), *Small Town and Rural Economic Development: A Case Studies Approach*, Westport, CT: Greenwood Press, pp 39–45.

Cleland, C. (1995) 'Measuring rurality', *Human Services in the Rural Environment*, 18, 4, pp 13–18.

Cloke, P. and Little, J. (1997) *Contested Countryside Cultures: Otherness, Marginalisation and Rurality*, London: Routledge.

Cloke, P., Doel, M., Matless, D., Phillips, M. and Thrift, N. (1994) *Writing the Rural: Five Cultural Geographies*, London: Paul Chapman.

Cloke, P., Goodwin, M. and Milbourne, P. (1997) *Rural Wales: Community and Marginalisation*, Cardiff: University of Wales Press.

Clyde, Lord J. (1992) *Report of the Inquiry into the Removal of Children from Orkney in February 1991*, Edinburgh: HMSO.

Coates, J., Gray, M. and Hetherington, T. (2006) 'An "ecospiritual" perspective: finally a place for indigenous approaches', *British Journal of Social Work*, 36, 3, pp 381–99.

Cody, P.J. and Welch, P.L. (1997) 'Rural gay men in Northern New England: life experiences and coping styles', *Journal of Homosexuality*, 33, 1, pp 51–67.

Cohen, A. P. (1982) *Belonging: Identity and Social Organisation in British Rural Cultures*, Manchester: Manchester University Press.

Coleman, M. (2000) *Online Therapy and the Clinical Social Worker – NASW Social Work Practice Update*, Washington DC: National Association of Social Workers.

Collier, K. (1984) *Social Work with Rural Peoples: Theory and Practice*, Vancouver: New Star Books.

Collings, J. and Murray, P. (1996) 'Predictors of stress among social workers: an empirical study', *British Journal of Social Work* 26, 3, pp 375–87.

Commission for Rural Communities (2006a) *Rural Services Standard – Fifth Progress Report 2005/6*, Cheltenham: CRC.

Commission for Rural Communities (2006b) *Challenging Government to Meet Rural Needs – Rural Proofing Monitoring Report 2006*, Cheltenham: CRC.

Community Development Foundation (2006) *An Analysis of the Rural Impacts of Public Sector Interventions to Tackle Social Exclusion*, Welshpool, Powys: Resources for Change, also available at: www.defra.gov.uk

Coorey, L. (1988) *Domestic Violence and the Police: Who is Being Protected? A Rural Australian View*, Sydney: University of Sydney Printing Service, University of Sydney.

Countryside Agency (2003) *The Rural Services Standard: Second Progress Report 2002/03*, Wetherby: Countryside Agency, also available at: www.countryside.gov.uk

Countryside Agency (2004) *Rural Proofing the Delivery Chain*, Cheltenham: Countryside Agency, available online at: www.ruralcommunities.gov.uk/files/CRN%2076.pdf

Coward, R.T., McLaughlin, D.K., Duncan, R.P. and Bull, C.N. (1994) 'An overview of health and aging in rural America', in R.T. Coward, C.N. Bull, G. Kukulka and J.M. Galliher (eds), *Health Services for Rural Elders*, New York: Springer, pp 1–32.

Craig, G. and Manthorpe, J. (1999) *Unfinished Business: Local Government Reorganisation and Social Services*, Bristol: The Policy Press.

CRE (Commission for Racial Equality) (2006) *Common Ground: Equality, Good Race Relations and Sites for Gypsies and Irish Travellers*, London: CRE.

Cribb, J. (1994) 'Farewell to the Heartland', *The Australian Magazine*, February 10-16, pp 12–13.

Crow, G. and Allan, G. (1994) *Community Life: An Introduction to Local Social Relations*, London: Harvester Wheatsheaf.

Crwydren, R. (1994) 'Welsh lesbian feminist: a contradiction in terms?', in J. Aaron, T. Rees, S. Betts and M. Vincentelli (eds), *Our Sister's Land: The Changing Identities of Women in Wales*, Cardiff: University of Wales Press, pp 294–300.

CSCI (Commission for Social Care Inspection) (2006) *Time to Care?*, London: CSCI.

Csepeli, G. and Simon, D. (2004) 'Construction of Roma identity in Eastern and Central Europe: perception and self-identification', *Journal of Ethnic and Migration Studies*, 30, 1, pp 129–50.

Cummins, R., Gentle, I. and Hull, C. (2008) 'Community: Aboriginal Australian perspectives', in J. Taylor, D. Wilkinson and B. Cheers (eds), *Working with Communities in Health and Human Services*, South Melbourne: Oxford University Press, pp 43–60.

Dabydeen, D., Gilmore, J. and Jones, C. (2007) *The Oxford Companion to Black British History*, Oxford: Oxford University Press.

Dahlstrom, M. (1996) 'Young women in a male periphery – experiences from the Scandinavian North', *Journal of Rural Studies*, 12, 3, pp 259–71.

Daley, M.R. and Avant, F.L. (2004) 'Rural social work: reconceptualizing the framework for practice', in T.L. Scales and C.L. Streeter (eds), *Rural Social Work: Building and Sustaining Community Assets*, Belmont, CA: Thomson Brooks/Cole, pp 34–42.

Dana, R., Behn, J. and Gonwa, T. (1992) 'Checklist for the examination of the cultural competence of social services agencies', *Research on Social Work Practice*, 2, 2, pp 220–33.

D'Augelli, A.R., Grossman, A.H. and Hershberger, S.L. (2001a) 'Aspects of mental health among older lesbian, gay and bisexual adults', *Ageing and Mental Health*, 5, 2, pp 149–58.

D'Augelli, A.R., Pilkington, N.W. and Hershberger, S.L. (2001b) 'Suicidality patterns and sexual orientation-related factors among lesbian, gay and bisexual youths', *Suicide and Life Threatening Behavior*, 31, 3, pp 250–64.

Davis, J. (2001) 'American Indian boarding school experiences: recent studies from native perspectives', *Magazine of History*, 15, Winter, pp 1–7, Organization of American Historians, available online at: www.oah.org/pubs/magazine/deseg/davis.html

Davis, V. (2007) *Democratic Processes and the Governance of Indigenous Communities*, Washington, DC: National Congress of American Indians, available online at: www.ncai.org

Davis, L.E. and Proctor, E.K. (1989) *Race, Gender and Class: Guidelines for Practice with Individuals, Families and Groups*, Englewood Cliffs, NJ: Prentice Hall.

Deaville, J. (2001) *The Nature of Rural General Practice in the UK – Preliminary Research*, Gregynog, Newtown, Powys: British Medical Association/Institute for Rural Health.

DEFRA (Department for Environment, Food and Rural Affairs) (2002) *The Way Ahead for Rural Services: A Guide to Good Practice in Locating Rural Services*, London: DEFRA, also available at: www.defra.gov.uk

DEFRA (2004a) *Survey of Rural Customers' Satisfaction with Services*, London: DEFRA, available at: www.defra.gov.uk

DEFRA (2004b) *Social and Economic Change and Diversity in Rural England*, London: DEFRA, also available at: www.defra.gov.uk

DEL (Department of Employment and Learning) (2007) *Attitudes to Migrant Workers: Results from the Northern Ireland Omnibus Survey*, Belfast: DEL and the Northern Ireland Statistics and Research Agency.

Delaney, R. and Brownlee, K. (1995) 'Ethical considerations for Northern social workers', in R. Delaney and K. Brownlee (eds), *Northern Social Work Practice*, Thunder Bay: Lakehead University Press, pp 162–81.

Delanty, G. (2003) *Community*, London: Routledge.

de Lima, P. (1999) 'Research and action in the Scottish Highlands', in P. Henderson and R. Kaur (eds), *Rural Racism in the UK*, London: The Community Development Foundation, pp 33–43.

de Lima, P. (2001) *Needs Not Numbers: An Exploration of Minority Ethnic Communities in Scotland*, London: Commission for Racial Equality and the Community Development Foundation.

de Lima, P. (2004) 'John O'Groats to Land's End: racial equality in rural Britain', in N. Chakraborti and J. Garland (eds), *Rural Racism*, Cullompton, Devon: Willan Publishing, pp 36-60.

de Lima, P. (2006) '"Let's keep our heads down and maybe the problem will go away": experiences of rural minority ethnic households in Scotland', in S. Neal and J. Agyeman (eds), *The New Countryside: Ethnicity, Nation and Exclusion in Contemporary Rural Britain*, Bristol: The Policy Press, pp 73–97.

de Lima, P., Jentsch, B. and Whelton, R. (2005) *Migrant Workers in the Highlands and Islands*, Inverness: Highlands and Islands Enterprise, available online at: hie.co.uk/migrant-workers-in-the-highlands-and-islands-report-2005.pdf

Dench, G., Gavron, K. and Young, M. (2006) *The New East End: Kinship, Race and Conflict*, London: Profile Books.

Denham, C. and White, I. (1998) 'Differences in urban and rural Britain', *Population Trends*, 91, Spring, pp 23–34.

Department of Corrections (2001) *About Time: Turning People Away From a Life of Crime and Reducing Re-offending*, Auckland, NZ: Department of Corrections, available online at: www.corrections.govt.nz/public/pdf/publications/abouttime.pdf

Department of Families, Youth and Community Care (1997) *RAATSICCP Calendar*, Brisbane: Department of Families, Youth and Community Care.

DePoy, E. and Butler, S. (1996) 'Health: elderly women's conceptions', *Affilia*, 11, 2, pp 207–20.

De Warren, D. (2008) 'A queer community study of gay men residing in a small city of regional Queensland, Australia', Unpublished PhD thesis, University of South Australia.

DFACS (Department of Families and Community Services) (1994) *RAATSICCP Services Progress Summary 1994*, Brisbane: DFACS.

DFACS (1995) *North Queensland Community Services Development Regional Profile*, Brisbane: DFACS.

Dhalech, M. (1999) 'Race equality initiatives in South-West England', in P. Henderson and R. Kaur (eds), *Rural Racism in the UK*, London: The Community Development Foundation, pp 11-21.

Dickson-Gilmore, J. and La Prairie, C. (2005) *Will the Circle be Unbroken: Aboriginal Communities, Restorative Justice, and the Challenge of Conflict and Change*, Toronto, ON: University of Toronto Press.

Dixon, J. and Scheurell, R. (1995) *Social Welfare with Indigenous Peoples*, London: Routledge.

Dobbs, J., Green, H. and Zealey, L. (2006) *Focus on Ethnicity and Religion*, Newport, Wales: Office of National Statistics, available online at: www.statistics.gov.uk

Dollard, M.F., Winefield, H.R. and Winefield, A.H. (1999) 'Burnout and job satisfaction in rural and metropolitan social workers', *Rural Social Work*, 4, pp 32–42.

Dominelli, L. (1988) *Anti-Racist Social Work*, Basingstoke: Macmillan.

Drennan, J., Treacy, M., Butler, M., Byrne, A., Fealy, G., Frazer, K. and Irving, K. (2008) 'The experience of social and emotional loneliness among older people in Ireland', *Ageing & Society*, 28, 8, pp 1113–32.

Eaton, S. (1995) *Multi-Agency Work with Young People in Difficulty*, Rowntree Research Findings, Social Care Research 68, York: Joseph Rowntree Foundation, available online at: www.jrf.org.uk

Edwards, J. and Cheers, B. (2007) 'Is social capital good for everyone? The case of same-sex attracted women in rural South Australian communities', *Health Sociology Review*, 16, 3, pp 226–36.

Edwards, B., Goodwin, M., Pemberton, S. and Woods, M. (1999) *Partnership Working in Rural Regeneration*, Rowntree Research Findings, York: Joseph Rowntree Foundation, available online at: www.jrf.org.uk

Ellen Walsh, M. (1989) 'Rural social work practice', in B. Compton and B. Galaway (eds), *Social Work Processes*, Pacific Grove: CA: Brooks/Cole Publishing, pp 586–94.

Emmett, I. (1964) *A North Wales Village: A Social Anthropological Study*, London: Routledge and Kegan Paul.

Esping-Anderson, G. (1990) *Three Worlds of Welfare Capitalism*, Princeton, NJ: Princeton University Press.

Evans-Campbell, T. (2008) 'Historical trauma in American Indian/Native Alaska communities', *Journal of Interpersonal Violence*, 23, 3, pp 316–38.

Eversole, R., McNeish, J. and Cimadamore, A.D. (eds) (2005) *Indigenous Peoples and Poverty: An International Perspective*, London: Zed Books.

Falk, W., Hunt, L. and Hunt, M. (2004) 'Return migrations of African-Americans to the South: reclaiming a land of promise, going home, or both?', *Rural Sociology*, 69, 4, pp 490–509.

Farber, N., Miller-Cribbs, J.E. and Reitmeier, M.C. (2005) 'Kin networks in the South: a comparison of low-income, rural African-American and white women', *Rural Social Work*, 10, 1, pp 52–62.

Findlay, R.A. and Sheehan, M.C. (2004) 'Utilisation of mental health services in rural and remote communities', *Journal of Rural Community Psychology*, 7, 1, only available online at: www.marshall.edu/jrcp/e62_findlay.htm

Fischer, C. (1982) *To Dwell Among Friends: Personal Networks in Town and City*, Chicago, IL: The University of Chicago Press.

Flora, J.L. (1998) 'Social capital and communities of place', *Rural Sociology*, 63, 1, pp 481–506.

Flora, J.L., Sharp, J., Flora, C. and Newlon, B. (1997) 'Entrepreneurial social infrastructure and locally initiated economic development in the nonmetropolitan United States', *The Sociological Quarterly*, 3, 4, pp 623–45.

Fluharty, C. (2002) Keynote speech at the 27th Annual National Rural Social Work Conference, Frostburg, MD, 17 July, cited in N. Lohmann and R.A. Lohmann (eds), *Rural Social Work Practice*, New York: Columbia University Press, pp xi–xxvii.

Fook, J. (1993) *Radical Casework: A Theory of Practice*, St Leonards, NSW: Allen and Unwin.

Fook, J. (2002) *Social Work: Critical Theory and Practice*, London: Sage.

Foster, S.J. (1997) 'Rural lesbians and gays: public perceptions, worker perceptions, and service delivery', in J. Smith and R. Mancoske (eds), *Rural Gays and Lesbians: Building on the Strengths of Communities*, New York: Haworth Press, pp 23–35.

FPC (The Foreign Policy Centre) (2002) *Independent Asylum Commission*, London: FPC.

Francis, D. and Henderson, P. (1992) *Working with Rural Communities*, Basingstoke: Macmillan.

Frank, F. and Smith, A. (1999) *The Community Development Handbook: A Tool to Build Community Capacity*, Quebec: Human Resources Development Canada, Government of Canada Publications, available online at: www.hrsdc.gc.ca/eng/epb/sid/cia/comm_deve/cdhbooke.pdf

Frankenberg, R. (1957) *Village on the Border*, London: Cohen and West.

Franklin Harbour Community Development Group (2002) *A Community Plan for the Franklin Harbour District*, Cowell, South Australia: Franklin Harbour Development Group.

Freedman, L. and Stark, L. (1993) 'When the white system doesn't fit', *Australian Social Work*, 46, 1, pp 29–36.

Freudenberg, W.R. and Jones, R.E. (1991) 'Criminal behaviour and rapid community growth: examining the evidence', *Rural Sociology*, 56, 4, pp 619–45.

Fryer, P. (1984) *Staying Power: The History of Black People in Britain*, London: Pluto Press.

Fuller-Thomson, E. and Minkler, M. (2005) 'American Indian/Alaskan Native grandparents raising grandchildren: findings from the Census 2000 Supplementary Survey', *Social Work*, 50, 2, pp 131–9.

Galbreath, W. (2005) 'Dual relationships in rural communities', in N. Lohmann and R. Lohmann (eds), *Rural Social Work Practice*, New York: Columbia University Press, pp 105–23.

Gallaway, B. (1996) 'Wrong question asked?', *The Social Worker*, 64 (Spring), p 14.

Ganguli, M., Gilby, J., Seaberg, E. and Belle, S. (1995) 'Depressive symptoms and associated factors in a rural elderly population: the MoVIES Project', *American Journal of Geriatric Psychiatry*, 3, 2, pp 144–60.

Giarchi, G. (ed) (2007) *Challenging Welfare Issues in the Global Countryside*, London: Blackwell.

Gibbs, J. (2001) 'Pre-service education and qualification – the impact on recruitment and retention in rural child protection', *Rural Social Work*, 6, 2, pp 19–28.

Gibbs, J. and Keating, T. (1999) 'Recruitment and retention of child protection workers in rural Victoria', Unpublished report to the Victorian Department of Human Services, La Trobe University, Albury/Wodonga Campus.

Gilbert, J. (1999) 'Responding to mental distress in the Third World: cultural imperialism or the struggle for synthesis', *Development in Practice*, 9, 3, pp 155–67.

Gilbert, A., Philip, L. and Shucksmith, M. (2006) 'Rich and poor in the countryside', in P. Lowe and L. Speakman (eds), *The Ageing Countryside: The Growing Older Population of Rural England*, London: Age Concern, pp 69–93.

Gilpin, N., Henty, M., Lemos, S., Portes, J. and Bullen, C. (2006) *The Impact of Free Movement of Workers from Central and Eastern Europe on the UK Labour Market*, Department for Work and Pensions Working Paper No 26, Leeds: Department for Work and Pensions.

Ginsberg, L.H. (1980) 'Foreword', in E. Martinez-Brawley (ed), *Pioneer Efforts in Rural Social Welfare: Firsthand Views Since 1908*, University Park, PA, and London: Pennsylvania State University Press.

Ginsberg, L.H. (ed) (1998) *Social Work in Rural Communities* (3rd edn), Alexandria, VA: Council on Social Work Education.

Glendinning, C., Clarke, S., Hare, P., Kotchetkova, I. Maddison, J. and Newbronner, L. (2006) *Outcomes Focused Services for Older People*, London: SCIE.

Goddard, C. and Liddell, M. (2002) 'Abuse in the desert', *Community Care*, May, p 45.

Goffman, E. (1968) *Stigma: Notes on the Management of Spoiled Identity*, Harmondsworth: Pelican.

Goodfellow, M. (1983) 'Reasons for use and nonuse of social services among the rural elderly', *Human Services in the Rural Environment*, 8, 4, pp 10–16.

Goodwin, M. (2000) 'The governance of rural areas: some emerging research issues and agendas', *Journal of Rural Studies*, 14, 1, pp 5–12.

Gottleib, M. (1993) 'Avoiding exploitative dual relationships: a decision-making model', *Psychotherapy: Theory, Research, Practice and Training*, 30, 1, pp 41–8.

Graham, J., Brownlee, K. and Ritchie, I. (1996) 'AIDS, social work, and the coming home phenomenon', *The Social Worker*, 64, 4, pp 74–84.

Grant, G. (1984) 'The rural–urban dichotomy in social care: rhetoric and reality', in J. Lishman (ed), *Social Work in Rural and Urban Areas*, Research Highlights 9, Aberdeen: Department of Social Work, Aberdeen University, pp 46–68.

Gray, M., Coates, J. and Yellow Bird, M. (2008) *Indigenous Social Work Around the World: Towards Culturally Relevant Education and Practice*, Aldershot: Ashgate.

Green, E.J. (2006) '"Staying bush" – a study of gay men who live in rural areas', Unpublished PhD thesis, University of New South Wales, available online at: www.library.unsw.edu.au/~thesis/adt-NUN/uploads/approved/adt-NUN20070102.145032/public/02whole.pdf

Green, J. (1999) *Cultural Awareness in the Human Services*, Needham Heights, MA: Allyn and Bacon.

Green, R. (2003a) 'Social work in rural areas: a personal and professional challenge', *Australian Social Work*, 56, 3, pp 209–19.

Green, R. (2003b) 'Only in exceptional circumstances! Education in Australia for rural social work and welfare practice', *Rural Social Work*, 8, 1, pp 50–7.

Green, J. and Thomas, R. (2005) 'Learning through our children, healing for our children: best practice in First Nations communities', in L. Dominelli (ed), *Communities in a Globalising World: Theory and Practice for Community Empowerment*, Aldershot: Ashgate, pp 1–34.

Green, J. and Thomas, R. (2009) 'Children in the centre: indigenous perspectives on anti-oppressive child welfare practice', in S. Strega and J. Carrière (eds), *Walking this Path Together: Anti-Oppressive Practice in Child Welfare*, Halifax, NS: Fernwood Publishing.

Green, R. and Lonne, B. (2005) 'Great lifestyle, pity about the job stress: occupational stress in rural human service practice', *Rural Society*, 15, 3, pp 252–66.

Green, R. and Mason, R. (2002) 'Managing confidentiality in rural welfare practice in Australia', *Rural Social Work*, 7, 1, pp 34–43.

Green, R., Gregory, R. and Mason, R. (2003) 'It's no picnic: personal and family safety for rural workers', *Australian Social Work*, 56, 2, pp 94–106.

Greenfield, L. and Smith, S. (1999) *American Indians and Crime*, Washington, DC: Department of Justice.

Greer, A. (2005) *Agricultural Policy in Europe*, Manchester: Manchester University Press.

Grewal, J. (2000) 'Pushing the limits and finding a center on the margins', *Diversity Digest*, available online at: www.umd.edu/DiversityWeb/Digest

Griffith, D.A. (1994) 'A Northern Territory approach to quantifying "Access Disadvantage" to educational services in remote and rural Australia', Issues Affecting Rural Communities: Proceedings of an International Conference held by the Rural Education Research and Development Centre, Townsville, Queensland, Australia, 10–15 July, pp 311–14, also available online at www.eric.ed.gov/

Gross, E.R. (2003) 'Native American family continuity as resistance', *Journal of Social Work*, 3, 1, pp 31–44.

Gumpert, J., Saltman, J.E. and Sauer-Jones, D. (2000) 'Toward identifying the unique characteristics of social work practice in rural areas: from the voices of practitioners', *The Journal of Baccalaureate Social Work*, 6, 1, pp 19–35.

Haase, T. (1999) 'Affluence and deprivation: a spatial analysis based on the 1991 census of population', in D. Pringle, J. Walsh and M. Hennessy (eds), *Poor People, Poor Places: Geography of Poverty and Deprivation in Ireland*, Dublin: Oak Tree Press and Geographical Society of Ireland, pp 13–36.

Hadley, R. and McGrath, M. (1980) *Going Local: Neighbourhood Social Services*, London: Bedford Square Press.

Hager, M.A., Brimer, A. and Pollak, T.H. (2005) 'The distribution of nonprofit social service organizations along the rural–urban continuum', in N. Lohmann and R. Lohmann (eds), *Rural Social Work Practice*, New York: Columbia University Press, pp 73–85.

Hague, G. (1997) 'Smoke screen or leap forward: interagency initiatives as a response to domestic violence', *Critical Social Policy*, 17, 53, pp 93-109.

Hague, G. (2000) *Reducing Domestic Violence: What Works – Multi-Agency Fora*, London: Home Office.

Halfacree, K. (1993) 'Locality and social representation: space, discourse and alternative definitions of rurality', *Journal of Rural Studies*, 9, 1, pp 23–34.

Halhead, V. (2007) 'Rural movements in Europe: Scandinavia and the Accession States', in G. Giarchi (ed), *Challenging Welfare Issues in the Global Countryside*, London: Blackwell, pp 18–33.

Hanson, G. (2007) 'Guest v gatecrashers: the uncomfortable economics of immigration reform', *The Economist*, 31 May, available online at: www.economist.co.uk

Harris. A.P. (2001) 'Foreword', in W.O. Weyrauch (ed), *Gypsy Law: Romani Legal Traditions and Culture*, Berkeley, CA: University of California Press, pp ix–xiv.

Harris, K., Cheers, B. and Hatte, E. (1993a) *South Townsville Inner City Village Project: Social Survey*, Townsville: Welfare Research and Studies Centre, James Cook University of North Queensland.

Harris, K., Cheers, B. and Hatte, E. (1993b) *South Townsville Inner City Village Project: Summary and Recommendations*, Townsville: Welfare Research and Studies Centre, James Cook University of North Queensland.

Harrop, A. and Palmer, G. (2000) *The Costs of the Joint Provision of Services in Rural Communities: A Report for the Countryside Agency*, London: New Policy Initiative.

Harrop, A. and Palmer, G. (2002) *Indicators of Poverty and Social Exclusion in Rural England: A Report for the Countryside Agency*, London: The New Policy Institute, also available online at: www.npi.org.uk/reports/rural%20indicators.pdf

Hart, M. (2002) *Seeking Mino-Pimatisiwin: An Aboriginal Approach to Helping*, Halifax, NS: Fernwood Publishing.

Hartwell, S., Kitchen, L., Milbourne, P. and Morgan, S. (2007) *Population Change in Rural Wales: Social and Cultural Impacts*, Cardiff: Wales Rural Observatory Research Report no 12, available online at: www.walesruralobservatory.org.uk

Haskins, C. (2003) *Rural Delivery Review – A Report on the Delivery of Government Policies in Rural England*, London: Department for the Environment, Food and Rural Affairs, available online at: http://homepages.rya-online.net/cumbriacanoeists/pdf/Haskins-Intro-and-Summary.pdf

Havemann, P. (1999) *Indigenous People's Rights in Australia, Canada and New Zealand*, Auckland: Oxford University Press.

Hawes, D. and Perez, B. (1996) *The Gypsy and the State: The Ethnic Cleansing of British Society*, Bristol: The Policy Press.

Hawton, K., Simkin, S., Malmberg, A., Fagg, J. and Harris, L. (1998) 'Methods used for suicide by farmers in England and Wales', *British Journal of Psychiatry*, 173, 4, pp 320–4.

Hayden, W. (1998) 'African-American Appalachians: barriers to equality', in L.H. Ginsberg (ed), *Social Work in Rural Communities*, Alexandria, VA: Council for Social Work Education, pp 177–97.

Heather, B., Skillen, L., Young, J. and Vladicka, T. (2005) 'Women's gendered identities and the restructuring of rural Alberta', *Sociologia Ruralis*, 45, 1/2, pp 86–97.

Heflin, C. and Pattillo, M. (2002) 'Kin effects on black–white account and home ownership', *Sociological Inquiry*, 72, 2, pp 220–39.

Help the Aged/Rural Development Commission (1996) *Growing Old in the Countryside*, London: Help the Aged and the Rural Development Commission.

Henshall Hansen Associates (1988) *Small Towns Study in Victoria*, Melbourne: Department of Agriculture and Rural Affairs.

Herbert-Cheshire, L. (2003) 'Translating policy: power and action in Australia's country towns', *Sociologica Ruralis*, 43, 4, pp 454–73.

Hering, S. and Waaldijk, B. (2006) *Guardians of the Poor – Custodians of the Public. Welfare History in Eastern Europe 1900–1960*, Opladen and Farmington Hills: Barbara Budrich Publishers.

Hernández-Plaza, S., Alonso-Morillejo, E. and Pozo-Muñoz, C. (2006) 'Social support interventions in migrant populations', *British Journal of Social Work*, 36, 7, pp 1151–69.

Hetherington, R., Cooper, A., Smith, P. and Wilford, G. (1997) *Protecting Children: Messages from Europe*, Lyme Regis: Russell House Publishing.

Hindle, T., Spollen, M. and Dixon, P. (2004) *Review of the Evidence on Additional Costs of Delivering Services to Rural Communities*, London: SECTA, available online at: www.defra.gov.uk

Hodgkin, S. (2002) 'Competing demands, competing solutions, differing constructions of the problem of recruitment and retention of frontline rural child protection staff', *Australian Social Work*, 55, 3, pp 193–203.

Hold, M., Korszon, S., Kotchekova, E. and Grzesiak, F. (2007) *Migrant Workers in Flintshire*, Penmaenmawr: North East Wales Race Equality Network.

Home Office (2007) *The Economic and Fiscal Impact of Immigration*, London: Home Office and Department of Work and Pensions.

Hooyman, N. and Gonyea, J. (1995) *Feminist Perspectives on Family Care: Policies for Gender Justice*, London: Sage.

HREOC (Human Rights and Equal Opportunity Commission) (1997) *Bringing Them Home: Report of the National Enquiry into the Separation of Aboriginal and Torres Strait Islander Children from their Families*, Sydney: HREOC, available online at: www.hreoc.gov.au/pdf/social_justice/bringing_them_home_report.pdf

HREOC (2001) *Frequently Asked Questions*, Sydney: HREOC, available online at: www.humanrights.gov.au/social_justice/bth_report/about/faqs.html#ques9

HREOC (2006) *A Statistical Overview of Aboriginal and Torres Strait Islander Peoples in Australia*, Sydney: HREOC, available online at: www.humanrights.gov.au/social_justice/statistics/index.html#toc4

Humpage, L. (2004) 'Indigenous affairs: old wine in new bottles', Address to RMIT Indigenous Studies students, 22 April, cited in L. Briskman (2007) *Social Work with Indigenous Communities*, Sydney: Federation Press.

Humphries, B. (2004) 'An unacceptable role for social work: implementing immigration policy', *British Journal of Social Work*, 34, 1, pp 93–107.

Hunter, S.V. (2008) 'Child maltreatment in remote Aboriginal communities and the Northern Territory Emergency response: a complex issue', *Australian Social Work*, 61, 4, pp 372–88.

Hurdle, D. (2002) 'Native Hawaiian traditional healing: culturally based interventions for social work practice', *Social Work*, 47, 2, pp 183–92.

IAC (Independent Asylum Commission) (2008) *Fit For Purpose Yet? The Independent Asylum Commission's Interim Findings*, London: IAC, available online at: www.independentasylumcommission.org.uk

ICGPSIA (Interorganizational Committee on Guidelines and Principles for Social Impact Assessment) (1993) 'Guidelines and principles for social impact assessment', ICGPSIA, unpublished manuscript.

Ife, J. and Tesoriero, F. (2006) *Community Development: Community Based Alternatives in an Age of Globalization*, French's Forest: Pearson Education Australia.

IFSW (International Federation of Social Workers) (2005) *International Policy on Indigenous Peoples*, Berne, Switzerland, available online at: www.ifsw.org/en/p38000138.html

IHS (Indian Health Service) (2008) *IHS Fact Sheets: Indian Health Disparities*, Washington, DC: IHS, available online at: http://info.ihs.gov

INAC (Indian and Northern Affairs Canada) (2004) *Words First: An Evolving Terminology Relating to Aboriginal Peoples in Canada*, Ottawa: INAC, available online at: www.cleonet.ca/instance.php?instance_id=1468

Innes, A., Blackstone, K., Mason, A. and Smith, A. (2005) 'Dementia care provision in Scotland: service users' and carers' experiences', *Health and Social Care in the Community*, 13, 4, pp 354–65.

Innes, A., Cox, S., Smith, A. and Mason, A. (2006) 'Service provision for people with dementia in rural Scotland: difficulties and innovations', *Dementia*, 5, 2, pp 249–70.

Institute for Public Policy Research (2007) *The Reception and Integration of New Migrant Communities*, London: Commission for Racial Equality.

ITK (Inuit Tapiriit Kanatami) (2007) *Inuit Statistical Profile*, ITK, Ottawa, Canada, available online at: www.itk.ca/publications/inuit-statistical-profile

Jacobsen, G.M. (1980) 'Rural communities and community development', in H.W. Johnson (ed), *Rural Human Services*, Itasca, IL: Peacock, pp 196–202.

Jay, E. (1992) *Keep Them in Birmingham: Challenging Racism in the South West*, London: Commission for Race Equality.

Jayaratne, S. and Chess, W.A. (1984) 'Job satisfaction, burnout, turnover: a national study', *Social Work*, 29, 5, pp 448–53.

Jedrej, C. and Nuttall, M. (1996) *White Settlers: The Impact of Rural Repopulation in Scotland*, Luxembourg: Harwood Academic Publishers.

Johnson, A. (1998) 'The revitalization of community practice; characteristics, competencies and curricula for community based services', *Journal of Community Practice*, 5, 3, pp 37–62.

Johnson, M. (1998b) 'Ethnic monitoring: bureaucratic construction of a "minority" entity or identity', in C. Williams, H. Soydan and M. Johnson (eds), *Social Work and Ethnic Minorities*, London: Routledge, pp 79–90.

Johnson, P., Wistow, G., Schulz, R. and Hardy, B. (2003) 'Interagency and interprofessional collaboration in community care: the interdependence of structures and values', *Journal of Interprofessional Care*, 17, 1, pp 69–83.

Kagel, J.D. and Giebelhausen, P.N. (1994) 'Dual relationships and professional boundaries', *Social Work*, 39, 2, pp 213–20.

Kahn, S. (1991) *Organizing: A Guide for Grassroots Leaders*, Washington, DC: NASW Press.

Kahn, S. (1994) *How People get Power*, Washington, DC: NASW Press.

Kasimis, C. and Papadopoulos, A. (2005) 'The multifunctional role of migrants in the Greek countryside', *Journal of Ethnic and Migration Studies*, 31,1, pp 99–127.

Kasimis, C., Papadopoulos, A.G. and Zacapoulou, E. (2003) 'Migrants in rural Greece', *Sociologia Ruralis*, 43, 2, pp 167–84.

Kelley, P. and Kelley, V. (1985) 'Supporting natural helpers: a cross-cultural study', *Social Casework*, 66, pp 358–67.

Kelly, S. and Bunting, J. (1998) 'Trends in suicide in England and Wales 1982–1986', *Population Trends*, 92 (Summer), pp 29–41.

Kendall, K. (2000) *Social Work Education: Its Origins in Europe*, Alexandria, VA: CSWE.

Kennedy, V. (2004) 'The relationship between community banking and community development in one rural township in New South Wales', Unpublished BSW (Hons) thesis, University of South Australia, Whyalla.

Kenny, S. (1994) *Developing Communities for the Future: Community Development in Australia*, Melbourne: Nelson.

Khinduka, S. (1971) 'Social work in the Third World', *Social Service Review*, 45, 1, pp 62–73.

Kivett, V.R. (1983) 'Affinal and consanguineal kin as a social support for the rural elderly', Paper of the Journal Series of the North Carolina Agricultural Research Services, Raleigh, NC.

Kohli, R. and Mather, R. (2003) 'Promoting psychosocial well-being in unaccompanied asylum seeking young people in the UK', *Child and Family Social Work*, 8, 3, pp 201–12.

Kornbeck, J. (2003) *Language Teaching in the Social Work Curriculum*, Mainz: Logophon Verlag.

Kretzman, J. and McKnight, J. (1993) *Building Communities From the Inside Out: A Path Toward Finding and Mobilizing a Community's Assets*, Chicago, IL: ACTA.

Kyonne, J. (2007) 'The role of teamwork in public welfare caseworker's intentions to leave', Unpublished PhD thesis, University of Missouri-Columbia, available online at: http://edt.missouri.edu/Summer2007/Dissertation/KyonneJ-071607-D8322/research.pdf

Laing, G. and Hepburn, M. (2006) 'Working with retrenched timber workers and impacted communities: use of a community development approach', *Rural Social Work and Community Practice*, 11, December, pp 18–29.

Laird, S. (2008) 'Social work practice in sub-Saharan Africa', *British Journal of Social Work*, 38, 1, pp 135–51.

Lane, J. (2000) *New Public Management*, London: Routledge.

Lawrence, G. and Share, P. (1993) 'Rural Australia: current problems and policy directions', *Regional Journal of Social Issues*, 27, pp 3–9.

Lea, D. and Wolfe, J. (1993) *Community Development Planning and Aboriginal Community Control*, Discussion Paper No 14, Darwin: Australian National University North Australia Research Unit.

Le Heron, R., Roche, M., Johnston, T. and Bowler, S. (1991) 'Pluriactivity in New Zealand's agro-commodity chains', in J. Fairweather (ed), *Proceedings of the Rural Economy and Society Section of the Sociological Association of Aotearoa (NZ)*, Discussion Paper No 129, Lincoln University, Agribusiness and Economics Research Unit, Canterbury, pp 41–56.

Lehmann, J. (2005) 'Human services management in rural contexts', *British Journal of Social Work*, 35, 3, pp 355–71.

Lemos, G. and Crane, X. (2004) *Community Conflict: Causes and Actions*, London, Lemos and Crane.

Leonard, P. (1997) *Postmodern Welfare, Reconstructing an Emancipatory Project*, London: Sage.

Levitas, R. (1998) *The Inclusive Society? Social Exclusion and New Labour*, London: Macmillan.

Lichter, D. and Johnson, K. (2006) 'Emerging rural settlement patterns and the geographic redistribution of America's new immigrants', *Rural Sociology*, 71, 1, pp 109–31.

Liégeois, J.-P. (1998) *School Provision for Ethnic Minorities: The Gypsy Paradigm*, Hatfield: University of Hertfordshire Press (originally published 1986).

Lifeline (1992) *A Response to the Drought: A Report of the Activities of Lifeline's Rural Support Unit*, Brisbane: Lifeline.

Lifeline Darling Downs and South West Queensland Ltd (2005) *Annual Report*, Toowoomba: Lifeline Darling Downs and South West Queensland Ltd.

Lindeman, E.C. (1921) *The Community: An Introduction to Community Leadership and Organization*, New York: Association Press.

Little, J. (2002) *Gender and Rural Geography*, Harlow: Prentice-Hall.

Little, J. (2003) '"Riding the rural love train": heterosexuality and the rural community', *Sociologica Ruralis*, 43, 4, pp 401–17.

Little, J. and Austin, P. (1996) 'Women and the rural idyll', *Journal of Rural Studies*, 12, 2, pp 101–11.

Lloyd, C., King, R. and Chenoweth, L. (2002) 'Social work, stress and burnout', *Journal of Mental Health*, 11, 3, pp 255–65.

Locke, B.L. (1991) 'Research and social work in rural areas: are we asking the "right" questions', *Human Services in The Rural Environment*, 15, 2, pp 12–15.

Locke, B.L. and Winship, J. (2005) 'Social work in rural America: lessons from the past and trends for the future', in N. Lohmann and R.A. Lohmann (eds), *Rural Social Work Practice*, New York: Columbia University Press, pp 1–24.

Loffreda, B. (2000) *Losing Matt Shepard: Life and Policy in the Aftermath of Anti-Gay Murders*, New York: University of Columbia.

Lohmann, N. and Lohmann, R.A. (eds) (2005) *Rural Social Work Practice*, New York: Columbia University Press.

Loney, M. (1983) *Community Against Government. The British Community Development Project 1968–78: A Study of Government Incompetence*, London: Heineman.

Lonne, B. (1990) 'Beginning country practice', *Australian Social Work*, 43, 1, pp 31–9.

Lonne, B. (2002) 'Retention and adjustment of social workers to rural positions in Australia: implications for recruitment, supports and professional education', Unpublished PhD thesis, University of South Australia, Whyalla.

Lonne, B. and Cheers, B. (1999) 'Recruitment, relocation and retention of rural social workers', *Rural Social Work*, December, pp 13–23.

Lonne, B. and Cheers, B. (2000) 'Rural social workers and their jobs: an empirical study', *Australian Social Work*, 53, 1, pp 21–8.

Lonne, B. and Cheers, B. (2004a) 'Retaining rural social workers: an Australian study', *Rural Society*, 14, 2, pp 163–77.

Lonne, B. and Cheers, B. (2004b) 'Practitioners speak – balanced account of rural practice recruitment and retention', *Rural Social Work*, 9, December, pp 244–54.

Lorenz, F.O., Conger, R.D., Montague, R.B. and Wickrama, K.A.S. (1993) 'Economic conditions, spouse support, and psychological distress of rural husbands and wives', *Rural Sociology*, 58, 2, pp 247–68.

Lowe, P. and Speakman, L. (2006) *The Ageing Countryside: The Growing Older Population of Rural England*, London: Age Concern.

Lucassen, L., Willems, W. and Cottaar, A. (1998) *Gypsies and Other Itinerant Groups. A Socio-Historical Approach*, London and New York: MacMillan/St Martin's Press.

Luloff, A.E. (1998) *What Makes a Place a Community?* The Fifth Sir John Quick Bendigo Lecture, Bendigo, Australia, La Trobe University.

Luloff, A.E. and Wilkinson, K.P. (1979) 'Participation in the National Flood Insurance Program: a study of community activeness', *Rural Sociology*, 44, Spring, pp 137–52.

Lumb, R. (1982) 'The demography of small communities: stable numbers and fragile structure,' in H. Jones (ed) *Recent Migration in Northern Scotland: Pattern, Process, Change*, London, Social Science Research Council.

Lundin, R. and Arger, G. (1994) 'Rural isolation: technologies for the delivery of education and training', in D. McSwan and M. McShane (eds), *Issues Affecting Rural Communities*, Townsville: Rural Education Research and Development Centre, James Cook University of North Queensland, pp 157–63.

Lupton, C. and Nixon, P. (1999) *Empowering Practice? A Critical Appraisal of the Family Group Conference Approach*, Bristol: The Policy Press.

Lynn, R. (2001) 'Learning from a "Murri" way', *British Journal of Social Work*, 31, 6, pp 903–16.

MacKay, A. (2000) *Reaching Out: Women's Aid in a Rural Area*, St Andrews, East Fife: Women's Aid.

MacKenzie, P. (2001) 'Ageing people in ageing places: addressing the needs of older adults in rural Saskatchewan', *Rural Social Work*, 6, 3, pp 74–83.

Mackey, W. F. (1977) 'Prolegomena to language policy analysis', *Word*, 30, 1–2, pp 5–14.

MacLean, M.J. and Kelley, M.L. (2001) 'Palliative care in rural Canada', *Rural Social Work*, 6, 3, pp 63–73.

MacPherson, S. (1994) 'Can we turn social science into social development studies?', in L. Jayasuriya and M. Lee (eds), *Social Dimensions of Development*, Proceedings of the Inaugural Conference of the WA Inter-University Consortium for Development Studies, Bentley: Paradigm Books, pp 185–203.

Malik, K. (1996) *The Meaning of Race. Race, History and Culture in Western Society*, Basingstoke: Macmillan.

Manning, C. and Cheers, B. (1995) 'Child abuse notification in a country town', *Child Abuse and Neglect: The International Journal*, 19, 4, pp 387–97.

Māori Health (2008) *Health Status Indicators*, Wellington, NZ: Ministry of Health, available online at: www.maorihealth.govt.nz/moh.nsf/indexma/health-status-indicators

Markiewicz, A. (1996) 'Recruitment and retention of social work personnel within public child welfare: a case study of a Victorian department', *Australian Social Work*, 49, 4, pp 11–17.

Marsh, P. and Crow, G. (1998) *Family Group Conferences in Child Welfare*, Oxford: Blackwell Science.

Marson, S.M. and Powell, R.M. (2000) 'Resolving the transportation problem in a rural community: a case study of Robeson County's (USA) solution to TANF (Temporary Aid for Needy Families)', *Rural Social Work*, 6, 1, pp 26–32.

Martel, J. and Brassard, R. (2006) 'Painting the prison "red": constructing and experiencing Aboriginal identities in prison', *British Journal of Social Work*, 38, 2, pp 340–61.

Martin, K.E. and Wilkinson, K.P. (1984) 'Local participation in the Federal Grant System: effects of community action', *Rural Sociology*, 49, 3, pp 374–88.

Martina, C.M.S. and Stevens, N.L. (2006) 'Breaking the cycle of loneliness? Psychological effects of a friendship enrichment program for older women', *Aging and Mental Health*, 10, 5, pp 467–75.

Martinez-Brawley, E. (undated) *Social Services in Spain: The Case of Rural Catalonia*, University Park: Department of Sociology, The Pennsylvania State University.

Martinez-Brawley, E. (1980) *Pioneer Efforts in Rural Social Welfare: Firsthand Views since 1908*, University Park, PA, and London: Pennsylvania State University Press.

Martinez-Brawley, E. (1982) *Rural Social and Community Work in the US and Britain*, New York: Praeger.

Martinez-Brawley, E. (1984) 'In search of common principles in rural social and community work', in J. Lishman (ed), *Social Work in Rural and Urban Areas*, Research Highlights 9, Department of Social Work, Aberdeen University, pp 69–95.

Martinez-Brawley, E. (1986) 'Community-oriented social work in a rural and remote Hebridean patch', *International Social Work*, 29, 4, pp 349–72.

Martinez-Brawley, E. (1990) *Perspectives on the Small Community: Humanistic Views for Practitioners*, Silver Spring, MD: NASW Press.

Martinez-Brawley, E. (1998) 'Community-oriented practice in rural social work', in L.H. Ginsberg (ed), *Social Work in Rural Communities* (3rd edn), Alexandria, VA: Council on Social Work Education, pp 99–113.

Martinez-Brawley, E. (2000) *Close to Home: Human Services and the Small Community*, Silver Spring, MD: NASW Press.

Martinez-Brawley, E. (2003) 'Putting "glamour" back into practice thinking: implications for social and community development work', *Australian Social Work*, 55, 4, pp 292-302.

Martinez-Brawley, E. (2006) 'Reinventing localism: the evolving nature of rural service principles', Opening address at the Rural Social Work Conference, Keele University, 30 November, available online at: www.keele.ac.uk/research/lcs/makingresearchcount/downloads/ Prof_Martinez_Brawley_keynote.pdf

Martinez-Brawley, E. and Blundall, J. (1989) 'Farm families' preferences toward the personal social services', *Social Work*, 34, 6, pp 513–22.

Martinez-Brawley, E. and Zorita, P. M.-B. (2001) 'Latino immigrants in the borderlands: transcultural issues from the academy', *International Social Work*, 44, 1, pp 57–73.

Marx, K. and Engles, F. (1972) *Manifesto of the Communist Party*, Peking, China: Foreign Languages Press.

McAllister, R.R.J., Cheers, B., Darbas, T., Davies, J., Richards, C., Robinson, C. J., Ashley, M., Fernando, D. and Maru, Y.T. (2008) 'Social networks in arid Australia: a review of concepts and evidence', *The Rangelands Journal – Desert Knowledge Special Issue*, 30, 1, pp 161–76.

McCarty, D. and Clancy, C. (2002) 'Telehealth: implications for social work practice', *Social Work*, 47, 2, pp 153–61.

McClure, L. and Cock, G. (undated) *Project Proposal: Measuring Rural Community Capacity and Capability*, Adelaide: RC&E Program, South Australia Department of Primary Industries and Resources.

McClure, L. and Cock, G. (2003) *Achieving Targets: Industries and Communities*, Adelaide: RC&E Program, Primary Industries and Resources (PIRSA).

McCullough, L.B. and Wilson, N.L. (1995) *Long-Term Care Decisions: Ethical and Conceptual Dimensions*, Baltimore, MD: Johns Hopkins University Press.

McDonagh, J., Varley, T. and Shortall, S. (2009) *A Living Countryside? The Politics of Sustainable Development in Rural Ireland*, Aldershot: Ashgate.

McGillivray, A. and Comaskey, B. (1999) *Black Eyes All of the Time: Intimate Violence, Aboriginal Women, and the Justice System*, Toronto, ON: University of Toronto Press.

McKay, S., Craw, M. and Chopra, D. (2006) *Migrant Workers in England and Wales: An Assessment of Migrant Worker Health and Safety Risks*, Norwich: Health and Safety Executive, available online at: www.hse.gov.uk/research/rrhtm/rr502.htm

McKnight, J.L. and Kretzman, J.P. (2004) 'Mapping community capacity', in M. Minkler (ed), *Community Organising and Community Building for Health* (2nd edn), New Brunswick: Rutgers University Press, pp 158–72.

McMahon, A. (2002) 'Writing diversity: ethnicity and race in Australian social work 1947–1997', *Australian Social Work*, 55, 3, pp 172–83.

Meert, H. (2000) 'Rural community life and the importance of reciprocal survival strategies', *Sociologica Ruralis*, 40, 3, pp 319–38.

Memmott, P., Stacey, R., Chambers, C. and Keys, C. (2001) *Violence in Indigenous Communities*, Canberra: Attorney-General's Department.

Mercier, J.M., Paulson, L. and Morris, E.W. (1988) 'Rural and urban elderly: differences in the quality of the parent–child relationship', *Family Relations*, 37, 1, pp 68–72.

Midgley, G., Munro, I. and Brown, M. (1997) *Integrating User Involvement and Multi-Agency Working to Improve Housing for Older People*, Rowntree Research Findings, Housing Research 205, York: Joseph Rowntree Foundation, available online at: www.jrf.org.uk

Midgley, J. (1981) *Professional Imperialism: Social Work in the Third World*, London: Heineman.

Midgley, J. (1990) 'International social work: learning from the Third World', *Social Work*, 35, 4, pp 295–301.

Midgley, J. (2001) 'Issues in international social work', *Journal of Social Work*, 1, 1, pp 21–35.

Midgley, J., Hall, A., Hardiman, M. and Narine, D. (1986) *Community Participation, Social Development and the State*, London: Methuen.

MIF (Migration Impact Forum) (2007) *Evidence from our Regional Consultation on the Impacts of Migration*, London: MIF, Home Office, available online at: www.ind.homeoffice.gov.uk

Milbourne, P. and Hughes, R. (2005) *Poverty and Social Exclusion in Rural Wales*, Cardiff: Cardiff University, Wales Rural Observatory, available online at: www.walesruralobservatory.org.uk

Miller, P.J. (1998) 'Dual relationships in rural practice: a dilemma of ethics and culture', in L.H. Ginsberg (ed), *Social Work in Rural Communities* (3rd edn), Alexandria, VA: CSWE, pp 55–62.

MIND (2008) *Fact Sheet on Rural Mental Health*, London: MIND, available online at: www.mind.org.uk/Information/Factsheets/Rural+issues+in+mental+health.htm

Minkes, J., Hammersley, R. and Raynor, P. (2005) 'Partnership in working with young offenders with substance misuse problems', *The Howard Journal*, 44, 3, pp 254–68.

Mishra, R. (1999) *Globalisation and the Welfare State*, Cheltenham: Edward Elgar.

Mmatli, T. (2008) 'Political activism as a social work strategy in Africa', *International Social Work*, 51, 3, pp 297–310.

MNC (Métis National Council) (2008) *National Definition of Métis*, MNC, Ottawa, Canada, available online at: www.metisnation.ca

Modood, T., Berthoud, R., Lakey, J., Nazroo, J., Smith, P., Virdee, S. and Beishin, S. (1997) *Ethnic Minorities in Britain: Diversity and Disadvantage*, London: Policy Studies Institute.

Mokuau, N., Garlock-Tuiali'i, J. and Lee, P. (2008) 'Has social work met its commitment to Native Hawaiians and other Pacific islanders?', *Social Work*, 23, 2, pp.115–21.

Molnar, J., Duffy, P., Claxton, L. and Bailey, C. (2000) 'Private food assistance in a small metropolitan area: urban resources and rural needs', *Journal of Sociology and Social Welfare*, 28, 3, pp 187–209.

Moor, C. and Whitworth, J. (2001) *All Together Now? Social Inclusion in Rural Communities*, London: Local Government Association, available online at: www.lga.gov.uk

Morgan, T. (1998) Address at the Opening of the Phoenix Indian School 1891, cited by the Archaeological Institute of America, available online at: www.archaeology.org/online/features/phoenix/

Morrisette, V., McKenzie, B. and Morrisette, L. (1993) 'Towards an Aboriginal model of social work practice', *Canadian Social Work Review*, 10, 1, pp 91–108.

Morse, H.N. (1919) 'The underlying factors of rural community development', in E. Martinez-Brawley (ed) (1980) *Pioneer Efforts in Rural Social Welfare: Firsthand Views since 1908*, University Park and London: Pennsylvania State University Press, pp 109–15.

Morton Consulting Services Pty Ltd (1990) *Rationalisation: Rural Local Government and Human Services*, Brisbane. The Local Government Association of Queensland (Inc).

Moseley, M. (2000) *Accessibility and Care in a Rural Area – The Case of Tewkesbury Borough*, Cheltenham: Countryside and Community Research Unit, Cheltenham and Gloucester College of Higher Education.

Moseley, M. and Parker, G. (1998) *The Joint Provision of Rural Services*, Wetherby: The Countryside Agency.

Mullaly, R. (1993) *Structural Social Work; Ideology, Theory and Practice*, Oxford: Oxford University Press.

Mungall, I. (2005) 'Trend towards centralisation of hospital services and its effect on access to care for rural and remote communities in the UK', *Rural and Remote Health*, 5, 2, pp 1–8.

Munn, P. (1990) 'Changing seats in a medium-sized remote community: the implications of this phenomenon', *Australian Social Work*, 43, 1, pp 40–3.

Munn, P. (2002) 'Human services coordination in rural South Australia', Unpublished PhD thesis, University of South Australia, Whyalla.

Munn, P., Cheers, B. and Petkov, J. (2003) 'Extent of service coordination in rural South Australia', *Rural Social Work*, 8, 1, pp 38–49.

Murdoch, J. and Marsden, T. (1994) *Reconstituting Rurality*, London: UCL Press.

Murdoch, J. and Pratt, A.C. (1997) 'From the power of topography to the topography of power', in P. Cloke and J. Little (eds), *Contested Countryside Cultures: Otherness, Marginalisation and Rurality*, London: Routledge, pp 51–69.

Murty, S. A. (2005) 'The future of rural social work', *Advances in Social Work*, 6, 1, Spring, pp 132–43.

Myers, P. (1995) 'Country mutters', *The Guardian*, March 21, pp 4–5.

Nagpaul, H. (1972) 'The diffusion of American social work education to India', *International Social Work*, 15, 1, pp 13–17.

Naryan, U. (1989) 'Working together across differences', in B. Compton and B. Galaway (eds), *Social Work Processes*, Pacific Grove, CA: Brooks-Cole, pp 317–28.

National Assembly for Wales (2003) *Review of Service Provision for Gypsy Travellers*, Cardiff: National Assembly for Wales.

National Association of Social Workers (2003) *Social Work Speaks: Rural Social Work*, Washington DC: NASW Press.

NCAI (National Congress of American Indians) (2008) *Health*, Washington, DC: NCAI, available online at: www.ncai.org

Newby, H. (1994) 'Introduction', in G. Crow and G. Allan, *Community Life: An Introduction to Local Social Relations*, London: Harvester Wheatsheaf, pp xi–xxi.

NFWI (National Federation of Women's Institutes) (1999) *The Changing Village*, London: NFWI.

Ní Laoire, C. (2001) 'A matter of life and death? Men, masculinities and staying behind in rural Ireland', *Sociologia Ruralis*, 4, 2, pp 220–36.

NIMHE (National Institute for Mental Health England) (2004) *Scoping Review on Mental Health Anti-Stigma and Discrimination: Current Activities and What Works*, Leeds: NIMHE.

Nizhar, P. (1995) *No Problem? Race Issues in Shropshire*, London: Commission for Racial Equality.

Norman, A. (1985) *Triple Jeopardy: Growing Old in a Second Homeland*, London: Centre for Policy Studies in Ageing.

Northern Territory Emergency Response Review Board (2008) *Report of the Northern Territory Emergency Response Review Board*, Canberra: Commonwealth of Australia.

NPS (National Probation Service) (2002) *Total Cost Survey*, London: NPS, Home Office.

Nuttall, M. (1992) *Arctic Homeland: Kinship, Community and Development in Northwest Greenland*, London: Belhaven Press.

Offe, C. (1993) 'Interdependence, difference and limited state capacity', in G. Drover and P. Kerans (eds), *New Approaches to Welfare Theory*, Aldershot: Edward Elgar, pp 235–41.

Office of Population Censuses and Surveys (1992) *Census 1991*, Newport: HMSO.

Okely, J. (1997) 'Cultural ingenuity and travelling autonomy: not copying, just choosing', in T. Acton and G. Mundy (eds), *Romani Culture and Gypsy Identity*, Hatfield: University of Hertfordshire Press.

Olaveson, J., Conway, P. and Shaver, C. (2004) 'Defining rural for social work', in T. L. Scales and C. L. Streeter (eds), *Rural Social Work: Building and Sustaining Community Assets*, Belmont, CA: Thomson Brooks/Cole, pp 9–20.

OMHD (Office of Minority Health and Health Disparities) (2008) *American Indians and Alaska Native Populations*, Atlanta, GA: OMHD, available online at: www.cdc.gov/omhd/populations/aian/aian.htm

OND (Office of Northern Development) (1994) *Towards the Development of a North Australia Social Justice Strategy: Final Report*, Darwin: Commonwealth Department of Housing and Regional Development, Office of Northern Development.

ONS (Office for National Statistics) (2002) *Population Density, Regional Trends, 38*, Newport: ONS, available online at: www.statistics.gov.uk/StatBase/Expodata/Spreadsheets/D7662.xls

ONS (2004) *Rural and Urban Area Classification: An Introductory Guide*, Newport: ONS, available online at: www.statistics.gov

Osborne, S. P., Beattie, R. S. and Williamson, A. P. (2002) *Community Involvement in Rural Regeneration Partnerships in the UK. Evidence from England, Northern Ireland and Scotland*, York: Joseph Rowntree Foundation, available online at: www.jrf.org.uk

O'Sullivan, D., Ross, D. and Young, S. (1997) 'Framework in the use of competencies in rural social work field practice units', *Australian Social Work*, 50, 1, pp 31–8.

Oswald, R. F. and Culton, L. S. (2003) 'Under the rainbow: rural gay life and its relevance for family providers', *Family Relations*, 52, 1, pp 72–81.

Parr, H., Philo, C. and Burns, N. (2002) *Visibility, Gossip and Intimate Neighbourly Knowledges*, Glasgow and Dundee: Universities of Glasgow and Dundee.

Parry, G., van Cleemput, P., Peters, J., Moore, J., Walters, S., Thomas, K. and Cooper, C. (2004) *The Health Status of Gypsies and Travellers in England*, Report of the Department of Health Inequalities in Health Research Initiative Project, University of Sheffield, Sheffield.

Parry-Jones, B. and Soulsby, J. (2001) 'Need-led assessment: the challenges and the reality', *Health and Social Care in the Community*, 9, 6, pp 414–28.

Pascal, G. (1996) *Social Policy: A New Feminist Analysis*, London: Routledge.

Patel,V., Mutambirwa,J. and Nhiwatiwa, S. (1995) 'Stressed or depressed? A perspective on mental health, culture and religion', *Developments in Practice*, 5, 3, pp 142–54.

Patterson, S.L., Germain, C.B., Brennan, E.M. and Memmott, J. (1988) 'Effectiveness of rural natural helpers', *Social Casework*, 69, 9, pp 272–9.

Pearson, N. (2001/2002) 'On the human right to misery, mass incarceration and early death', *Arena Magazine*, 56, January/February, pp 22–31.

Pelech, W. (1993) 'A return to the circle', in K. Feehan and D. Hannis (eds), *From Strength to Strength: Social Work Education and Aboriginal People*, Edmonton: Grant MacEwan Community College, pp 147–62.

Pennell, J. and Burford, G. (1994) 'Widening the family circle; family group decision making in Canada', *Journal of Child and Youth Care*, 9, 1, pp 1–11.

Perkin, H. (1969) *The Origins of Modern English Society, 1780–1880*, London: Routledge and Kegan Paul.

Petrova, D. (2003) 'The Roma: between myth and the future', *Social Research*, 70, 1, pp 111–61.

Pettersen, L. and Solbakken, H. (1998) 'Empowerment as a strategy for change for farm women in western industrialised countries', *Sociologica Ruralis*, 38, 3, pp 318–31.

Phillips, L.F. (1983) 'Recruiting and retaining social workers in small town practice', *Human Services in the Rural Environment*, 8, 2, pp 32–4.

Philo, C. (1992) 'Neglected rural geographies: a review', *Journal of Rural Studies*, 8, 2, pp 193–207.

Philo, C., Parr, H. and Burns, N. (2003) *Social Geographies of Rural Mental Health: Experiencing Inclusion and Exclusion*, Glasgow and Dundee: Universities of Glasgow and Dundee.

Pickering, J. (2003) *Innovative Methods of Service Delivery in Rural Scotland: A Good Practice Guide*, Good Practice in Rural Development, No 8, Cardiff: Centre For Advanced Studies, University of Cardiff, also available at: www.scotland.gov.uk/library5/rural/gprd-08.asp

Pinderhughes, E. (1997) 'Developing diversity competence in child welfare and permanency planning', *Journal of Multicultural Social Work*, 5, 1–2, pp 19–38.

Piven, F.F. and Cloward, R.A. (1982) *The New Class War*, New York: Pantheon.

Plaice, E. (1990) *The Native Game: Settler Perceptions of Indian/Settler Relations in Central Labrador*, St Johns: Institute for Social and Economic Research Press.

Poole, D.L. (2005) 'Rural community building strategies', in N. Lohmann and R.A. Lohmann (eds), *Rural Social Work Practice*, New York: Columbia University Press, pp 124–43.

Poole, D.L. and Daley, J.M. (1985) 'Problems of innovation in rural social services', *Social Work*, 30, 4, pp 338–44.

Pope, K.S. and Vetter, V.A. (1992) 'Ethical dilemmas encountered by members of the American Psychological Association: a national survey', *American Psychologist*, 47, 3, pp 397–411.

Postle, K. and Beresford, P. (2007) 'Capacity building and the reconception of political participation: a role for social workers?', *British Journal of Social Work*, 37, 1, pp 143–58.

Pozzuto, R., Aruass Juska, A., Angel, B. and Johnstone, P. (2004) 'Social work opportunities in rural development: Lithuania 1991–2004', *Rural Social Work*, 9, December, pp 42–8.

Pray, K. (1949) *Social Work in a Revolutionary Age*, Philadelphia, PA: University of Pennsylvania Press, cited in R. Smalley (1967) *Theory for Social Work Practice*, New York: Columbia University Press.

Price, L. and Evans, N. (2006) 'From "good as gold" to "gold diggers": farming women and the survival of British family farming', *Sociologia Ruralis*, 46, 4, pp 280–98.

Prinsen, G., Maruatona, T., Mbaiwa, N., Youngman, F., Bar-On, N., Maundeni, T., Modie, T. and Mompati, T. (1996) *PRA: Contract and Commitment for Village Development, Report on the Ministry of Finance and Development Planning's Participatory Rural Appraisal Pilot Project*, Gaborone: Government Printer.

Proulx, C. (2003) *Reclaiming Aboriginal Justice: Identity and Community*, Saskatoon: Purich Publishing.

Prugl, E. (2004) 'Gender orders in German agriculture: from the patriarchal welfare state to liberal environmentalism', *Sociologia Ruralis*, 44, 4, pp 349–72.

Puckett, T. and Frederico, M. (1992) 'Examining rural welfare practice: differences and similarities between rural and urban settings', *Australian Social Work*, 45, 2, pp 3–10.

Pugh, R. (1996) *Effective Language in Health and Social Work*, London: Chapman and Hall.

Pugh, R. (1997) 'Considering social difference', in J. Bates, R. Pugh and N. Thompson (eds), *Child Protection: Challenges and Change*, Aldershot: Arena, pp 7–24.

Pugh, R. (1998) 'Attitudes, stereotypes and anti-discriminatory education: developing themes from Sullivan', *British Journal of Social Work*, 28, 6, pp 939–59.

Pugh, R. (2000) *Rural Social Work*, Lyme Regis: Russell House Publishing.

Pugh, R. (2001) 'Globalisation and social change; the fragmentation thesis and the analysis of difference in rural social work', *Rural Social Work*, 6, 3, pp 41–53.

Pugh, R. (2003) 'Considering the countryside: is there a case for rural social work?', *British Journal of Social Work*, 33, 1, pp 67–85.

Pugh, R. (2004a) 'Difference and discrimination in rural areas', *Rural Social Work*, 9, 1, pp 255–64.

Pugh, R. (2004b) 'Responding to racism: delivering local services', in N. Chakraborti and J. Garland (eds), *Rural Racism*, Cullompton: Willan Publishing, pp 176–203.

Pugh, R. (2007a) 'Dual relationships: professional and personal boundaries in rural communities', *British Journal of Social Work*, 37, 8, pp 1405–23.

Pugh, R. (2007b) 'Rurality and the Probation Service', *Probation Service Journal*, 54, 2, pp 145–59.

Pugh, R. and Richards, M. (1996) 'Speaking out: a practical approach to empowerment', *Practice*, 8, 2, pp 35–44.

Pugh, R. and Thompson, N. (1999) 'Social work, citizenship and constitutional change in the UK', *International Perspectives on Social Work: Social Work and the State*, Brighton: Pavilion Publishing, pp 19–30.

Pugh, R. and Williams, D. (2006) 'Language policy and provision in social service organisations', *British Journal of Social Work*, 36, 7, pp 1227–44.

Pugh, R., Scharf, T. and Williams, C. (2007) *Obstacles to Using and Providing Rural Social Care*, Research Briefing 22, London: Social Care Institute for Excellence, available online at: www.scie.org.uk

Rawsthorne, M. (2003) 'Social work and the prevention of sexual violence in rural communities: the ties that bind', *Rural Social Work*, 8, 1, pp 4–11.

RDC (Rural Development Commission) (1996) *Rural Transport: The Vital Link*, Salisbury: RDC.

Read, J. and Baker, S. (1996) *Not Just Sticks and Stones: A Survey of the Stigma, Taboos and Discrimination Experienced by People with Mental Health Problems*, London: MIND, available online at: www.leeds.ac.uk/disability-studies/archiveuk/Baker/MIND.pdf

Reamer, F.G. (1998) *Ethical Standards in Social Work: A Critical Review of the NASW Code of Ethics*, Washington, DC: NASW Press.

Rees, G. (1984) 'Rural regions in national and international economies', in T. Bradley and P. Lowe (eds), *Locality and Rurality*, Norwich: Geobooks, pp 27–44.

Reisch, M. (2000) 'Social work and politics in the new century', *Social Work*, 45, 4, pp 293–7.

Riggs, R. and Kugel, L. (1976) 'Transition from urban to rural mental health practice', *Social Casework*, 57, November, pp 562–7.

Roberts, J., Boyington, D. and Kazarian, S. (2008) *Diversity and First Nations Issues in Canada*, Toronto: Edmond Montogomery Publications.

Robertson, B. (2000) *The Aboriginal and Torres Strait Islander Women's Task Force on Violence Report*, Brisbane: Queensland Department of Aboriginal and Torres Strait Islander Policy and Development.

Robinson, G. (1990) *Conflict and Change in the Countryside*, Chichester: Wiley.

Robinson, V. and Gardner, H. (2006) 'Place matters: exploring the distinctiveness of racism in rural Wales', in S. Neal and J. Agyeman (eds), *The New Countryside. Ethnicity, Nation and Exclusion in Contemporary Rural Britain*, Bristol: The Policy Press, pp 47–72.

Rogers, G. (1998) *Alberta Social Work Degree Accessibility Plan: Virtual Learning Circles*, Report submitted to Alberta Advanced Education and Career Development by the University of Calgary, Faculty of Social Work, Calgary.

Rolley, F. and Humphreys, J. (1993) 'Rural welfare – the human face of Australia's countryside', in T. Sorensen and R. Epps (eds), *Prospects and Policies for Rural Australia*, Cheshire, Melbourne: Longman, pp 241–57.

Rollinson, P. A. and Pardeck, J. T. (2006) *Homelessness in Rural America: Policy and Practice*, New York: The Haworth Press.

Romans, S.E., Walton, V.A., Herbison, G.P. and Mullen, P.E. (1992) 'Social networks and psychiatric morbidity in New Zealand women', *Australian and New Zealand Journal of Psychiatry*, 26, 3, pp 485–92.

Ross, M.G. (1955) *Community Organization: Theory, Principle and Practice*, New York: Harper Row.

Rothenberg, J. (1961) *Measurement of Social Welfare*, Englewood Cliffs, NJ: Prentice-Hall.

Rothman, J. (1968) Three models of community organization practice', *Social Work Practice 1968*, New York: Columbia University Press, pp 16–47; also available in F.M. Cox, J.L. Erlich, J. Rothman and J.E. Tropman (eds), *Strategies of Community Organization*, Itasca, IL: Peacock, pp 22–39.

Rothman, J. (1974) *Planning and Organizing for Social Change: Action Principles from Social Science Research*, New York: Columbia University Press.

Rounds, K. (1988) 'AIDS in rural areas: challenges to providing care', *Social Work*, 33, 3, pp 218–29.

Royal Commission (1996) *Report of the Royal Commission on Aboriginal Peoples: People to People, Nation to Nation*, Ottawa: Indian and Northern Affairs Canada, available online at: www.ainc-inac.gc.ca/ap/pubs/rpt/rpt-eng.asp

Rubin, H. and Rubin, I. (1986) *Community Organizing and Development*, Columbus, OH: Merrill.

Sacred Circle (2005) *Restoration of Safety for Native Women*, Rapid City, SD: Restoration of Native Sovereignty, available online at: www.ncai.org/ncai/advocacy/hr/docs/dv-sovereignty_restoration.pdf

Said, E. (1993) *Culture and Imperialism*, London: Chatto and Windus.

Sakamoto, I. (2007) 'A critical examination of immigrant acculturation: towards an anti-oppressive social model of immigrant adults in a pluralistic society', *British Journal of Social Work*, 37, 3, pp 515–35.

Salt, B. (1992) *Population Movements in Non-metropolitan Australia*, Rural and Provincial Policy Unit, Department of Primary Industries and Energy, Bureau of Immigration Research, Department of Immigration, Local Government and Ethnic Affairs, Canberra: Australian Government Publishing Service.

Salt, B. (2001) *The Big Shift: Welcome to the Third Australian Culture*, South Yarra, Victoria: Hardie Grant Books.

Saltman, J., Gumpert, J., Allen-Kelly, K. and Zubrzycki, J. (2004) 'Rural social work practice in the United States and Australia', *International Social Work*, 47, 4, pp 529–45.

Sanders, M.R. (1999) 'Triple P – Positive Parenting Program: towards an empirically validated multilevel parenting and family support strategy for the prevention of behavior and emotional problems in children', *Clinical Child and Family Psychology Review*, 2, 1, pp 71–90.

Sanders, M. (2003) *Language Support Strategy for Tower Hamlets: A Literature Review*, London: Praxis.

Sanders, M.R. and Markie-Dadds, C. (1996) 'Triple P: a multilevel family intervention program for children with disruptive behaviour disorders', in P. Cotton and H. Jackson (eds), *Early Intervention and Prevention in Mental Health*, Melbourne: Australian Psychological Society, pp 59–85.

Save the Children (2002) *Refugee Children Parliamentary Briefing: Asylum Seeking Children and the Reservation to the UNCRC*, London: Save the Children, cited in S. Cemlyn and L. Briskman (2003) 'Asylum, children's rights and social work', *Child and Family Social Work*, 8, 3, pp 163–78.

Scales, T.L. and Streeter, C.L. (eds) (2004) *Rural Social Work: Building and Sustaining Community Assets*, Belmont, CA: Thomson Brooks/Cole.

Scharf, T. and Bartlam, B. (2006) *Rural Disadvantage: Quality of Life and Disadvantage Among Older People – A Pilot Study*, Cheltenham: Commission for Rural Communities.

Schenck, C. (2003) 'Rural social work in South Africa: the perception and experiences of practitioners', Unpublished report, Pretoria: University of South Africa.

Schilde, K. and Schulte, D. (2005) *Need and Care: Glimpses into the Beginnings of Eastern Europe's Professional Welfare*, Opladen and Bloomfield Hills: Barbara Budrich Publishers.

Schmidt, G. (2000) 'Remote northern communities: implications for social work practice', *International Social Work*, 43, 3, pp 337–49.

Schmidt, G. (2005) 'Geographic context and northern child welfare practice', in K. Brownlee and J. Graham (eds), *Readings and Research from Northern and Rural Canada*, Toronto: Canadian Scholars Press, pp 16–29.

Schmidt, G. (2009) Information from personal correspondence, 26 January.

Schmidt, G. and Klein, R. (2004) 'Geography and social worker retention', *Rural Social Work*, 9, pp 235–43.

Schneider, R. and Lester, L. (2002) *Social Work Advocacy*, Belmont, CA: Brooks Cole.

Schulte, D. (2006) 'The history of social work in eight Eastern European countries from 1909–1960 – an overview', in S. Hering and B. Waaldijk (eds), *Guardians of the Poor – Custodians of the Public: Welfare History in Eastern Europe 1900–1960*, Opladen and Farmington Hills: Barbara Budrich Publishers, pp 83–139.

Scott, J.P. and Roberto, K.A. (1985) 'Use of informal and formal support networks by rural elderly poor', *The Gerontologist*, 25, 6, pp 624–30.

Scott, J.P. and Roberto, K.A. (1987) 'Informal supports of older adults: a rural–urban comparison', *Family Relations: Journal of Applied Family and Child Studies*, 36, 4, pp 444–9.

Senkpiel, A. (1997) 'Side by side in the Yukon: the development of the northern human service worker/BSW program', in K. Brownlee, R. Delaney and J.R. Graham (eds), *Strategies for Northern Social Work Practice*, Thunderbay: Lakehead University Centre for Northern Studies, pp 9–44.

Sheldon, B. (1982) 'A romantic illusion', *Social Work Today*, 13, 46, pp 10–12; cited in E. Martinez-Brawley (1984) 'In search of common principles in rural social and community work', in J. Lishman (ed), *Social Work in Rural and Urban Areas*, Research Highlights 9, Aberdeen: Department of Social Work, Aberdeen University, pp 69–95.

Sher, J. and Sher, K.R. (1994) 'Beyond the conventional wisdom: rural development as if Australia's rural people really mattered', in D. McSwan and M. McShane (eds), *Issues Affecting Rural Communities*, Townsville: Rural Education Research and Development Centre, James Cook University of North Queensland, pp 9–32.

Shewell, H. (2004) *'Enough to Keep Them Alive': Indian Welfare in Canada 1873–1965*, Toronto: University of Toronto Press.

Shucksmith, M. (2003) *Social Exclusion in Rural Areas: A Review of Recent Research*, Aberdeen: Arkleton Centre, available online at: www.defra.gov.uk

Shucksmith, M., Shucksmith, J. and Watt, J. (2007) 'Rurality and social inclusion: a case of pre-school education', in G. Giarchi (ed) *Challenging Welfare Issues in the Global Countryside*, London: Blackwell, pp 97–110.

Sibley, D. (1997) 'Endangering the sacred: nomads, youth cultures and the countryside', in P. Cloke and J. Little (eds), *Contested Countryside Cultures: Otherness, Marginalisation and Rurality*, London: Routledge, pp 218–31.

Simard, M. (2009) 'Retention and departure factors influencing highly skilled immigrants in rural areas: medical professions in Quebec, Canada', in B. Jentsch and M. Simard (eds), *International Migration and Rural Areas*, Aldershot: Ashgate, pp 43–76.

Slack, T. and Jensen, L. (2002) 'Race, ethnicity, and underemployment in nonmetropolitan America: a 30-year profile', *Rural Sociology*, 67, 2, pp 208–33.

Smale, G. and Bennett, W. (1989) *Community Work in Scotland: Pictures of Practice: Volume 1*, London: National Institute for Social Work.

Smale, G., Tuson, G. and Statham, D. (2000) *Social Work and Social Problems: Working Towards Social Inclusion and Social Change*, Basingstoke: Macmillan.

Smalley, R.E. (1967) *Theory for Social Work Practice*, New York: Columbia University Press.

Smith, A. (2007) *Soul Wound: The Legacy of Native American Schools*, New York: Amnesty International USA, available online at: www.amnestyusa.org/amnestynow/soulwound.html

Smith, G. and Smith, W. (1987) 'Mobile counselling', in A. Blanchard and M. Lin (eds), *Social Work in a Changing Society*, Proceedings of the 20th National Conference of the Australian Association of Social Workers, Canberra: AASW Pty Ltd.

Smith, J. and Mancoske, R. (1997) *Rural Gays and Lesbians: Building on the Strengths of Communities*, New York: Haworth Press.

Smith, M.K. (2005) 'Community organization', *The Encyclopedia of Informal Education*, available online at: www.infed.org/community/b-comorg.htm

Smith, M.K. (2006) 'Community work', *The Encyclopaedia of Informal Education*, available online at: www.infed.org/community/b-comwrk.htm

Snipp, C. M. (1996) 'Understanding race and ethnicity in rural America', *Rural Sociology*, 61, 1, pp 125–42.

Soliman, H. (2005) 'Rural families' response to chronic technological disasters: the case of the Pigeon River', *Rural Social Work and Community Practice*, 10, 1, pp 18–31.

Soydan, H. (1999) *The History of Ideas in Social Work*, Birmingham: SWRA/Venture Press.

Stalford, H., Baker, H. and Beveridge, F. (2003) *Children and Domestic Violence in Rural Areas: A Child-Focused Assessment of Service Provision*, London: Save the Children.

Stanley, J., Tomison, A. and Pocock, J. (2003) *Child Abuse and Neglect in Indigenous Australian Communities*, National Protection Clearing House, Issues Paper 19, Melbourne: Australian Institute of Family Studies.

Stannard, D. E. (1992) *American Holocaust: The Conquest of the New World*, New York: Oxford University Press.

Statistics Canada (2008) *Aboriginal Peoples in Canada in 2006: Inuit, Métis and First Nations, 2006 Census: Inuit*, Ottawa, available online at: www12.statcan.ca/english/census06/analysis/aboriginal/index.cfm

Statistics New Zealand (2007) *QuickStats About Culture and Identity*, Wellington, available online at: www.stats.govt.nz

Stedman, R., Parkins, J. and Beckley, T. (2004) 'Resource dependence and community well-being in rural Canada', *Rural Sociology*, 69, 2, pp 213–34.

Steiner, J.F. (1925) *Community Organisation: A Study of its Theory and Practice*, New York: The Century Co.

Stockdale, A. (2004) 'Rural out-migration: community consequences and individual migrant experiences', *Sociologia Ruralis*, 44, 2, pp 167–86, cited in S. Hartwell, L. Kitchen, P. Milbourne and S. Morgan (2007) *Population Change in Rural Wales: Social and Cultural Impacts*, Cardiff: Wales Rurual Observatory, available online at: www.walesruralobservatory.org.uk/reports/english/MigrationReport_Final.pdf.

Sundet, P.A. and Cowger, C.D. (1990) 'The rural community environment as a stress factor for rural child welfare workers', *Administration in Social Work*, 14, 3, pp 97–110.

Swain, P.A. (2006) 'A camel's nose under the tent? Some Australian perspectives on confidentiality and social work practice', *British Journal of Social Work*, 36, 1, pp 91–107.

SWIA (Social Work Inspection Agency) (2005) *An Inspection into the Care and Protection of Children in Eilean Siar*, Edinburgh: Scottish Executive.

Taylor, J. (1999a) 'Community services development in social work practice', South Australia Centre for Rural and Remote Health, University of South Australia Whyalla Campus, South Australia.

Taylor, J. (1999b) 'Rural social service provision and competitive tendering: against the heart', *Rural Social Work*, 4, April, pp 20–5.

Taylor, J. (2002) 'Understanding community participation in rural health service development', *Rural Social Work*, 7, 2, pp 36–46.

Taylor, J., Cheers, B., Weetra, C., Gentle, I. and Miller, G. (2001) *Grief, Shame and Pride: A Study of the Impact of Family Violence and the Strengths of the Ceduna Community to Act Against it*, Ceduna, SA: Weena Mooga Gu Gudba, Inc.

Taylor, J., Cheers, B., Weetra, C. and Gentle, I. (2004) 'Supporting community solutions to family violence', *Australian Social Work*, 57, 1, pp 71–83.

Taylor, J., Wilkinson, D. and Cheers, B. (2008) *Working with Communities in Health and Human Services*, South Melbourne: Oxford University Press.

Taylor, R.J., Chatters, L.M. and Mays, V.M. (1988) 'Parents, children, siblings, in-laws, and non-kin as sources of emergency assistance to Black Americans', *Family Relations*, 37, 3, pp 298–304.

Te Ara (2008) *The Encyclopedia of New Zealand,* Wellington: Ministry for Culture and Heritage, available online at: www.teara.govt.nz

Thomas, R., Green, J., Richardson, C. and Ormiston, T. (2008) 'Indigenous specializations: dreams, development, delivery and vision', Paper presented at *World Indigenous People's Conference on Education,* Melbourne, Australia.

Thompson-Cooper, I. and Moore, G. (2009) *Walking in the Good Way: Aboriginal Social Work Education,* Toronto: Canadian Scholars Press.

Thornicroft, G. (2006) *Shunned: Discrimination against People with Mental Illness,* Oxford: Oxford University Press, extracts available online at: www.mentalhealthcare.org.uk/content/?id=190

Tonna, A., Kelly, B., Crockett, J., Greig, J., Buss, R., Roberts, R. and. Wright, M. (in press, expected December 2009) 'Improving the mental health of drought affected communities: an Australian model', *Rural Society,* 19, 4, special edition on rural mental health.

TRC (Treaty Resource Centre) (2008) *Government Breaches of Te Tiriti o Waitangi,* Aotearoa, New Zealand: TRC, available online at: www. trc.org.nz/sites/trc.org.nz/files/Treaty%20Violations.pdf and further information available at: www.trc.org.nz/resources/media.htm

Tropman, J.E., Erlich, J.L. and Rothman, J. (1995) *Tactics and Techniques of Community Intervention,* Itasca, IL: F. E. Peacock.

Trudgen, R.I. (2000) *Why Warriors Lie Down and Die: Towards an Understanding of Why the Aboriginal People of Arnhem Land Face the Greatest Crisis in Health and Education since European Contact: Djambatj Mala,* Darwin: Aboriginal Resource and Development Services Inc.

Truth Commission into Genocide in Canada (2001) *Hidden From History: The Canadian Holocaust. The Untold Story of the Genocide of Aboriginal Peoples by Church and State in Canada,* available online at: http://canadiangenocide.nativeweb.org/

TUC (Trades Union Congress) (2004) *Propping Up Rural and Small Town Britain – Migrant Workers in Britain,* London: TUC.

Turbett, C. (2002) 'Calling the shots: innovations in joint working at a local level', unpublished MSc dissertation, University of Paisley, Paisley.

Turbett, C. (2004) 'A decade after Orkney: towards a practice model for social work in the remoter areas of Scotland', *British Journal of Social Work,* 34, 7, pp 981–95.

Turton, J., De Maio, F. and Lane, P. (2003) *Interpretation and Translation Services in the Public Sector: Findings Summary,* London: HARP/ University of East London.

UN (2004) *United Nations World Populations Prospects Report,* New York: UN, available online at: www.un.org/esa/population/unpop.htm

UNESCO (1996) Universal Declaration of Linguistic Rights, Paris: UNESCO, available online at http://www.unesco.org/most/lnngo11.htm

Ungar, M. (2008) 'Resilience across cultures', *British Journal of Social Work*, 38, 2, pp 218–35.

US Census Bureau (2000a) *US Census of Population*, Washington, DC: US Census Bureau.

US Census Bureau (2000b) *Urban and Rural Classification Census*, Washington, DC: US Census Bureau, cited in F.L. Avant (2004) 'African Americans in rural areas', in T.L. Scales and C.L. Streeter (eds), *Rural Social Work: Building and Sustaining Community Assets*, Belmont, CA: Thomson Brooks/Cole.

US Census Bureau (2001) *Urban and Rural Classification 2000*, US, available online at: www.nysdot.gov/divisions/policy-and-strategy/darb/dai-unit/ttss/repository/ua_2k.pdf

US Census Bureau (2002) *The American Indian and Alaska Native Population: 2000*, Washington, DC: US Census Bureau, available online at: www.census.gov

Valentich, M. and Gripton, J. (2003) 'Dealing with non-sexual professional–client dual relationships in rural communities', Paper presented at Rural Human Services Conference: Beyond Disciplinary Boundaries, Halifax, Canada, available in a revised version: Gripton, J. and Valentich, M. (2004) 'Dealing with non-sexual professional–client dual relationships in rural communities', *Rural Social Work*, 9, pp 216–25.

Valtonen, K. (2001) 'Social work with immigrants and refugees: developing a participation based framework for anti-oppressive practice', *British Journal of Social Work*, 31, 6, pp 955–60.

van Cleemput, P. (2000) 'Health care needs of travellers', *Archives of Diseases of Childhood*, 82, 1, pp 32–7.

Van der Ploeg, J. D., Renting, H., Brunori, G., Knickel, K., Mannion, J., Marsden, T., De Roest, K., Sevilla-Guzmá, E. and Ventura, F. (2000) 'Rural development: from practices and policies towards theory', *Sociologica Ruralis*, 40, 4, pp 391–408.

Villa, M. (1999) 'Born to be farmers? Changing expectations in Norwegian farmers' life courses', *Sociologia Ruralis*, 39, 3, pp 328–42.

Waites, C., Macgowan, M., Pennell, J., Carlton-LaNey, I. and Weil, M. (2004) 'Increasing the cultural responsiveness of family group conferencing', *Social Work*, 49, 2, pp 291–300.

Wales Rural Observatory (2006a) *Scoping Study on Eastern and Central European Migrant Workers in Rural Wales*, Cardiff: Wales Rural Observatory, available at: www.walesruralobservatory.org.uk

Wales Rural Observatory (2006b) *A Survey of Rural Services in Wales*, Cardiff: Wales Rural Observatory, available online at: www.walesruralobservatory.org.uk

Walsh, C., Este, D. and Krieg, B. (2008) 'The enculturation experience of Roma refugees: a Canadian perspective', *British Journal of Social Work*, 38, 5, pp 900–17.

Walsh, K. (1995) *Public Services and Market Mechanisms: Competition, Contracting and the New Public Management*, London: Macmillan.

Walsh, P. (1993) *Community Participation in Planning: A Human Services Perspective*, Brisbane: Queensland Council of Social Service Inc.

Walton, R. and El Nasr, A. (1988) 'Indigenization and authentization in terms of social work in Egypt', *International Social Work*, 31, 2, pp 135–44.

Warner, M.E. (2007) 'Market-based governance and the challenge for rural governments: US trends', in G. Giarchi (ed), *Challenging Welfare Issues in the Global Countryside*, London: Blackwell, pp 34–52.

Warner, M. and Hefetz, A. (2003) 'Rural–urban differences in privatization: limits to the competitive state', *Environment and Planning: Government and Policy*, 21, 5, pp 703–18.

Warren, R.L. (1963) *The Community in America*, Chicago, IL: Rand McNally.

Wasko, N.H. (2005) 'Wired for the future? The impact of information and telecommunications technology on rural social work', in N. Lohmann and R.A. Lohmann (eds), *Rural Social Work Practice*, New York: Columbia University Press, pp 41–72.

Weaver, H.N. (1998) 'Indigenous people in a multicultural society: unique issues for human services', *Social Work*, 43, 3, pp 203–11.

Weaver, H.N. (1999) 'Indigenous people and the social work profession: defining culturally competent services', *Social Work*, 44, 3, pp 217–25.

Webster, L. and Millar, J. (2001) *Making a Living: Social Security, Social Exclusion and New Travellers*, Bristol: Joseph Rowntree Foundation/ The Policy Press, available online at: www.jrf.org.uk

Wendt, S. (2005) 'Grapevines, church steeples, family history ... stories of local culture and domestic violence in South Australian wine country: feminist poststructural understandings', Unpublished PhD thesis, University of South Australia, Adelaide.

Wendt, S. and Cheers, B. (2004) 'Rural cultures and domestic violence: stories from human service workers living in South Australian wine country', *Rural Social Work*, 9, pp 97–105.

Wenger, C. (1994a) *Support Networks of Older People: A Guide for Practitioners*, Bangor: Centre for Social Policy Research and Development, University of Wales.

Wenger, C. (1994b) 'Old women in rural Wales: variations in adaptation', in J. Aaron, T. Rees, S. Betts and M. Vincentelli (eds), *Our Sisters' Land: The Changing Identities of Women in Wales*, Cardiff: University of Wales Press, pp 61–85.

Wenger, C. (2001) 'Myths and realities of ageing in rural Britain', *Ageing and Society*, 21, 1, pp 117–30.

Weyrauch, W. O. (2001) *Gypsy Law: Romani Legal Traditions and Culture*, Berkeley, CA: University of California Press.

Whatmore, S., Marsden, T. and Lowe, P. (1994) *Gender and Rurality*, London: David Fulton.

Whitaker, W. H. (1986) 'A survey of perceptions of social work practice in rural and urban areas', *Human Services in the Rural Environment*, 9, 3, pp 12–19.

Whitbeck, L., Adams, G., Hoyt, D. and Chen, X. (2004) 'Conceptualizing and measuring historical trauma among American Indian people', *American Journal of Community Psychology*, 33, 3–4, pp 119–30.

White, C. (2001) *Who Gets What, Where, and Why the NHS is Failing Rural and Disadvantaged Areas*, Cheltenham: Countryside Agency.

Whiteside, M., Tsey, K., McCalman, J., Cadet-James, Y. and Wilson, A. (2006) 'Empowerment as a framework for Indigenous workforce development and organisational change', *Australian Social Work*, 59, 4, pp 422–34.

Wilkinson, K. P. (1989) 'Community development and industrial policy', *Research in Rural Sociology and Development*, 4, pp 241–54.

Wilkinson, K. P. (1991) *The Community in Rural America*, New York: Greenwood.

Williams, C. J. and McHugh, J. (1993) 'Growing old in rural North Queensland', *Rural Society*, 3, 2, pp 2–6.

Williams, F. (1989) *Social Policy: A Critical Introduction – Issues of Race, Gender and Class*, Cambridge: Polity Press.

Williams, J. (1996) 'Policy and planning in community services – a role for government', in T. Dalton, M. Draper, W. Weeks and J. Wiseman (eds), *Making Social Policy in Australia: An Introduction*, St Leonards: Allen and Unwin, pp 181–94.

Wilson, F. (2002) *Key Issues for Rural Areas in Northumberland*, Unpublished paper, Newcastle, North Tyneside and Northumberland Mental Health Trust, Hexham.

Woods, M. (2006) 'Redefining the "rural question": the new "politics of rural" and social policy', *Social Policy and Administration*, 40, 6, pp 579–95.

World Bank (1994) *The World Bank and Participation*, Washington DC: World Bank, Operations Policy Development.

Yamamoto, T. (1992) 'Contemporary social problems in Japan: a study of the suicide and depopulation problems', *International Journal of Japanese Sociology*, 1, 1, pp 19–33.

York, R., Denton, R. and Moran, J. (1998) 'Rural and urban social work practice: is there a difference?', in L.H. Ginsberg (ed), *Social Work in Rural Communities* (3rd edn), Alexandria, VA: Council on Social Work Education, pp 83–97.

Younggren, J. (2002) *Ethical Decision-Making and Dual Relationships*, only available online at: http://kspope.com/dual/younggren.php

Zapf, M.K. (1985) 'Home is where the target group is: role conflicts facing an urban-trained worker in a remote Northern Community', in W. Whitaker (ed), *Social Work in Rural Areas: A Celebration of Rural People, Place and Struggle,* Proceedings of the Ninth National and Second International Institute on Social Work in Rural Areas, Orono, ME, University of Maine, 28–31 July 1984.

Zapf, M.K. (1993) 'Remote practice and culture shock: social workers moving to isolated northern regions', *Social Work*, 38, 6, pp 694–704.

Zembylas, M. and Bekerman, Z. (2008) 'Education and the dangerous memories of historical trauma: narratives of pain, narratives of hope', *Curriculum Inquiry*, 38, 2, pp 125–54.

Zekeri, A. and Wilkinson, K. (1995) 'Suicide and rurality in Alabama communities', *Social Indicators Research*, 36, 2, pp 177–90.

Zur, O. (2006) 'Therapeutic boundaries and dual relationships in rural practice: ethical, clinical and standard of care considerations', *Journal of Rural Community Psychology*, 9, 1, pp 1–40, available online at: www.marshall.edu/jrcp/9_1_Zur.htm or via www.zurinstitute.com

Index

W

Y

Z